Genesis, Isaiah and Psalms

Supplements

to

Vetus Testamentum

Edited by the Board of the Quarterly

VOLUME 135

Portrait of Professor John Emerton by
John Edwards

Genesis, Isaiah and Psalms

A Festschrift to honour Professor John Emerton
for his eightieth birthday

Edited by

Katharine J. Dell
Graham Davies
Yee Von Koh

BRILL

LEIDEN • BOSTON
2010

This book is printed on acid-free paper.

Library of Congress Cataloging-in-Publication Data

Genesis, Isaiah, and Psalms : a festschrift to honour Professor John Emerton for his eightieth birthday / edited by Katharine Dell, Graham Davies, Yee Von Koh.
    p. cm. — (Supplements to Vetus Testamentum ; v. 135)
    Includes bibliographical references and index.
    ISBN 978-90-04-18231-8 (hardback : alk. paper) 1. Bible. O.T. Genesis—Criticism, interpretation, etc. 2. Bible. O.T. Isaiah—Criticism, interpretation, etc. 3. Bible. O.T. Psalms—Criticism, interpretation, etc. I. Emerton, John Adney. II. Dell, Katharine J. (Katharine Julia), 1961– III. Davies, Graham I. IV. Koh, Y. V. (Yee-Von) VI. Title. VII. Series.

BS1235.52.G475 2010
221.06—dc22

2009051878

ISSN 0083-5889
ISBN 978 90 04 18231 8

Copyright 2010 by Koninklijke Brill NV, Leiden, The Netherlands.
Koninklijke Brill NV incorporates the imprints BRILL, Hotei Publishing, IDC Publishers, Martinus Nijhoff Publishers and VSP.

Mixed Sources
Productgroep uit goed beheerde bossen
en andere gecontroleerde bronnen.
www.fsc.org Cert no. CU-COC-803902
FSC © 1996 Forest Stewardship Council

PRINTED BY DRUKKERIJ WILCO B.V. - AMERSFOORT, THE NETHERLANDS

For John, from his colleagues, former pupils and friends

CONTENTS

PART C

PSALMS

PREFACE

On Thursday 5th June, 2008 a one-day symposium was held at St John's College, Cambridge, to honour John Emerton on the very day of his eightieth birthday. He and Norma were the honoured guests. Friends, colleagues and others came and enjoyed four learned papers, all from close friends of John's – Rudolf Smend, Arie van der Kooij, Ora Lipschitz and Bertil Albrektson – and a very good lunch by courtesy of St John's College! A toast was proposed to John by William Horbury, a colleague of many years standing, and John replied. Three of those papers are reproduced in this volume, which therefore in part springs out of the symposium but was already in mind as a separate venture.

This volume focuses on three biblical books that have long been of interest to John and on all of which he has published key articles. These books are Genesis, Isaiah and Psalms, three central books in the Old Testament canon. The contributions diverge in approach and focus, but these texts remain a starting-point and a point of cohesion. The essays are from scholars from all around the world – from Europe, Israel, the Far East and America. Some of John's own students have contributed, others are colleagues and friends with whom John has had close academic relationships over the years. There are Jewish and Christian scholars from a range of universities and institutions.

It is a great privilege for the editors, all of whom know John through different connections, to dedicate this volume to him. He is one of the leading Hebraists and biblical scholars of our time. He has already been honoured by the presentation of a volume on the occasion of his retirement (J. Day, R. P. Gordon and H. G. M. Williamson [eds.], *Wisdom in Ancient Israel: Essays in honour of J. A. Emerton* [Cambridge, 1995]), in which further words of appreciation, biographical information and a list of his many earlier publications can be found. The list of his publications since 1996 contained in this new volume shows his considerable ongoing contribution to Old Testament studies. Our wish is that he go on to enjoy plenty more years of good health and good scholarship, despite what the Psalmist says about "four score years"!

Katharine J. Dell
Graham Davies
Yee Von Koh

Cambridge, July 2009

BIBLIOGRAPHY OF THE WORKS OF
JOHN ADNEY EMERTON, 1996–2008

(for details of publications before 1996 see J. Day, R. P. Gordon and H. G. M. Williamson [eds.], *Wisdom in Ancient Israel: Essays in honour of J. A. Emerton* [Cambridge, 1995], pp. 289–99).

1996
"Are There Examples of Enclitic *mem* in the Hebrew Bible", in M. V. Fox, V. A. Hurowitz, Avi Hurvitz, M. L. Klein, B. J. Schwartz, and Nili Shupak (eds.), *Texts, Temples and Traditions: A Tribute to Menahem Haran* (Winona Lake, IN, 1996), pp. 321–38.

1997
"Further comments on the use of tenses in the Aramaic inscription from Tel Dan", *VT* 47 (1997), pp. 429–40.
"The house of Baal in I Kings xvi 32", *VT* 47 (1997), pp. 293–300.
"The Biblical High Place in the Light of Recent Study", *PEQ* 129 (1997), pp. 116–31.
Review of Diana V. Edelman (ed.), *The Triumph of Elohim: From Yahwisms to Judaism*, *VT* 47 (1997), pp. 393–400.
Review of J. Trebolle Barrera and L. Vegas Montaner (eds.), *The Madrid Qumran Congress: Proceedings of the International Congress on the Dead Sea Scrolls, Madrid 18–21 March, 1991*, *VT* 47 (1997), pp. 402–09.

1998
Review of L. Koehler and W. Baumgartner, *Hebräisches und aramäisches Lexikon zum Alten Testament*, 3rd edn., Lieferungen IV and V; also the two volumes of the whole *Lexikon*, *VT* 48 (1998), pp. 111–17.
Review of *The Hebrew and Aramaic Lexicon of the Old Testament*, 3rd edn., vols. I–III, translated by M. E. J. Richardson, *VT* 48 (1998), pp. 118–20.

1999

"'Yahweh and his Asherah': the goddess or her symbol?", *VT* 49 (1999), pp. 315–37.

"How Many Months are Mentioned in the Gezer Calendar?", *PEQ* 103 (1999), pp. 20–27.

2000

"The Hebrew Language" in A. D. H. Mayes (ed.), *Text in Context: Essays by Members of the Society for Old Testament Study* (Oxford, 2000), pp. 171–99.

"The problem of Psalm lxxxvii", *VT* 50 (2000), pp. 183–89.

"Two issues in the interpretation of the Tel Dan inscription", *VT* 50 (2000), pp. 27–37.

"Was there an epicene pronoun *Hū'* in early Hebrew?", *JSS* 45 (2000), pp. 267–76.

2001

"Godfrey Rolles Driver 1892–1975", in C. Edmund Bosworth (ed.), *A Century of British Orientalists 1902–2001* (Oxford, 2001), pp. 102–119. (A reprint of the memoir in *PBA* 63 (1977), pp. 345–62).

"Samuel Rolles Driver 1846–1914" in C. Edmund Bosworth (ed.), *A Century of British Orientalists 1902–2001* (Oxford, 2001), pp. 122–38.

"Some Difficult Words in Isaiah 28:10 and 13", in Ada Rapoport-Albert and Gillian Greenberg (eds.), *Biblical Hebrew, Biblical Texts: Essays in Memory of Michael P. Weitzman* (The Hebrew Bible and Its Versions 2, JSOTSup 333; London and New York, 2001), pp. 39–56.

"Looking on one's enemies", *VT* 57 (2001), pp. 186–96.

"The Teaching of Amenemope and Proverbs xxii 17–xxiv 22: further reflections on a long-standing problem", *VT* 57 (2001), pp. 431–65.

"Were the Lachish letters sent from Lachish?", *PEQ* 133 (2001), pp. 2–15.

2002

"S. R. Driver as an exegete of the Old Testament", in C. Bultmann, W. Dietrich and C. Levin (eds.), *Vergegenwärtigung des Alten Tes-*

taments: Beiträge zur biblischen Hermeneutik. Festschrift für Rudolf Smend zum 70. Geburtstag (Göttingen, 2002), pp. 285–95.

"The value of the Moabite stone as an historical source", *VT* 52 (2002), pp. 483–92.

2003

"A Phrase in a Phoenician Papyrus and a Problem in Isaiah 5:14", in J. Cheryl Exum and H. G. M. Williamson (eds.), *Reading from Right to Left: Essays on the Hebrew Bible in Honour of David J. A. Clines* (JSOTSup 373; Sheffield, 2003), pp. 121–27.

"Introduction: Ernest Nicholson's Contribution to Old Testament Studies", in A. D. H. Mayes and R. B. Salters (eds.), *Covenant as Context: Essays in Honour of E. W. Nicholson* (Oxford, 2003), pp. xvii–xxxvi.

"Treading the bow", *VT* 53 (2003), pp. 465–86.

2004

"Some Problems in Psalm 88:16", in Carmel McCarthy and J. F. Healey (eds.), *Biblical and Near Eastern Essays: Studies in Honour of Kevin J. Cathcart* (JSOTSup 374; London and New York, 2004), pp. 95–103.

"The Date of the Yahwist", in J. Day (ed.), *In Search of Pre-Exilic Israel: Proceedings of the Oxford Old Testament Seminar* (JSOTSup 406; London and New York 2004), pp. 107–29.

"A Problem in Proverbs 3:25", in C. Cohen, A. Hurvitz and S. M. Paul (eds.), *Sefer Moshe: The Moshe Weinfeld Jubilee Volume: Studies in the Bible and the Ancient Near East, Qumran and Post-Biblical Judaism* (Winona Lake, IN, 2004), pp. 9–24.

2005

"A Questionable Theory of Egyptian Influence on a Genre of Hebrew Literature", in G. Khan (ed.), *Semitic Studies in Honour of Edward Ullendorf* (Studies in Semitic Languages and Linguistics 47; Leiden, 2005) pp. 189–202.

2006

"George Wishart Anderson 1913–2002", *PBA* 138 (Biographical Memoirs of Fellows 5; 2006), pp. 39–48.

"The Kingdoms of Judah and Israel and Ancient Hebrew History Writ-ing", in S. E. Fassberg and Avi Hurvitz (eds.), *Biblical Hebrew and its Northwest Semitic Setting: Typological and Historical Perspectives* (Publication of the Institute for Advanced Studies I, The Hebrew University of Jerusalem; Jerusalem, 2006), pp. 33–49.

"The Problem of Criteria for the Dating of Biblical Books", *Jewish Studies* 43 (2005–6), pp. 9*–19*.

2008

"Abraham and Damascus in Some Greek and Latin Texts of the Hell-enistic Period", in Shawna Dolansky (ed.), *Sacred History, Sacred Literature: Essays on Ancient Israel, the Bible and Religion in Honour of R. E. Friedman on his Sixtieth Birthday* (Winona Lake, IN, 2008), pp. 179–93.

ABBREVIATIONS

AB	Anchor Bible
ADAJSup	Annual of the Department of Antiquities of Jordan Supplements
AfO	*Archiv für Orientforschung*
AnOr	Analecta Orientalia
ANET	J. B. Pritchard (ed.), *Ancient Near Eastern Texts relating to the Old Testament* (3rd ed.; Princeton, 1969)
AOAT	Alter Orient und Altes Testament
ATD	Das Alte Testament Deutsch
BASOR	*Bulletin of the American Schools of Oriental Research*
BDB	F. Brown, S. R. Driver and C. A. Briggs, *A Hebrew and English Lexicon of the Old Testament* (Oxford, 1906)
BETL	Bibliotheca Ephemeridum Theologicarum Lovaniensium
BiOr	*Bibliotheca Orientalis*
BJSUCSD	Biblical and Judaic Studies, University of California at San Diego
BKAT	Biblischer Kommentar: Altes Testament
BSt	Biblische Studien
BWANT	Beiträge zur Wissenschaft vom Alten und Neuen Testament
BZ	*Biblische Zeitschrift*
BZAW	Beihefte zur Zeitschrift für die alttestamentliche Wissenschaft
CBSC	Cambridge Bible for Schools and Colleges
CBET	Contributions to Biblical Exegesis and Theology
CBQ	*Catholic Biblical Quarterly*
CIG	*Corpus Inscriptionum Graecarum*
CIS	*Corpus Inscriptionum Semiticarum*
COS	W. W. Hallo and K. L. Younger Jr. (eds.), *The Context of Scripture*, 3 vols. (Leiden, New York and Köln, 1997–2002)
CRAIBL	*Comptes Rendus de l'Academie des Inscriptions et Belles Lettres*
CSEL	Corpus Scriptorum Ecclesiasticorum Latinorum

DDD	K. van der Toorn, B. Becking and P. W. van der Horst, *Dictionary of Deities and Demons in the Bible* (2nd ed.; Leiden and Grand Rapids, 1999)
DJD	*Discoveries in the Judaean Desert (of Jordan)* (Oxford, 1955)
DNP	*Der Neue Pauly* (Stuttgart, 1996–)
DUL	G. del Olmo Lete and J. Sanmartin, *A Dictionary of the Ugaritic Language in the Alphabetic Tradition*, 2 vols. (2nd ed.; Leiden and Boston, 2004)
ET	English Translation
ExpT	*Expository Times*
FAT	Forschungen zum Alten Testament
FIOTL	Formation and Interpretation of Old Testament Literature
Gesenius[18]	W. Gesenius, *Hebräisches und Aramäisches Handwörterbuch über das Alte Testament*, 18th ed. by H. Donner, R. Meyer and U. Rüterswörden (Berlin and Heidelberg, 1987–)
GK	*Gesenius' Hebrew Grammar* as edited and enlarged by the late E. Kautzsch and A. E. Cowley (2nd ed.; Oxford, 1910 = 28th German ed.; Leipzig, 1909)
FRLANT	Forschungen zur Religion und Literatur des Alten und Neuen Testaments
FS	Festschrift
HBS	Herders Biblische Studien
HdO	Handbuch der Orientalistik
Heb.	Hebrew
HKAT	Handkommentar zum Alten Testament
HNT	Handbuch zum Neuen Testament
HTKAT	Herders Theologischer Kommentar zum Alten Testament
HTR	*Harvard Theological Review*
ICC	International Critical Commentary
JBL	*Journal of Biblical Literature*
JBQ	*Jewish Biblical Quarterly*
JBTh	*Jahrbuch für Biblische Theologie*
JNES	*Journal of Near Eastern Studies*
JPS	Jewish Publication Society
JSOT	*Journal for the Study of the Old Testament*

JSOTSup	Journal for the Study of the Old Testament Supplement Series
JSS	*Journal of Semitic Studies*
JSSM	Journal of Semitic Studies Monographs
JSSSup	Journal of Semitic Studies Supplements
JTS	*Journal of Theological Studies*
KAT	Kommentar zum Alten Testament
KeHAT	Kurzgefasstes exegetisches Handbuch zum Alten Testament
KHAT	Kurzer Hand-Commentar zum Alten Testament
KTU	M. Dietrich, O. Loretz and J. Sanmartin, *The Cuneiform Alphabetic Texts from Ugarit, Ras Ibn Hani and Other Places* (2nd enlarged ed.; Münster, 1995)
LCL	Loeb Classical Library
LXX	Septuagint
MSU	Mitteilungen des Septuaginta-Unternehmens
MT	Mas(s)oretic Text
MVEOL	Mededelingen en Verhandelingen van het Vooraziatisch-Egyptisch Genootschap "Ex Oriente Lux"
NCAB	*National Cyclopedia of American Biography*, 55 vols. (New York, 1892–1974)
NEchtB	Die Neue Echter Bibel
N.S.	New Series
NumC	*Numismatic Chronicle*
OBO	Orbis Biblicus et Orientalis
OG	Old Greek
OTL	Old Testament Library
PBA	*Proceedings of the British Academy*
PEQ	*Palestine Exploration Quarterly*
RB	*Revue Biblique*
RES	*Répertoire d'épigraphie sémitique*
RevQ	*Revue de Qumran*
RGG	H. Gunkel and L. Zscharnack (eds.), *Die Religion in Geschichte und Gegenwart* (2nd ed., Tübingen, 1927–31; 3rd ed. by K. Galling; Tübingen, 1957–65)
RlA	*Reallexikon der Assyriologie* (Berlin, 1928–)
SAA	State Archives of Assyria
SBLAB	Society of Biblical Literature Academia Biblica
SBLDS	Society of Biblical Literature Dissertation Series

SBLSympS   Society of Biblical Literature Symposium Series
SDSSRL   Studies in the Dead Sea Scrolls and Related Literature
SJT   *Scottish Journal of Theology*
SSN   Studia Semitica Neerlandica
ThLZ   *Theologische Literaturzeitung*
ThR   *Theologische Rundschau*
ThT   *Theologisk Tidsskrift*
ThW   Theologische Wissenschaft
ThWAT   G. J. Botterweck, H. Ringgren and H.-J. Fabry (eds.), *Theo-logisches Wörterbuch zum Alten Testament* (Stuttgart, 1970–)
UCOP   University of Cambridge Oriental Publications
UF   *Ugarit-Forschungen*
VT   *Vetus Testamentum*
VTSup   Supplements to Vetus Testamentum
WMANT   Wissenschaftliche Monographien zum Alten und Neuen Testament
ZAW   *Zeitschrift für die alttestamentliche Wissenschaft*

LIST OF CONTRIBUTORS

Bertil Albrektson, formerly Professor of Old Testament Exegetics at Åbo Akademi, Åbo (Turku), formerly member of the Swedish Bible Translation Commission, Uppsala

Graham Davies, Professor of Old Testament Studies, Faculty of Divinity, University of Cambridge, and Fellow of Fitzwilliam College

Katharine J. Dell, Senior Lecturer in Old Testament, Faculty of Divinity, University of Cambridge, and Fellow of St Catharine's College

Terry Fenton, Senior Lecturer in the Department of Biblical Studies, University of Haifa

Anthony Gelston, Reader Emeritus in Theology at the University of Durham

Menahem Haran, formerly Yehezkel Kaufmann Professor of Bible Studies at the Hebrew University, Jerusalem

John Healey, Professor of Semitic Studies, School of Languages, Linguistics and Cultures (Middle Eastern Studies), University of Manchester

Knud Jeppesen, Vice-rector emeritus, Ecumenical Institute for Theological Studies, Tantur, Jerusalem, former Associate Professor, University of Aarhus

Yee Von Koh, former Ph.D. student, University of Cambridge

Arie van der Kooij, Professor of Old Testament Studies in the Leiden Institute of Religious Studies, Leiden University

Alan Millard, Emeritus Rankin Professor of Hebrew and Ancient Semitic Languages, The University of Liverpool

Patrick D. Miller, Professor of Old Testament Theology Emeritus, Princeton Theological Seminary

Stefan C. Reif, Emeritus Professor of Medieval Hebrew Studies and Fellow of St John's College, University of Cambridge

Joachim Schaper, Professor in Hebrew, Old Testament and Early Jewish Studies at the University of Aberdeen

Rudolf Smend, Professor Emeritus of Old Testament at the University of Göttingen

Ina Willi-Plein, Professor Emerita of Old Testament and Late Israelite Religious History, Department of Protestant Theology at the University of Hamburg

PART A

GENESIS

THE STORY OF PARADISE IN THE LIGHT OF MESOPOTAMIAN CULTURE AND LITERATURE

Arie van der Kooij

I

It is a great pleasure indeed to contribute to this Festschrift in honour of John Emerton. Since Genesis is one of the major areas of his interest I would like to present some of my thoughts about a most interesting narrative in this part of the Hebrew Bible – the Story of Paradise.

Beside numerous articles published in recent times, a number of important and stimulating books on this story have also appeared in the last two decades. I have in mind the works by E. van Wolde, J. Barr, T. Stordalen, M. Arneth, P. Kübel, and T. N. D. Mettinger.[1] It is not my intention to give a survey of these and other publications, rather, I will focus on some of the motifs in the story of paradise. In doing so, I will pay special attention to the question of how the culture and literature of Mesopotamia might help us better understand specific elements of the narrative. Through the years scholars have taken into account points of (supposed) agreement between the Paradise narrative and myths from Mesopotamia,[2] but recent studies, such as by Stordalen, M. Dietrich, and Mettinger, provide more detailed discussions in this regard, especially pertaining to the garden of Eden, to

---

[1] E. van Wolde, *A Semiotic Analysis of Genesis 2–3. A Semiotic Theory and Method of Analysis Applied to the Story of the Garden of Eden* (SSN 25; Assen, 1989); J. Barr, *The Garden of Eden and the Hope of Immortality. The Read-Tuckwell Lectures for 1990* (London, 1992; Minneapolis, 1993); T. Stordalen, *Echoes of Eden. Genesis 2–3 and Symbolism of the Eden Garden in Biblical Hebrew Literature* (CBET 25; Leuven, 2000); M. Arneth, *Durch Adams Fall ist ganz verderbt... Studien zur Entstehung der alttestamentlichen Urgeschichte* (FRLANT 217; Göttingen, 2007), pp. 97–147; P. Kübel, *Metamorphosen der Paradieserzählung* (OBO 231; Fribourg/Göttingen, 2007); T. N. D. Mettinger, *The Eden Narrative. A Literary and Religio-historical Study of Genesis 2–3* (Winona Lake, 2007).

[2] See e.g. C. Westermann, *Genesis 1–11* (BKAT; Neukirchen-Vluyn, 1970), pp. 279, 286, 291–292, 301–302.

the four rivers, and to links between the Paradise narrative, on the one hand, and the myth of Adapa and the Gilgamesh Epic, on the other.[3]

Before entering the garden, a remark on the question of the literary unity of Gen. 2:4b–3:24 is in order. A number of studies, such as those by O. H. Steck and E. Otto, and recently by Arneth and Mettinger, have made it clear, and convincingly so in my view, that the Paradise narrative makes perfect sense if taken as a literary unity.[4]

The following topics which, in my view, are crucial to the story will make up the structure of this essay: A. The prohibition, B. The garden of Eden, C. The frame of the narrative, and D. The two trees. I will conclude with some summarizing statements, including a brief discussion about the theme of the story.

II

A. *The Prohibition*

As soon as "the man" is in the garden of Eden, the Lord God commands him, saying:

> You may freely eat of every tree of the garden; but of the tree of the knowledge of good and evil you shall not eat, for on the day you eat of it you shall certainly die. (Gen. 2:17)

This verse raises the following well-known questions: What does the expression "the knowledge of good and evil" mean? How is one to interpret the phrase "on the day that…"? And what about the expres-

---

[3] Stordalen, *Echoes of Eden*, pp. 94–98, 111–116, 139–155; M. Dietrich, "Das biblische Paradies und der babylonische Tempelgarten. Überlegungen zur Lage des Gartens Eden", in B. Janowski und B. Ego (eds.), *Das biblische Weltbild und seine altorientalische Kontexte* (FAT 32; Tübingen, 2001), pp. 281–323; Mettinger, *Eden Narrative*, pp. 100–122. See also A. S. Kapelrud, "You Shall Surely Not Die", in A. Lemaire and B. Otzen (eds.), *History and Traditions of Early Israel. Studies presented to Eduard Nielsen* (VTSup 50; Leiden, 1993), pp. 50–61, and A. Schüle, "Made in the 'Image of God'. The Concepts of Divine Images in Gen. 1–3", *ZAW* 117 (2005), pp. 1–20.

[4] O. H. Steck, *Die Paradieserzählung. Eine Auslegung von Genesis 2,4b–3,24* (BSt 60; Neukirchen-Vluyn, 1970); E. Otto, "Die Paradieserzählung Genesis 2–3: Eine nachpriesterschriftliche Lehrerzählung in ihrem religionshistorischen Kontext", in A. A. Diesel et al. (eds.), *"Jedes Ding hat seine Zeit…" Studien zur israelitischen und altorientalischen Weisheit: Diethelm Michel zum 65. Geburtstag* (BZAW 241; Berlin, 1996), pp. 167–192; Arneth, *Adams Fall*. For other views, see e.g. M. Witte, *Die biblische Urgeschichte. Redaktions- und theologiegeschichtliche Beobachtungen zu Genesis 1,1–11,26* (BZAW 265; Berlin, 1998); Kübel, *Metamorphosen*.

sion "you shall die"? I leave aside the first issue for a moment; I will come back to it later (section D). As to the interpretation of Hebrew ביום in the verse, opinions differ. Some argue that the word "day" should not be taken in the strict sense of a (one) day,[5] but rather in a more global sense (a period of time). Mettinger is of the opinion that "on the day" should be taken in a rather loose sense.[6] He further notes that this expression is "not necessarily temporal". "Here, and in some other instances as well, it carries more of a conditional sense" (p. 22). Hence his translation runs as follows: "for *if* you eat of it you shall certainly die" (p. 23). Regarding the phrase "you shall certainly die" he states that it is not to be understood in the light of death sentences occuring in the hophal, as other scholars do. On the contrary, the plot of the whole story, he argues, revolves around a test of the first two humans: Will they obey the divine commandment or not? When they fail the test, it is stated in 3:19 that they will die: man "must return to the dust". Mettinger thus sees a close relationship between 2:17 and 3:19b ("In the sweat of your face you shall eat bread till you return to the ground", that is to say, till you die).

This interpretation reminds me of the way the narrative was read in Antiquity. The understanding of the passage in Early Judaism seems to have been that it was the disobedience of Adam and/or Eve that led to the state of man's mortality. For instance, Ben Sira 25:24 reads: "In a woman was sin's beginning: on her account we all die".[7] There are also pertinent passages in the New Testament such as Romans 5:12, and 1 Tim. 2:13–14. The underlying idea is that man was created as an immortal being (cf. Enoch 69:11 ["created as the angels"]; Wisd. 2:23).

Another example of this interpretation is to be found in the version of Symmachus; his rendering of the final part of Gen. 2:17 reads: "on the day on which you will eat of the tree you will be mortal (θνητός)".[8] The phrase "on the day that" is taken here in a temporal sense: from that day on you will be mortal. In this way Symmachus solved the problem that man did not die on the day that he ate of the tree of

---

[5] So e.g. J. Skinner, *Genesis* (ICC; Edinburgh, 1910), p. 67.

[6] Cf. e.g. Westermann, *Genesis*, p. 305.

[7] On the allusions to Gen. 2–3 in the Wisdom of Ben Sira, see J. J. Collins, "Interpretations of the Creation of Humanity in the Dead Sea Scrolls", in M. Henze (ed.), *Biblical Interpretation at Qumran* (SDSSRL; Grand Rapids, 2005), pp. 31–34.

[8] See A. Salvesen, *Symmachus in the Pentateuch* (JSSM 15; Manchester, 1991), pp. 9–10.

knowledge. It is interesting to see how the author of Jubilees dealt with this issue. Jub. 4:30 comments on the high lifespan of Adam (930 years) as follows: "He lacked seventy years from one thousand years because one thousand years are one day in the testimony of heaven. For this reason it was written regarding the tree of knowledge: 'On the day that you eat from it you will die'. Therefore he did not complete the years of this day because he died during it".[9] This passage too reflects the idea that the clause "you shall die" was understood as referring to natural death, i.e. to man's mortality.

A famous scholar of Antiquity, Philo of Alexandria, held a different view on the expression "you shall die". "Wherever Moses speaks of 'dying the death', he means the penalty-death, not that which takes place in the course of nature" (*Leg. Alleg.* I 107). This observation is well taken because the Hebrew phrase *môt tāmût* is related to the well-known expression in the hophal as attested in the laws, *môt yûmāt*. The difference is due to the fact that in Gen. 2:17 it is part of a direct speech in the sense of a verdict conveying the notion of death penalty. For a parallel see 1 Sam. 22:16: "And the king said, 'You shall surely die (*môt tāmût*), Ahimelech, you and all your father's house'". And so it happens in the next verse. Hence the pertinent phrase in Gen. 2:17 is best understood as referring to a death sentence.

But what about the expression "on the day"? It conveys a temporal meaning, although it also carries a conditional notion because, if man obeys, the punishment will not be carried out. The idea that "on the day" should not be taken in the strict sense, but rather in a more global way (after some time), is not convincing. The story of Genesis itself contains clear evidence that it should be taken strictly. In Gen. 3:5 it is said by the serpent to the woman: "For God knows that *on the day* you eat of it your eyes will be opened…". As is clear from what follows in vv. 6–7, as soon as they had eaten of the tree, their eyes were opened, that is to say, on the same day.

If taken this way, 2:17 warns us that the day man eats of the tree of knowledge he will receive the death penalty. In other words, man is threatened with instantaneous death as soon as he eats of the forbidden tree. This reading is confirmed by a passage in the book of Kings which provides a fitting parallel to our verse – 1 Kings 2:37, 42. These

---

[9] J. C. VanderKam, *The Book of Jubilees Translated* (Leuven, 1989), p. 30. For this explanation, see also Justin Martyr, *Dialogue*, 81.

verses are about King Solomon who said to Shimei that he should stay in Jerusalem, and should not leave this city. "For *on the day* that you go forth, and cross the brook Kidron, know for certain that you shall die (*môt tāmût*)" (v. 37). The same wording is also found in v. 42. As the story goes, Shimei did not obey the command of the king, and died the same day (v. 46).

In sum, I agree with those scholars who understand Gen. 2:17 as referring to the death penalty, in the sense of an instant punishment.[10] This raises, of course, the question of why the death penalty was not carried out in our story, but that is another matter.[11]

As noted above, Mettinger is of the opinion that the verse under discussion is related to 3:19b. This however is not plausible since, according to 3:19, man will die because he was made out of dust: at the end of his life he will "return to the ground, *for* out of it you were taken; you are dust, and to dust you shall return". This passage is not referring to 2:17, but to the creation of man in 2:7 (cf. "taken out of the ground" and "dust").[12] Thus, man was created as a mortal being. Gen. 3:19b does not refer to the death penalty in 2:17, but is about natural death, which is not seen as punishment,[13] but which is due to the fact that "man is taken from the ground".

B. *The Garden of Eden*

I now want to discuss a major element of the Paradise narrative – the garden of Eden. In Gen. 2:8–9 we read:

> And the LORD God planted a garden in Eden, in the east; and there he put the man whom he had formed. And out of the ground the LORD God made to grow every tree that is pleasant to the sight and good for food; and the tree of life was in the midst of the garden as well as the tree of knowledge of good and evil.

The garden is depicted as a place full of wonderful trees, a wonderful place to be, all the more so since one may freely eat of (nearly)

---

[10] See e.g. Skinner, *Genesis*, pp. 67, 95; Barr, *Garden of Eden*, p. 10.

[11] For comments on this issue, see e.g. Skinner, *Genesis*, p. 67; Westermann, *Genesis*, p. 377; O. Procksch, *Die Genesis übersetzt und erklärt*. 2. und 3. Aufl. (KAT; Leipzig/Erlangen, 1924), p. 37; P. A. Bird, "Genesis 3 in der gegenwärtigen biblischen Forschung", *JBTh* 9 (1994), p. 21.

[12] Cf. Arneth, *Adams Fall*, p. 104.

[13] Cf. Barr, *Garden of Eden*, p. 9. For another view, see Arneth, *Adams Fall*, p. 103.

every tree (2:16f.). The text of verses 8–9 raises the following questions: What kind of garden does it refer to? Where is the garden of Eden located? And since the text has it that God planted a garden "in" Eden, the relationship between "the garden" and "Eden" is to be discussed as well.

In his book *Echoes of Eden*, Stordalen offers an extensive discussion of the issue of the "Eden Garden" (as he calls it).[14] He distinguishes three types of gardens: royal gardens, cultic gardens, and gardens in mythic stories. The first type is well known from Neo-Assyrian sources: kings like Assurnasirpal II, Sargon, and Sennacherib planted royal parks which are best understood as symbolizing their royal power. The second type includes gardens as cultic sites as attested in Mesopotamian sources. As to the third type, Stordalen points to gardens such as the Cedar Forest (or Forest Garden) and the Jewel Garden in the Gilgamesh Epic – two gardens which "were located at the borders between the divine and the human world" (p. 285). He reaches the conclusion that the third type provides the most likely backdrop to the Eden Garden in Gen. 2–3.

A crucial issue at stake here is the identification of the four rivers in Gen. 2:10–14. According to Stordalen, the four rivers are best understood as four cosmic rivers. Pishon is identified by him as the Red Sea and the Arabian Ocean. "Pishon would then extend water from the cosmic ocean at the rim of the earth. A similar apprehension would be presumed for the Nile (his identification of the Gihon, vdK), Tigris and Euphrates" (p. 285). What does this mean for the location of the Eden Garden? In the light of the Babylonian world map which depicts the way the world was perceived at that time, Stordalen answers this question as follows: "Eden is a land outside the terrestrial disc" – as depicted on the Babylonian world map – "The river emerging in Eden first waters the garden, then forms the cosmic ocean round the earth, and subsequently forms four rivers extending blessing from the corners of the earth to its central region. This places the Eden Garden outside the regular world, probably at the far shore of the cosmic ocean" (p. 299; cf. p. 474). He then continues by saying that this "coincides with mythic literature presenting gardens as cosmic border areas between the human and the divine world" (p. 299), and here he refers,

---

[14] Stordalen, *Echoes of Eden*, pp. 94–104, 111–116.

among other things, to the two gardens mentioned above – the Forest Garden and the Jewel Garden in the Gilgamesh Epic.

Stordalen's work provides an important and stimulating contribution to the topic. I like his idea that the Eden Garden is a place outside the terrestrial disc (see below), but his theory raises further questions. First, the two gardens in the Gilgamesh Epic, the Forest Garden and the Jewel Garden, do not fit the picture provided in Gen. 2. Both gardens differ from the one in Gen. 2 because they are not places with trees "pleasant to the sight and good for food". One could argue that the Jewel Garden was a place "pleasant to the sight" because of the jewels involved, but certainly not a place with trees good for food. Second, the location of both gardens in Gilgamesh does not concur with the place proposed by Stordalen for the Eden Garden because they are not located at the other side of the ocean surrounding the earth. And thirdly, one wonders whether his identification of the four rivers is plausible.

Consequently, as to the question which type of garden in ancient Near Eastern sources suits best as a parallel, we are left with the temple garden, and the royal park. Recently, Dietrich has argued that the garden of Gen. 2–3 should be seen in the light of the temple garden as known from Babylonian sources.[15] Although this view makes sense in some respects, the difficulty is that it is based on the assumption that man was created *in* the garden (p. 294). According to the story of Gen. 2, however, man was created outside the garden as is clear from vv. 8, 15: he was put in the garden after he was created (on this aspect, see further below). In my view, the so-called royal garden provides the most appropriate parallel. Assyrian kings like Sargon II and Sennacherib planted wonderful parks outside their capital cities, Dur-Sharruken and Nineveh respectively. These were places full of all kinds of trees. The park of Sargon II is described thus:

> Einen Park, eine genaue Nachbildung des Amanus-Gebirges, in dem alle aromatische Bäume des Hatti-Landes (und) sämtliche Obstbaumsorten des Gebirges angepflanzt sind, legte ich um sie (i.e. the new city) herum an (Bull Inscription).[16]

According to one of the letters from the correspondence of Sargon II, the people of Suhu were collecting saplings of almond, quince and

---

[15] Dietrich, "Paradies", pp. 293–301.
[16] A. Fuchs, *Die Inschriften Sargons II. aus Khorsabad* (Göttingen, 1994), p. 304.

plum trees and were transporting them to Dur-Sharruken. In another letter we read that cedar and cypress saplings should be pulled and brought, as commanded by the king.[17] Regarding its symbolism Stordalen points out that "[t]he ideology of Assyrian royal gardens stands firmly within general Assyrian royal ideology" (p. 98).[18]

Seen from this perspective it can be said that in Gen. 2–3 God is the king who planted his royal garden.[19] It is only natural then to read in Gen. 3:8, that God was walking in his garden, in the cool of the day. The garden in Eden is a royal park. It is interesting to note that the LXX rendering, *paradeisos* for Hebrew *gan*, is in line with this idea because the Greek word actually means a park, including among other things, the gardens of oriental kings.[20]

However, Stordalen would object that this idea is not convincing since the concept of royal garden does not have a "mythical significance" as he considers is the case in the story of Gen. 2–3, seen by him rightly as a myth.[21] This is the main reason why he prefers to look for gardens in mythic stories as parallels. Here we touch on an important issue. In line with what is generally taken for granted, Stordalen adheres to the view that the garden of Eden, though consisting of two elements – "garden" and "Eden" – represents one motif, the result being that one has to look for parallels for the "Eden Garden". For myself, I doubt whether this assumption is right. This leads to the following question: What about Eden?

According to Gen. 2:8, "The Lord God planted a garden in Eden, in the east". The garden is located "in" Eden, and that is why it is called the garden "of" Eden in the rest of the narrative.[22] As the text of 2:8 differentiates between the garden and Eden the question arises, Where and what is Eden? Eden is located "in the east",[23] and the name carries the notion of delight and happiness.[24] In Gen. 2:10 it is said that

---

[17] For both letters, see S. Parpola, *The Correspondence of Sargon II, Part I: Letters from Assyria and the West* (SAA 1; Helsinki, 1987), pp. 176–178.

[18] On the issue of symbolism, see also M. Novák, *Herrschaftsform und Stadtbaukunst* (Saarbrücken, 1999), pp. 347–349.

[19] Compare Eccl. 2:5 where Solomon the king is supposed have said, "I made myself gardens and parks, and planted in them all kinds of fruit trees".

[20] Cf. Eccl. 2:5 (*pardēs* // *gan*). See *RlA*, X, pp. 332–333.

[21] Stordalen, *Echoes of Eden*, p. 104.

[22] Cf. Westermann, *Genesis*, p. 286.

[23] Contra Stordalen, *Echoes of Eden*, pp. 268–270, who opts for a reading of *miqqedem* in the temporal sense.

[24] See Stordalen, *Echoes of Eden*, p. 257.

"a river flowed out of Eden to water the garden", which means that Eden is seen as a source of water for the garden, that is to say, sweet water.

It is an old question where Eden might have been located. The story of Genesis contains a clue which, as far as I know, has been overlooked by most scholars.[25] I have in mind the terminology used in 2:8 and in 2:15:

> "and there he put the man whom he had formed" (v. 8);
> "The Lord God took the man and put him in the garden of Eden (to till it and to keep it)" (v. 15).

Man was created outside the garden of Eden and later on the beasts as well as the woman were created in the garden. This raises the question how he got to the garden. The answer is that God "took" him, and "put" him there. This seems to imply that the place where the garden is located (Eden) is an area which is not accessible to man. Interestingly, we touch here upon a concept that is also found in Mesopotamian literature.

As is well known, the eleventh tablet of the Gilgamesh Epic (Standard Version) offers the story of the flood as told by Utnapishtim to Gilgamesh. At the end of this moving tale Utnapishtim reveals to Gilgamesh how he and his wife became immortal beings (XI, 198–205). It reads thus:

> Ellil came up into the boat,
> And seized my hand and led me up.
> He led up my woman and made her kneel down at my side.
> He touched our foreheads, stood between us, blessed us:
> "Until now Ut-napishtim was mortal,
> But henceforth Ut-napishtim and his woman shall
> be as we gods are.
> Ut-napishtim shall dwell far off at the mouth of the rivers".
> They took me and made me dwell far off, at the mouth of the rivers.[26]

So the gods took Utnapishtim and his wife and put them in a place far off, designated as "the mouth of the rivers". As is clear from the rest of the epic, this is a place at the other side of the ocean; a place where

---

[25] But see Schüle, "Image of God", pp. 12–13, who regards this element as belonging to a set of allusions to the making of a divine image in Mesopotamia according to the *mis pi* ritual.

[26] Translation according to S. Dalley, *Myths from Mesopotamia. Creation, The Flood, Gilgamesh, and others* (Oxford, 1998), pp. 115–116.

man cannot come, although an exception is made for Gilgamesh. It
is the place where Utnapishtim and his wife live their eternal lives, as
immortals. According to the Babylonian world map this place is one
of the isles at the other side of the bitter sea, called "okeanos" by the
Greeks, surrounding the terrestrial disc.

   Which isle might be meant here? In the Sumerian flood story we are
told that king Ziusudra, the hero of this story, also became immortal:
"(Who) gave him life, like a god, Elevated him to eternal life, like a
god". In line 206 it reads, "They (the gods) settled (him, Ziusudra) in
an overseas country, in the orient, in Dilmun".[27]

   It seems plausible that the location referred to in Gilg XI is the same
as mentioned in the Sumerian text – Dilmun.[28] On that isle, far away,
in the orient, the gods settled the hero of the flood, as someone with
eternal life.[29]

   As may be clear, these Mesopotamian texts shed light on the terminology employed in Gen. 2:8, 15. This applies not only to the verbs
"to take" and "to put", but also to the phrase "in the east". It strongly
suggests that Eden is a location like Dilmun, or even is Dilmun. Furthermore, the fact that the Mesopotamian texts speak of this as a place
of eternal life is helpful in understanding another feature of the story
in Gen. 2–3 – the presence of the tree of life, i.e., of life in the sense of
immortality (on this tree, see further below).

   Notably, the passage in Gilg XI contains yet another element which
seems to provide a further clue for a better understanding of the narrative in Genesis, namely, the expression "the mouth of the rivers". It
reminds me of the picture evoked in Gen. 2:10 where one reads about
"the river" flowing out of Eden, a river from which "the four rivers"
originate. Before dealing with this possible link between Mesopotamia
and Genesis, a few remarks on the identification of the four rivers
mentioned in Gen. 2:11–14 are in order.

---

   [27] M. Civil, "The Sumerian Flood Story", in W. G. Lambert and A. R. Millard, *Atra-
hasis. The Babylonian Story of the Flood* (Oxford, 1969), p. 145.
   [28] See A. R. George, *The Babylonian Gilgamesh Epic: Introduction, Critical Edition
and Cuneiform Texts*. Vol. 2 (Oxford, 2003), p. 520.
   [29] For parallels in Greek literature, see Homer, *Od.* 4.561–569 ("the Elysian plain"),
and Hesiod, *Works and Days* 167–173 ("the isles of the blessed"). Cf. M. L. West, *The
East Face of Helicon. West Asiatic Elements in Greek Poetry and Myth* (Oxford, 1997),
pp. 166–167. This concept is also attested in Early Jewish sources; see 1 Enoch 32:2–3,
and Josephus, *War* II, 156 ("an abode beyond the ocean").

The number four is usually taken as symbolizing the four corners of the earth, and hence the four rivers are often regarded as encompassing the earth. As we have seen, Stordalen thinks these are cosmic rivers. Mettinger holds the same opinion because, as he puts it, we do not have "a real-geography world here" (p. 16). The idea that the four rivers symbolize the four corners of the earth makes good sense, but this does not necessarily imply that they are to be seen as rivers encompassing the earth, as cosmic rivers. To give an illustration of this point of view: In Gen. 10:10–12 we read about four cities, in Babylonia, and in Assyria, respectively. Also in this case the number four is symbolic, referring to the four corners of the earth, but the cities involved are not at the rim of the terrestrial disc. On the contrary, they are cities in Mesopotamia. The same may well apply to the four rivers in Gen. 2. Two rivers are well known – the Tigris and the Euphrates. But what about the Gihon and the Pishon? According to an ancient tradition, the Gihon is often equated with the Nile, and the Pishon with the Ganges.[30] Recently, however, Dietrich has argued, on good grounds, that these two rivers are to be taken as the Ulay (Greek: Eulaios; now Karcheh) and the Uqnu (now Karun).[31] If so, the text of Gen. 2:10–14 refers to four rivers mentioned in an order ranging from east to west, ending up with the Euphrates as the westernmost one.

Be that as it may, the picture of a river flowing out of Eden, in Gen. 2:10, may well go back to the expression "the mouth of the rivers" in Gilg XI because the latter designates, just as in Gen. 2, a special place, a place where man is "put" by the gods. It has been suggested by scholars that the phrase in Gilg XI refers to the mouth of the Apsu, the source of sweet water.[32] According to the myth of Enki and Ninhursag, Dilmun is depicted as a place where the sweet waters are flowing out

---

[30] So e.g. Josephus, *Antiquities* I,38–39.

[31] Dietrich, "Paradies", pp. 308–314. So already G. Hölscher, *Drei Erdkarten. Ein Beitrag zur Erdkenntnis des Hebräischen Altertums* (Heidelberg, 1949), p. 39. For the river Ulay, see also Dan. 8:2,16. As pointed out by Dietrich ("Paradies", p. 314), the name Cush in Gen. 2:13 refers to the area called Kassu which in Neo-Assyrian times is the name of the mountaneous region nord of Susiana. For Gihon in connection with Cush – Cassites, see also E. Noort, "Gan-Eden in the Hebrew Bible", in G. P. Luttikhuizen (ed.), *Paradise interpreted. Representations of Biblical Paradise in Judaism and Christianity* (Themes in Biblical Narrative, 2; Leiden, 1999), p. 30.

[32] See George, *Gilgamesh Epic*, p. 520. On this phrase, see also W. Horowitz, *Mesopotamian Cosmic Geography* (Winona Lake, 1998), pp. 104–105.

of the ground.[33] This is in line with the idea in Gen. 2:10 that the river flowed out "to water the garden".

To summarize this section on the Garden of Eden: the expression "the garden of Eden" turns out to represent a combination of two different elements known from Mesopotamia: a royal park, on the one hand, and a location outside the terrestrial disc (Dilmun), on the other. Interestingly, the passage in Gilg XI quoted above sheds light on three components of the narrative in Gen. 2–3: first, the use of the verbs "to take" and "to put", related to a location far away; second, the motif of eternal life, and thirdly, the picture of a river flowing out of that special location.[34] However, the idea of a royal park planted in a location as Eden is not attested in Mesopotamian sources. This feature of the story of paradise is due, in my view, to the literary creativity of its author. The same may apply to the idea of the four rivers as being related to a river flowing out of Eden in Gen. 2:10, although the link between the one river and the four rivers might have been evoked by the phrase "the mouth of the *rivers*".

C. *The Frame of the Narrative*

Gen. 2:4b–7
In the day that the Lord God made the earth and the heavens,
(5) when no shrub of the field was yet in the earth
      and the plants (greens, cereals) of the field had not yet sprung up –
      for the Lord God had not caused it to rain upon the earth
      and there was no man to till the ground;
(6) but a flood went up from the earth and watered the whole face of
      the ground
(7) then the Lord God formed man of dust from the ground,
      and breathed into his nostrils the breath of life;
      and man became a living being.

And the Lord God planted a garden in Eden...
(Gen. 2:8–3:22)

Genesis 3:23
therefore the Lord God sent him forth from the garden of Eden,
to till the ground from which he was taken.

---

[33] Enki and Ninhursag, 56 (cf. *ANET*, p. 38).

[34] According to the Gilgamesh Epic, Gilgamesh was "clad only in a lionskin" (see X. 6) on his journey at the rim of the earth, trying to find his way to the place where Utnapishtim and his wife are living. This element may shed light on Gen. 3:21 (God made for the man and his wife garments of skin).

Both passages, 2:4b–7 and 3:23(–24), can be seen as the beginning and ending of the story because they are clearly related to each other by way of an inclusio.[35] In 2:5 we are told that, although earth and heaven had been made, it was not yet raining on earth and man was not yet there "to till the ground". The same expression, "to till the ground", also occurs in 3:23: "to till the ground from which he was taken". The latter part, "from which he was taken", refers back to 2:7. Man is not only "taken from the ground" / "formed of dust from the ground" (2:7), but "the ground" is also basic to his destination. According to the story of Gen. 2–3 man was created in order "to till the ground".

The text of 2:5–6 refers a situation which is marked by the idea of "not yet". No shrub of the field was yet in the earth, because God had not (yet) caused it to rain. No plants (greens, cereals) of the field had yet sprung up, because there was no man to till the ground. According to v. 6 a flood watered the surface of "the ground" making it a fertile area. Then the story goes on to tell that God formed man of dust from the ground and made him a living being. So everything seems in place now: man is there in order to till the (fertile) ground so that plants might grow. However, and this comes as a surprise, one has to wait until the end of the story before man is going to actually till the ground. Before that situation is reached, one which according to 2:5 is considered to be normal reality of life, it is said that God planted a garden in Eden and that he put man in that garden. As argued above, man is brought to a location far away, somewhere outside the terrestrial disc.

What does all this imply? It implies that man does not belong in the garden of Eden. He is put there for one reason or another, but as is clear from the outset (2:5) he cannot stay on there; he has to leave the garden, at a certain moment, in order to fulfil his real duty, namely, to till the ground. This raises of course the question of how to understand the last part of 2:15 where we read that man was put in the garden "to till it and to keep it". Usually, this phrase is taken as being in line with the expression about tilling the ground, but I do not think this is right.[36] Verse 15 contains a motif – that of the gardener of a royal

---

[35] Cf. Van Wolde, *Semiotic Analysis*, p. 84.

[36] The feminine suffix in both infinitives of v. 15b does not refer to the Hebrew *gan* (which is masc.), but presumably to the "ground" of the garden (v. 9). For other suggestions, see D. Carr, "The Politics of Textual Subversion: A Diachronic Perspective on the Garden of Eden Story", *JBL* 112 (1993), p. 578.

park (cf. the verb "keep") – which is different from the notion of tilling the ground by a farmer. Here again we touch on an element which we know from Mesopotamia: the idea of the king as gardener, which fits the image of the garden as a royal park.[37]

In short, the whole section on the garden of Eden turns out to be an intermezzo, an interlude one might say. To be more precise, being marked by the idea of "not yet" it is a prelude, a pre-history. This raises the question of why this prelude is part of the story. Why was a garden planted in Eden, and why was man put there?

D. *The Two Trees*

Among the many wonderful trees in the park of Eden two trees are mentioned in particular: "and the tree of life was in the midst of the garden as well as the tree of knowledge of good and evil" (2:9b). The latter one, the tree of knowledge, has a crucial role to play in the story: It is the tree of which it is said that man should not eat otherwise he would be sentenced to death. However, at the end of the story the *two* trees do show up again, in Gen. 3:22–23:

> Then the Lord God said, "Behold, the man has become like one of us, knowing good and evil; and now, lest he put forth his hand and take also of the tree of life, and eat, and live for ever". Therefore the Lord God sent him forth from the garden of Eden, to till the ground from which he was taken.

I will not deal with the issue of the one-tree hypothesis in an earlier version of the story. As has been argued by a growing number of scholars, the story as it stands, including the two trees, makes perfect sense.[38]

In the passage just quoted (3:22), both trees are related to each other: having eaten of the tree of knowledge man should not eat of the tree of life as well. In his recent study, Mettinger offers a new view on the relationship between the two trees. In line with his idea that the story

---

[37] Cf. Stordalen, *Echoes of Eden*, pp. 97–98. See also M. Hutter, "Adam als Gärtner und König (Gen. 2,8.15)", *BZ* 30 (1986), pp. 258–262. For examples of the theme of the gardener who becomes king, see R. Drews, "Sargon, Cyrus and Mesopotamian Folk History", *JNES* 33 (1974), pp. 387–393.

[38] See the literature referred to in n. 4. As to the issue of the two trees, see also e.g. Mettinger, *Eden Narrative*, pp. 5–10; J. Krispenz, "Wie viele Bäume braucht das Paradies? Erwägungen zu Gen. ii 4b–iii 24", *VT* 54 (2004), pp. 301–318; Kübel, *Metamorphosen* (passim).

of paradise is to be seen as presenting a divine test, he argues that the trees have different functions in this test: "the tree of knowledge served as the test case; the tree of life was the potential reward if the humans passed the test" (p. 60). I think the idea of a divine test is well taken. I will come back to it below.

The two trees each symbolize a particular motif. The tree of life is the tree by which one can attain everlasting life (3:22), that is to say, eternal life in the sense of immortality. The issue of immortality is part of the story.[39] As argued above, this motif fits Eden as a location in the east because, according to Mesopotamian traditions, this is a place where humans live an eternal life (i.e. Utnapishtim, and his wife; Ziusudra).

The tree of the knowledge of good and evil has raised a lot of discussion about what kind of knowledge is implied here. The main possibilities are: 1. the acquisition of human qualities; 2. sexual consciousness; 3. ethical knowledge; 4. universal knowledge.[40] The last one seems to be widely accepted nowadays. I agree with Mettinger that this interpretation is the most plausible one. Good and evil, or even better, good and *bad*, are best understood as referring to a totality. Hence, the phrase is about encompassing knowledge and wisdom.

The wisdom as presented in our story does not seem to be ordinary wisdom, but rather divine wisdom because in 3:5 and 3:22 this knowledge is presented as wisdom like that of the gods. According to the serpent, who is depicted as an animal possessing great wisdom, if man eats of the tree of knowledge he will be "like the gods". Notably, the serpent got it right because at the end of the story God says, "Behold, man has become like one of us".[41]

There is reason to believe that the knowledge and wisdom in the Paradise narrative has to do with kingship. In his dissertation Vriezen drew attention to 2 Sam. 14:17, 20 where David as king is depicted

---

[39] Cf. Barr, *Garden of Eden*, p. 4. The view that the Tree of Life symbolizes rejuvenation (see Stordalen, *Echoes of Eden*, p. 292; Kübel, *Metamorphosen*, pp. 112–114) is not plausible since it is hardly in line with Gen. 3:22.

[40] See Mettinger, *Eden Narrative*, pp. 62–63 (with bibl.). He does not refer to magical knowledge as an explanation for the phrase; for (criticism of) this interpretation see e.g. Skinner, *Genesis*, p. 96.

[41] On this issue, see R. W. L. Moberly, "Did the serpent get it right?", *JTS* N.S. 39 (1988), pp. 1–27.

as having wisdom like the angel of the Lord.[42] In v. 17 the woman of Tekoa says, "for my lord the king is like the angel of the Lord to discern good and evil". In v. 20 she puts it this way, "But my lord has wisdom like the wisdom of the angel of God to know all things that are on the earth".

The wisdom of David as king, which has to do with discerning good and evil and which is characterized as knowing all things, is said to be a wisdom like that of the angel of the Lord. This concept is very similar to the motif of divine wisdom in our story. The link between kingship and divine wisdom is also attested in Mesopotamian sources. The myth of Adapa is important in this regard. One of the first lines of this text, often cited in relation to the Genesis story, reads thus:

> To him he (Ea) had given wisdom,
> eternal life he had not given him.

This passage is interesting because it is about the two motifs which are also found in our story – wisdom (cf. the tree of knowledge), and eternal life (cf. the tree of life).[43] The (divine) wisdom of Adapa was proverbial as is clear from Mesopotamian sources.[44] Kings of Mesopotamia were eager to compare themselves with Adapa, the wise. So, for instance, Sargon II:

> Der König, offenen Sinnes (eig. offenen Ohres), befähigt zu jeglichem Beruf, (darin) dem Weisen (i.e. Adapa, vdK) gleich; der in Rat und Weisheit Grosse erreichte und an Einsicht hoch hinauswuchs.[45]

All this is not meant to deny that man in Gen. 2–3 is humankind in general. The words spoken by God to the woman and to the man in Gen. 3:15–19 are about daily life. At the same time, however, the aspect of divine knowledge seems best understood against the backdrop of kingship and royal ideology.[46]

---

[42] T. C. Vriezen, *Onderzoek naar de paradijsvoorstelling bij de oude Semietische volken* (Wageningen, 1937). See also H. Pfeiffer, "Der Baum in der Mitte des Gartens. Zum überlieferungsgeschichtlichen Ursprung der Paradieserzählung (Gen. 2,4b–3,24). Teil II: Prägende Traditionen und theologische Akzente", *ZAW* 113 (2001), p. 10.

[43] Cf. Mettinger, *Eden Narrative*, p. 108.

[44] See A. Picchioni, *Il poemetto di Adapa* (Budapest, 1981), pp. 82–101.

[45] See Fuchs, *Inschriften*, p. 292.

[46] The serpent as presented in Gen. 3 evokes also the idea of kingship (great wisdom). For the serpent symbolizing a king, see Isa. 14:29!

III

In the final section, I would like to make the following summarizing statements and concluding remarks.

1. In the light of Mesopotamian culture and literature, the expression "the garden in/of Eden" represents a combination of two distinct elements – the garden as a royal park, and Eden as the place far off, overseas, in the orient, Dilmun, where immortal humans were supposed to live.[47] Furthermore, the story of paradise betrays a great familiarity with motifs known from the Gilgamesh Epic: the idea of taking someone and putting him at a special place, the motif of eternal life as related to that place, and the picture of a river flowing out of Eden (cf. "the mouth of the rivers").

2. The story about the garden of Eden (Gen. 2:8–3:22) turns out to be a particular episode in the narrative as a whole. Man was created to till the ground, but before he did so God planted a garden in Eden and put man there. The garden episode is presented as an interlude, or even better, as a prelude, or pre-history, in line with the notion of "not yet" in 2:5.

3. As to the two special trees in the garden: in the light of Mesopotamian traditions the tree of life fits Eden as place of immortality, whilst the tree of knowledge, symbolizing divine and royal wisdom, is best understood as being related to the idea of the garden as a royal park. Both trees visualize two motifs that are also found in the myth of Adapa – wisdom and immortality. The fact that our story presents these motifs as "trees" is due to the concept of the royal park being a place full of trees.

4. The issue of immortality is part of the story. According to Mesopotamian belief, the gods, when creating humankind, established for humankind death, and for themselves, life.[48] The idea that man was created as a mortal being is also basic to Gen. 2–3, since he was

---

[47] Hence, the garden-Eden symbolism of Gen. 2–3 is different from that of Ezek. 28 and other places in the Hebrew Bible (for a detailed discussion of the passages involved, see Stordalen, *Echoes of Eden*, pp. 321–454). The garden of Eden as depicted in Gen. 2 is not related to the idea of the garden as a sacred mountain as in Ezek. 28. Ezek. 28 reflects mythic traditions of West Semitic origins (cf. Ugaritic literature), whereas Gen. 2–3 is better understood in light of the literature and culture of Mesopotamia.

[48] See Mettinger, *Eden Narrative*, p. 110.

formed out of the "dust of the ground". The difference between
Mesopotamian myths and Gen. 2–3 is that in the latter the decision
that man must remain mortal, was made for a particular reason –
namely, because man had acquired divine wisdom.

5. The tree of knowledge of good and evil plays a crucial role in the
   story of paradise. It was forbidden to eat of this tree, under penalty
   of death. However, for one reason or another, this penalty was
   not implemented when the woman and man ate of the tree. The
   knowledge of good and evil is quite special: it is divine wisdom,
   and it has to do with the great wisdom of kings, wisdom like that
   of Adapa (as in Mesopotamian sources). The underlying interest of
   the story concerns the wisdom and power of kingship. However, in
   contrast to 2 Sam. 14 and the Mesopotamian sources, in Gen. 2–3
   this knowledge is presented and viewed as being bad and dangerous; otherwise, it would not have been forbidden.

6. One wonders why the story of the garden in Eden was created as the
   main element of the narrative as a whole. According to Mettinger,
   this story is about a divine test of obedience to the commandment;
   its theme is the issue of disobedience and its consequences, which
   "should be seen as being inspired by Deuteronomistic theology"
   (p. 64).[49] I like his idea of viewing the story of the garden as a test,
   but, as argued above, I do not think his interpretation that "obedience to the commandment leads to life (i.e. eternal life), disobedience to death" (p. 64), is convincing. Instead, I would suggest
   that our story is better understood as a test like the one found in
   2 Chron. 32:31. There we read, about king Hezekiah:

> And so in the matter of the envoys of the princes of Babylon, who had
> been sent to him to inquire about the sign that had been done in the
> land, God left him to himself, in order to test him and to know all that
> was in his heart.

In the light of this passage, it can be stated that the garden episode is
meant to provide a particular insight into human nature – to know
what is in the heart of man – by way of an event of pre-history, before
real history starts. Quite similar to what is told in Chronicles, the test
of Gen. 2–3 is arranged, and fully so, by God.

---

[49] For the idea of a "test", see also Stordalen, *Echoes of Eden*, p. 248. The assumption that Deuteronomistic thinking is implied here is shared by Arneth (*Adams Fall*,
p. 147).

7. This raises, finally, the question of what turned out to be in the heart of man. As noted above, the knowledge of good and evil is viewed negatively, quite differently from 2 Sam. 14 as well as from the references to the divine wisdom of kings in Mesopotamian sources. One is led to ask why? The story of Gen. 2–3 is made up by using major motifs and concepts going back to Mesopotamian culture and literature. At the same time, however, the story as it stands, marked by a combination of a royal park and Eden as a special place, reflects a critical stance towards the royal ideology of Mesopotamian kings, particularly the Assyrian ones.[50] There is a passage in the Hebrew Bible which may help us to answer the question of what is in the heart of man – Isa. 10:13–14. This passage, which may also provide a historical background to the story of paradise, is part of the taunt of the king of Assyria (Isa. 10:5–15), a prophecy dating to the end of the eighth century B.C. The crucial point is that this passage contains a negative view of the wisdom of (Assyrian) kingship:

> For he – the king of Assyria – says, "By the strength of my hand I have done it, and by my wisdom, for I have understanding; I have removed the boundaries of peoples, and have plundered their treasures; like a bull I have brought down those who sat on thrones. My hand has found like a nest the wealth of the peoples; and as men gather eggs that have been forsaken so I have gathered all the earth; and there was none that moved a wing, or opened the mouth, or chirped".

Epilogue

Dear John, I want to congratulate you most heartily on your eightieth birthday. I wish you all the best, good health, and many happy returns now and in the future, together with your wife, Norma, and many others. Your age reminds me of a great man in the Old Testament – Barzillai, friend of king David (2 Sam. 19). When David returned to Jerusalem, Barzillai the Gileadite "went with the king to the Jordan, to escort him over the Jordan". David then invited him to become a member of the court, in Jerusalem, but Barzillai declined, by saying, "I am this day eighty years old. Can I know good from evil? Can your

---

[50] This also applies, in my view, to the story of Gen. 11:1–9; see A. van der Kooij, "The City of Babel and Assyrian Imperialism: Genesis 11:1–9 Interpreted in the Light of Mesopotamian Sources", in A. Lemaire (ed.), *Congress Volume Leiden 2004* (VTSup 109; Leiden, 2006), pp. 1–17.

servant taste what he eats or what he drinks? Can I still listen to the voice of singing men and singing women?" (2 Sam. 19:35).

John, you too are a great man and scholar, as well as a very kind and helpful person. Like Barzillai, you are this day eighty years old. It is my sincere wish that you, unlike what Barzillai was saying, will still be able, in many years to come, to provide us with your wisdom in our field of research and beyond, to taste what you eat and drink at the high tables in Cambridge and elsewhere, to listen to singing men and women in the courts and colleges of this lovely city, and to walk in the paradisiacal gardens of St. John's.

NIMROD'S CITIES: AN ITEM FROM THE ROLLING CORPUS

Terry Fenton

Some years ago I read a paper at an IOSOT congress on Genesis 10:8–12 ("Nimrod's Cities") in which I made four main points. Firstly, of all the ancient historical or mythological figures proposed as the source of the Nimrod tale, only the god Ninurta is appropriate. He, however, has undergone a process of polemical demythologization in Genesis 10 (I would now use a term such as reconceptualization). Secondly, the information concerning the cities he ruled and/or built reflects partially sound knowledge of Babylonian and Assyrian realities but also serious error or fantastic invention. The explanation of this paradox lies in accidents of transmission and consequent conjecture. When analysed the text is found originally to have told of only six cities in balancing sets of three, first for Babylonia, then for Assyria, and an attempt was made to demonstrate the process by which they became pairs of four. Thirdly, as had often been noticed, there must be a connection between the description of Nineveh as "the great city" in the Book of Jonah and the words "that is the great city" at the end of the passage under discussion, where Nineveh occurs. A new account of just what that connection is was proposed. Fourthly, the "name" Resen, or rather the Hebrew consonants רסן, are the mangled remains of the third Assyrian city, the great new capital of Sargon II, Dur-Sharrukin, Sargonsburg. This proposal has now been made again, independently.

The paper was not published at that time because I could not find solutions to problems which, unsolved, left the entire approach in an unsatisfactory condition. None of the explanations of the "Cushite problem" (what was Nimrod the son of an Ethiopian doing as an over-lord in Mesopotamia?) seemed convincing. No remedy was forthcoming for the impossible entity Rehovot-ir, and attempts to separate out the elements of a clearly composite text in terms of J, P, R or the like would not hang together. However, recent publications have some-times seemed to support the notions described and they, as well as fur-ther ponderings, seem to indicate ways of encountering the difficulties. Accordingly I attempt to re-engage the issue and am honoured to offer the outcome to John Emerton, an eminent colleague and good friend who has not avoided coming to grips with thorny questions.

The complex of problems which our passage presents will be addressed by discussing the four main points adumbrated above, following up their implications and dealing with residual issues as appropriate.

The "Ninurta-Nimrod" equation has now been dealt with so exhaustively and with such clarity of argumentation by Karel Van der Toorn[1] that it would be superfluous to add further discussion. There are, however, important implications for the dating of the original Hebrew Nimrod story before its insertion in the "Table of the Nations" framework in Genesis 10. Ninurta became a leading deity in Assyria, practically, if not "theologically", on a par or almost on a par with Ashur himself, after the adoption of Kalhu/Kalah by Ashur-nasir-pal as his capital after 883 B.C. (Ninurta being the patron deity of Kalhu). This pre-eminence lasted until Sargon built his new capital Dur-Sharrukin, magnificent, but unfinished at Sargon's death in 705. It would seem reasonable to surmise that "Ninurta-tales" could only arise in far-away Israel or Judah between these dates – or just possibly a little after 705 – when the fame of Ninurta continued to exist. During this period relations between Assyria and Israel seem to have been conditioned by the growing expansion of the Assyrian Empire and the increasing erosion of the northern state. Since Judah was also under threat and fast becoming Assyria's vassal, one would not expect Hebrew folklore reflecting positive attitudes to Assyrian figures, whether deities or otherwise, to come into existence at such a time. Indeed, some researchers regard the Nimrod passage, together with the Tower of Babel story of Genesis 11, as a comment on Assyrian hubris. The Nimrod passage, however, seems to be free of emotional charge and to present foreign historical and cultural phenomena with dispassionate curiosity rather than with political rancour. Since we have no knowledge of "culture contact" beyond the jejune reports of political events on both sides, no more can be said on such matters, but the dating of the material which lies behind our passage would seem to be established. If there is polemic in the passage it is theological, though earlier than the introduction of the Nimrod theme to the Table of Nations. Verse 9

---

[1] In K. van der Toorn and P. W. der Horst, "Nimrod before and after the Bible", *HTR* 83 (1990), pp. 1–29 (pp. 1–16, "Nimrod before the Bible").

has long been regarded as an interpretation which changes the intention of v. 8. Formally the nature of the addition is betrayed by the clumsy repetition of "He" without copula and the awkward limitation of the sense of גבור (not exactly "hero", rather "man of power") by the attachment of ציד, "powerful hunter". A translation of verses 8b–9a which brings out the nuances and the awkwardness of the two sentences might run: "He was the first man of power on Earth. He was a powerful hunter before Yahweh". Of course, "before Yahweh" is not intended to indicate any relationship between Yahweh and Nimrod. It means neither "unique" nor "in the estimation of" nor "in despite of" nor "with the assistance of" nor "in the constant presence of" (i.e. Nimrod is the constellation Orion), according to the choices collected by J. Skinner.[2] It constitutes a statement that Nimrod-Ninurta is no god. Yahweh is God, anything before Yahweh is not God, Nimrod is not God: by no means a syllogism but a statement of monotheism or at the least, monolatry. Admittedly Ninurta is "reconceptualized" already in v. 8 but this was evidently not sufficient for the interpolator. Several scholars have seen a similarity between לפני יהוה here and לאלהים in Jonah 3:3. There is a similar vagueness of expression but here the intention is that Nineveh is an object of concern to God and should be so also to Jonah. That there ever was a popular saying "Like Nimrod, a powerful hunter before Yahweh" would seem dubious. This is not home-grown Israelite folklore: it is a theological statement. We have here, therefore, either a "Yahweh-alone" gloss which facilitated the very acceptance of the Nimrod story, or a much later monotheistic one. The phrase החל להיות, as has been noted, connects v. 8 with the literary ambience of J and its natural continuation with the "cities" theme is found at v. 10. In accord with what has been said of Ninurta-Nimrod, this stream of J material cannot be much later then 700 B.C. and is probably earlier.

We now turn to the cities themselves. What is striking in the account of the cities which constituted the "beginning" of Nimrod's kingdom (whether he is purported to have built them or not) in Babylonia and those which he built in Assyria is the mixture of place-names familiar from Mesopotamian history and geography, arranged in a consistent manner, with others which defy identification – one of which is not a city-name at all! A concluding phrase, further, seems to inform us that

---

[2] J. Skinner, *Genesis* (ICC; Edinburgh, 1910), p. 208.

one of the unknown cities was "the great city". Clearly we have before us a severely disturbed text.

The first three names of v. 10 reflect some acquaintance with ancient and contemporary Babylonian culture, but not expertise. This is what we should expect of a Hebrew writer having some contact with Assyrians (or, with less likelihood, Babylonians) in the eighth or seventh century. Babylon had been the principal city of Babylonia for a millennium or so but not longer. If the writer were thinking firstly of the time when urban culture commenced in the Mesopotamian area, to designate Babylon as the leading city, as it was and had long been in his own time, was an egregious error, but of remote antiquity he could have little ken. His informants, however, had evidently imparted some information of ancient periods: Akkad is of no importance in the first millennium but the writer learned apparently that it was the seat of the first great Mesopotamian empire and of the speakers of the languages to which it gave its name. Uruk was always a large and powerful city. The absence of Ur is interesting and possibly significant. And then we come to Calneh, elsewhere in the Old Testament the designation of a northern Syrian city. As Assyriologists have remarked, had there been a significant Mesopotamian city of similar name we should have known of it. It has sometimes been suggested that the received spelling is a corrupted form of the city named Kullab(a), but that city was never of any importance and is quite out of place in the presence of the other three. W. F. Albright's emendation *kullānāh*, "all of them",[3] is widely accepted and has received impressive confirmation from the fact that the Samaritan tradition has always read and understood the word in this sense, as shown by J. A. Thompson, with reference to its Samaritan Targumic and Arabic renderings and its Hebrew pronunciation.[4] The understanding of the vocable כלנה as a place-name was, therefore, erroneous and the original sense of v. 10 was "And the beginning of his kingdom was Babylon, Uruk (mispointed "Erek" in MT) and Akkad and all of them were in the land of Babylonia". (It is clear that שנער denotes lower Mesopotamia in contrast to Assyria. For a full discussion of this name we are indebted, once again, to Van der Toorn.)[5]

---

[3] W. F. Albright, "The End of 'Calneh in Shinar'", *JNES* 3 (1944), pp. 254–55.

[4] J. A. Thompson, "Samaritan Evidence for 'All of them in the land of Shinar'", *JBL* 90 (1971), pp. 99–102.

[5] Van der Toorn, 1990, pp. 2–4.

Verse 10, then, contained only three city names and herein lies the clue to the peculiarities of vv. 11–12. There would appear to be a certain symmetry between vv. 10 and 11. "And the beginning of his kingdom was…in the land of Babylonia. From that land he went forth to Assyria and built…" Into this balanced framework were fitted the city names – three for Babylonia and three therefore for Assyria. There are indeed, at least apparently, three Assyrian place-names in v. 11, but one is of very strange appearance: רחבת עיר. It is not really a place-name, but since complicated problems arise here we shall postpone the discussion of it for the moment. On the other hand v. 12 supplies a fourth city, together with a note on its location and, apparently, the statement that it was "the great city". If רחבת עיר is "disallowed" it might appear that this additional city "Resen" is, in fact, the third city required to complete the Assyrian trio. There is, however, no Mesopotamian city of that name and the same reasoning as was applied in the case of "Calneh" applies here also. Even if *Resen* were the Hebrew reflection of Assyrian *Resh-eni* "fountain-head" (to which there could be no objection on phonetic grounds, since Akkadian vocables spelt with a *sh* were pronounced with an *s* in Neo- [and Middle] Assyrian), places with such a name are naturally of very limited size and could not be partnered with the other two great Assyrian cities of v. 11 – Nineveh and Kalah. Further consideration at this point, however, invites attention to the consonants רסן from a different viewpoint. Nineveh was a large and important city from very early times, often used by Assyrian monarchs. Kalhu was of comparable size and status and its function as the capital has already been noted. If a third city of similar size and magnificence is to be sought the choice must fall on the great new capital with its magnificent palace which Sargon II failed to complete before his death in battle in 705, the city which he named Dur-Sharrukin, "Fort Sargon". Scholars have considered this possibility on general and political grounds, notably Van der Toorn, who however was perplexed by the lack of harmony with the Hebrew name, and especially A. van der Kooij, who regards *resen*, in Hebrew "bridle", as a symbolic name for Dur-Sharrukin, the embodiment of Assyrian imperialist oppression.[6] While van der Kooij has offered a

---

[6] Van der Toorn, 1990, pp. 5–6; A. van der Kooij, "The City of Babel and Assyrian Imperialism", in A. Lemaire (ed.), *Congress Volume Leiden 2004* (VTSup 109; Leiden, 2006), pp. 14–15.

fascinating interpretation of the Babel and Nimrod episodes as profound critiques of the Assyrian regime, it is difficult to envisage the
listing of a group of cities, all bastions of an imperialist regime, by a
writer who invests only one of these cities with a symbolic name. In
the paper referred to above I suggested that רסן is all that has survived of an original דר-סרגן, as Dur-Sharrukin would have been written about 700 B.C. in Hebrew script. This implies considerable textual
damage. One can imagine typical scribal errors and perhaps physical
accidents harming manuscripts over a period of time. Such misfor-
tunes are by no means unknown in textual history. For MT I would
invite comparison of 2 Sam. 6:5 with 1 Chr. 13:8. This solution has
now been proposed independently by Y. Levin.[7]

We now have the desired two sets of three cities and it is suggested
that רחבת עיר was no part of the original Nimrod passage, which
concluded with the sentence "and he built Nineveh and Kalah and
Dur-Sargon". Subsequent expansion was contingent on the acceptance
of kullānāh in v. 10 as kalnēh, thus producing a fourth "Babylonian"
city. At this point a copyist noticed the imbalance between the Babylonian and Assyrian cities. (Of course one might think of a dissatisfied
reader who turned glossator – but to effect the further expansion as
it now exists he would have but little space at his disposal. A copyist would have far more scope.) The fourth Assyrian city inserted to
balance the numbers is the mysterious רחבת עיר, which, as we have
claimed, was not a city name at all. For the moment we suggest the
translation "city outskirts, suburbs" and will return to the matter after
a discussion of the expanded structure of the entire passage. The new
addition is really an attachment to the name "Nineveh", "Nineveh and
its outlying districts" or the like. Balancing the number of cities is not
the copyist/interpolator's only purpose: he adds that Dur-Sharrukin is
between Nineveh and Kalah and that the entire complex – Nineveh
and its outlying districts, Kalah and Dur-Sharrukin between Nineveh
and Kalah – is the great city. His purpose is to explain the prodigious
size of Nineveh in the Book of Jonah, where nearly every mention
of Nineveh is accompanied by the phrase "the great city". It was not
just Nineveh itself which took three days to cross – it was the great
Nineveh complex. This of course is the old idea of the "tetrapolis",

---

[7] Y. Levin, "Nimrod the Mighty, King of Kish, King of Sumer and Akkad", VT 52
(2002), pp. 350–66.

once very popular but now much out of favour. However, a little careful thought (and attention to the Book of Jonah) will reveal that this idea provides a satisfactory solution, whereas the attribution of greatness to any one of the individual cities is pointless.

As the text stands the clause "that is the great city" might refer to Dur-Sargon (if the corruption had not yet taken place) or to Kalah. In this case there would be an implication that there was a general notion that there existed a great city but there was uncertainty as to its identity: not a very likely situation. Further, it is unlikely that either of these cities should be singled out for its grandeur as against Nineveh. Indeed, it is sometimes suggested that the phrase is misplaced and should be attached to Nineveh. That also is pointless. At no time could any Mesopotamian, Israelite or other denizen of the area need to be informed of Nineveh's greatness, or superior greatness. The only other syntactic possibility is that the phrase should refer to the entire chain of cities built by Nimrod, as detailed from v. 11b to the end of 12a, with the intention described above. Further, the purpose of stating that Dur-Sharrukin was situated between Nineveh and Kalah was to stress that the four cities – or locations, if the copyist did not intend that רחבת עיר should be understood as a city – constituted a cohesive, tightly-knit complex. We cannot know whether the copyist was aware that Dur-Sharrukin could be considered to be situated between Nineveh and Kalah only in the vaguest of senses.

This section cannot be concluded without a word on the size of Nineveh according to the Book of Jonah. There were no cities in the ancient world which took three days to cross. Nineveh was 16 km. in circumference with an area of 1550 or 1850 acres according to various conjectures. The author wished to portray a city of immense proportions. His purpose must be the subject of another paper. At any rate such a city could not be a familiar one. If it had long lain in ruins there could be no assertion of disbelief. At every mention of Nineveh the phrase "the great city" is affixed except in Jonah 3:3–7 where the multiple repetitions would have been intolerable. Even there, when Jonah arrives at Nineveh it is again asserted: "and Nineveh was a great city...". Besides the occurrence discussed in this article the phrase appears elsewhere in the Old Testament only with reference to Jerusalem at Jer. 22:8 (and this would appear to be of significance for Jonah). Without the article the phrase appears at Josh. 10:2, but differently. Evidently the highly symbolic significance of Nineveh has escaped our copyist of Gen. 10. His understanding is literal and he is at great pains to show that the size of Nineveh, when correctly understood, is not an element of a tall story or a deception. The extreme rarity of the phrase "the great city" would seem to strengthen our explanation of its use in the Nimrod passage.

Of the residual problems concerning the Nimrod passage the most intractable would still appear to be the "Cushite issue". The problem of the entity רחבת עיר seems a little easier to handle once it is accepted that despite the עיר element, or perhaps because of it, one should not seek to find the actual name of a city, or some equivalent to it, behind the constituent words, in view of the inconsistency with the other place-names and in the realization that the element has been introduced owing to the faulty understanding of a copyist. Once, finally, the desire to find a rational relationship of composition and redaction is relaxed in favour of the notion of a rolling corpus, the stages leading to the final form of the passage are easier to discern.

None of the attempts to solve the Cush-Nimrod relationship seem to me any easier to accept. It has occurred to me that if the writer who knew something of Akkad, whose primordial ties with the city of Kish were well known, were thinking of the Mesopotamian flood stories as he wrote about the emergence of Nimrod's kingdom after the Biblical deluge, he might have remembered that after the Mesopotamian flood the kingship was again lowered from heaven – at Kish! But, as with similar possible connections, the Kish-Cush mechanism, if it existed, is now concealed from view behind the text which lies before us.

After looking at the texts again it does seem as though *rebītu* did mean both "streets" and "outlying suburbs" or the like. Whether the inventor of רחבת עיר really derived inspiration from this source cannot be made out. Our posited copyist worked after the composition of the Book of Jonah. Could he possibly have known that Dur-Sharrukin was erected in the *rebītu* of Nineveh? Or was there an intermediate stage in the development of the rolling corpus which I have failed to discern?

This brings us back to the process by which our passage assumed its final form. Without including the last possibility just adumbrated I offer the following stages:

1. In the days of the supremacy of Ninurta but possibly towards the end of those days, when Dur-Sharrukin had been built but left uncompleted, a writer of Yahwist persuasions wrote of a hero (incidentally, a title of Ninurta) named Nimrod, who founded a king-

dom in Babylonia with three main cities and then moved to Assyria and built three more.

2. A later Yahwist added a verse removing all hint of possibly divine traits in the persona of Nimrod.

3. A word in the text was misunderstood and an imbalance in the number of cities thus created.

4. A copyist, strongly influenced by the Book of Jonah, but concerned with the alleged prodigious size of Nineveh, revised the portion of the text concerned with the Assyrian cities, redressing the balance by creating a new place-name and editing in order to produce a tetrapolis which he then asserted to be the "great city", Nineveh, of Jonah.

5. By scribal error or physical damage, or both, the name of the city Dur-Sharrukin/דר סרגן was reduced beyond recognition.

POWER OR INHERITANCE: A CONSTRUCTIVE COMPARISON OF GENESIS 16 AND GENESIS 21*

Ina Willi-Plein

I

The two tales of Hagar's expulsion from Abraham's family in Gen. 16 and 21 have generally been regarded as (literary) doublets going back to the same oral tradition or motif. Even so, there are still various options to explain their relation to each other. Following the classical documentary hypothesis, most scholars have found a "J"-text in Gen. 16 and a separate "E" version in Gen. 21. Those who harbour doubts about an independent "E"-narration would still regard Gen. 21 as part of a consistent layer or at least of a group of texts that were added to "J" in order to complete a new literary unity "JE" or the like.[1] More recent discussions about the formation of the Pentateuch have focused more on form-critical problems, on the transmission of oral or literary tradition complexes, and on the process of "redaction".[2] Only a strictly "synchronic" reading of the final edited form of Genesis would, however, avoid any hypothesis as to how the texts came together; but even

---

* The desire to honour a great scholar whose work has lastingly advanced the international study of the Old Testament is stronger than the embarrassment of doing so in my poor English.

[1] We will not discuss the current debate about Pentateuchal criticism here. For a recent survey including most of the new approaches see E. Zenger et al., *Einleitung in das Alte Testament*, 5th ed. (Stuttgart, 2004), pp. 60–187. A thorough discussion (and a new hypothesis) was presented by R. N. Whybray, *The Making of the Pentateuch: A Methodological Study* (JSOTSup 53; Sheffield, 1987): cf. the fair review by J. A. Emerton, *VT* 39 (1989), pp. 110–16, who rightly comments that (p. 113) "within each of the postulated sources the alleged additional repetitions…add further information". Recently J. Jeremias, "Gen. 20–22 als theologisches Programm", in M. Beck and U. Schorn (eds.), *Auf dem Wege zur Endgestalt von Genesis bis II Regum* (FS H.-Ch. Schmidt 65; Berlin and New York, 2006), pp. 59–73, has observed a conceptual unity or even a parallelism (p. 60) in Gen. 20; 21:8–21; 22:1–14, 19.

[2] For a harsh criticism of an exegetical concept of "redaction" see J. Van Seters, *The Edited Bible. The Curious History of the "Editor" in Biblical Criticism* (Winona Lake, Ind., 2006).

then it would be necessary to understand their divergent views on the patriarchal tradition and their position in the biblical book as such.

Leaving aside the recent discussions about Pentateuchal criticism, in what follows I will compare the focus of the two narratives, which I regard as part of a literary unity composed before the addition of the "P"-material. In calling this layer a "JE"-stratum I hope not to deviate too much from John Emerton's ideas.[3]

Whether or not one accepts the general view of the formation of the patriarchal narrative presupposed in this article is of little importance for the following argument. Any methodological approach requires a comparison of both texts in order to come to a better understanding of each of them, but also to elucidate their historical and social implications and the pathways they open to the readers' understanding. Such a search for the implicit reader will allow us to take a fresh look at the authors' own world and time.

II

To begin with Genesis 16:1–2, 4–9, 11–15,[4] the narrative as part of the basic Genesis story ("J") ties in with the end of chapter 13, Abraham's separation from Lot and God's promise to give him the land through which he is walking (Gen. 13:14a, 17).[5] Within this basic frame the plot is rather simple: "Sarai, Abram's wife, had not borne a child..."; so, on seeing that she was barren and would probably not bear a son

---

[3] J. A. Emerton, "The Priestly Writer in Genesis", *JTS* N.S. 39 (1988), pp. 381–400.

[4] Verse 3, which aims to present the chronological context of v. 2, is probably due to the or a Priestly writer ("P"). Verse 10, too, seems to be a later addition, as is indicated by the *inclusio* of "and YHWH's messenger said unto her" in v. 10 and v. 11. The promise הרבה ארבה את זרעך is an adapted quotation of Gen. 22:17aα.

[5] Even if, as J. A. Emerton, "The Origin of the Promises to the Patriarchs in the Older Sources of the Book of Genesis", *VT* 32 (1982), pp. 14–32, argues with good reason (p. 19), one has to accept that it "has been widely recognized that the promises in vv. 14–17 are not original", I think vv. 13, 14a, 17 should not be excluded from the basic text; Abraham settled in the land of Canaan (13:12), and after Lot was separated from him, God told him (vv. 14a, 17) to "walk through the land...", and (v. 18) "then" (narrative tense) "he camped/put his tent up and dwelt at the oaks of Mamre...", i.e. at the centre of the Abraham tradition, where we find him in Gen. 18. But if Gen. 13:13–17 were secondary, the plot of Gen. 16 would be even more simple. In any case the reader would learn what happened after Lot's family had disappeared.

to her husband – as is expressed in her first speech to Abraham[6] (v. 2) – she decided to offer him her handmaid Hagar as a surrogate mother. That Hagar[7] is called "Egyptian" may in this context be a rather general description of her (or her descendants') affinity to Egyptian-dominated territory in the southern desert area. In the description of her characteristics a special Ishmaelite history of transmission connected with their descent from Abraham may have left its mark. Under the given circumstances the expression cannot be interpreted as indicating that Hagar was a "foreigner"; for in Gen. 16 Abraham would be a foreigner himself.

The possibility of surrogate mothership, different from adoption, is indicated in Mesopotamian sources as well as in the Jacob narrative of the Old Testament (Gen. 30:3, 9). Although it is no personal shame[8] to remain childless, it is a cause of sorrow and of course a severe problem for an isolated couple in foreign surroundings. A second marriage would be possible for a man, but certainly not for Abraham as he is depicted here.

Sarah hopes to "be built up" (בנה nif'al) by the birth of a son (בן), as she puts it in her first speech to Abraham, perhaps citing a common folk-etymology. At any rate, it is Sarah's wish to give birth to a son of Abraham's, and there is no doubt that the handmaid's son will be regarded as hers. Sarah takes the initiative to decide on her own and avoid the risk of being confronted with an uncertain future. She will remain the mistress of the future family as much as Abraham will remain their "lord" (אדון, Gen. 18:12):[9] The story has to be interpreted against the background of patriarchal family law.

The difference between שפחה and אמה has often been discussed, one of the most satisfactory explanations still being that provided by

---

[6] Except in direct quotations I shall use the forms "Abraham" and "Sarah" consistently.

[7] This is not the place to discuss onomastic questions, but Hagar is certainly not an Egyptian name.

[8] As is sometimes wrongly suggested in exegetical literature. In Isa. 54:4, בשת עלומיך "the shame of thy youth" and חרפת אלמנותיך "the reproach of thy widowhood" cannot be interpreted as a reproach for having remained childless. It is Zion who is addressed here, and in the following verses (5–7) the metaphor is decoded: The idea is the shame of having been left by her husband.

[9] ואדני זקן in Gen. 18:12 refers to Abraham as her husband and the "lord" of the family.

A. Jepsen.[10] According to Jepsen the main difference lies in the fact that a שפחה is an unmarried maid belonging to the housewife, whereas an אמה is a female slave under the dominion and even the sexual disposition of the housefather or his sons. So an אמה may be or become a concubine, while the term שפחה has no such connotation. Although Jepsen's observations work in most cases, there are still some doubts left in others which cannot be explained by a late usage that no longer marked the difference, as for instance in Abigail's speech to David (1 Sam. 25). Far from listing a range of synonyms, Abigail employs a variety of terms as a rhetorical device.[11] After initially presenting herself as "your female slave" (אמה) in the established manner of self-abasing courtesy, in v. 27 and in her last reply to David's proposal of marriage (v. 4) she changes her role to that of a שפחה – a term which is either ambiguous in the present context or otherwise slightly out of place; for the שפחה in Gen. 16 is a woman's servant.

To complete the argument, one may highlight the etymological connection between שפחה and משפחה, the latter being the term for a family in the widest sense, a group of relatives, kinship beyond the narrow limits of a single family as a "father's house": משפחה seems to be the equivalent of a "clan" or a still larger group of relatives and, as is also important, an entity of potential endogamy. In Amos 3:1, 2 it is nearly synonymous to "people" (עם). The same meaning seems to be represented in Ugaritic by šph,[12] which shares the same etymological root. There is something like a cross reference between Ugaritic šph and Hebrew משפחה and vice versa, inasmuch as *špht would be the single example of what šph means.

Thus we may presume that שפחה is a rather unspecific term for a female person of kin who is living without a position of her own in the family, and under the power of her and the whole house's mistress. What the שפחה does will be regarded as the mistress's business. Even

---

[10] A. Jepsen, "Amah und Schiphchah", *VT* 8 (1958), pp. 293–97, with the postscript, ibid., p. 426.

[11] For further discussion see I. Willi-Plein, "Abigajil und die Kunst der Rede. Zum Informationsgehalt der wörtlichen Reden in der Davidshausgeschichte", in Th. Naumann and R. Hunziker-Rodewald (eds.), *Diasynchron. Beiträge zur Exegese, Theologie und Rezeption der Hebräischen Bibel* (FS W. Dietrich 65; Stuttgart, 2009), pp. 417–32.

[12] G. del Olmo Lete and J. Sanmartín, *A Dictionary of the Ugaritic Language in the Alphabetic Tradition*, 2nd ed. (= DUL), (HdO 1/67; Leiden and Boston, 2004), p. 835.

the father of the family, the patriarch, cannot and will not take charge of his wife's שפחה (16:6).

Why, then, does Sarah grow angry about Hagar? In order to understand this development, we have to look at the other side of the coin, the position of the "mistress" (גבירה). In the historical context of the pre-exilic Judaean monarchy the term is used as a title for the queen mother who holds some sort of informal, yet well established, office in the royal family, and in the state.[13] It is not the king's wife but his mother who has the highest rank after him, and he has to pay obeisance to her as the only person of higher status within the family (1 Kings 2:19). Thus, the family from which the גבירה is descended will have influence upon, and hidden control of, the actual king's politics, so that the leading families and their tradition will be respected.[14] In general the גבירה is the mother of the firstborn or the eldest surviving son of his father/predecessor. The suspense in David's history is maintained by the open question, "Who will sit on your majesty's throne?" (1 Kings 1:20), for there are many sons and several mothers of possible successors. In the end Bathsheba wins out and takes her place on the throne of the king's mother, at the right hand of her son Solomon (1 Kings 2:19).

In contrast to the root שפח a noun of a root *gbr* corresponding to גבירה is not attested at Ugarit.[15] At first glance one might conclude that the social conditions in that Late Bronze Age city kingdom differed from those in the early monarchy of Judah and Jerusalem. But the feminine *'adt* is rather widely attested.[16] The king's mother is referred to as *(l) mlkt 'umy 'adty*, "(to) the queen, my mother and my lady" (*KTU* 2.82:2), and to her obeisance is paid (*KTU* 2.12:12).[17] Ugaritic *'adn*, which etymologically and semantically corresponds to Hebrew אדון,[18] is derived from the root 'DN, which is present in

---

[13] H. Donner, "Art und Herkunft des Amtes der Königinmutter im Alten Testament" (1958), in Donner, *Aufsätze zum Alten Testament aus vier Jahrzehnten* (BZAW 224; Berlin and New York, 1994), pp. 1–24.

[14] Cf. R. Kessler, *Staat und Gesellschaft im vorexilischen Juda vom 8. Jh. bis zum Exil* (VTSup 47; Leiden, 1992) and M. Niemann, *Herrschaft, Königtum und Staat. Skizzen zur soziokulturellen Entwicklung im monarchischen Israel* (FAT 6; Tübingen, 1993).

[15] Only perhaps as part of a personal name: *DUL*, p. 293.

[16] *DUL*, p. 23.

[17] For the formula "I bow before my lady" (*KTU* 2.12:7 etc.) and its pragmatic meaning see Donner, p. 16.

[18] For אדון in our context (Gen. 18:12) see above, n. 9.

Ugaritic *'idn* ("authorization, full powers"),[19] and in *'adt.* Ugaritic *'adn* means "lord", "father (of a family)", or "master".[20] Thus, the Ugaritic root 'DN has, with respect to social relations in a family, the same connotation as Hebrew גבר.

In Hebrew the root גבר denotes the power of a chief position in the family. The masculine adjective – morphologically an (adjectival) verbal noun of the pattern qaṭīl or qiṭīl[21] which here "refers to the state proper",[22] especially of holders of established functions (e.g. נגיד, נשׂיא, משׁיח) – describes a person as head of the family: "Be a גביר for your brothers, may your mother's sons pay obeisance to you" is part of the blessing for the firstborn who will take his father's position (Gen. 27:29).

Essentially, then, the role of the queen mother is nothing but the role of any family "lord"'s mother, albeit of course in a very special family. In Genesis 16 Sarah has been the גבירה for the female part of the household although she is not yet mother of a family. That is why the problem of her own dignity arises when her handmaid is pregnant from her husband: will the position of the גבירה pass on to Hagar once she has possibly given birth to a son? Hagar seems to think so and no longer feels herself subordinated to Sarah; she despises her mistress (v. 4). But then Abraham clarifies the situation; nothing has changed: Hagar will remain Sarah's maid, Sarah Hagar's mistress (and, we may add, the maid's son will be regarded as the son of the mistress).

Hagar does not need to be expelled; she flees in order to be free. YHWH's messenger finds her in the wilderness, and addresses her as "Hagar, Sarai's maid". When she explains that she is fleeing from her

---

[19] *DUL*, p. 19.

[20] For the meaning of Ugaritic *'adn* see *DUL*, pp. 18–19, and J. Huehnergard, *Ugaritic Vocabulary in Syllabic Transcription* (Atlanta, GA, 1987), p. 104, referring to *'adn* (or *'ad*), "father", and his commentary, 24.3 with note 2 (p. 48), to the effect that he is "not convinced by the suggestion of M. Weippert, UF 6, 415–19, that Ugaritic distinguished /*'addānu/ 'father' from /'adānu/ 'lord'." He then sums up that "Ugar. adn reflects a single word /*'adānu/ which means both 'lord' and 'father'." We may add here that Ug. *'adānu as well as Hebrew אדון means a "father" or "head of the family (including servants, brothers, and unmarried sisters etc.)". Social structures are thus shaped by family structures.

[21] See H. Bauer and P. Leander, *Historische Grammatik der hebräischen Sprache* (Halle 1922; repr. Hildesheim etc. 1991), §61C.g.2 (p. 470) and 3 (p. 471).

[22] B. K. Waltke and M. O'Connor, *An Introduction to Biblical Hebrew Syntax* (Winona Lake, 1990), 37.4.e (p. 620).

mistress, he demands that she surrender herself[23] to ("under the hand of") her mistress, who will remain her גבירה. Only after giving this order does he announce to Hagar that she will have a son, and he does so by using the pattern of a birth oracle, combined with a tribal saying on Ishmael.

Hagar's answer is the aetiological naming of the place where she has "seen" what in similar cases, when experienced by a patriarch, would be a typical revelation of "the god of the father". In this respect the happy ending may perhaps reflect traditions of a queen's extraordinary position in proto-Arabian society. In fact, Hagar will not be the גבירה of Abraham's family, but the head of her own.

Genesis 16:1–2, 4–9, 11–15 is narrated from Sarah's point of view. Despite using her maid as a surrogate mother she will not lose her position as גבירה. On the way a potential problem of matrimonial law has been solved. To be sure, "the struggle between the women is a regular power struggle, unaffected by love inasmuch as it is centered round motherhood and its attendant benefits",[24] but this summary by A. Brenner fits only Genesis 16, not Genesis 21. What will happen after the parents' death? Who will be the heir? What about changing social conditions with different constellations of family law? These are some of the questions that the author of Genesis 21 is considering. Above all he has to do so because, according to the basic narrative ("J"), Isaac's birth has been announced in Genesis 18, and in 21:1–2 ("J") we learn that finally Sarah has given birth to the promised son. Obviously, 21:3–5 are a P addition to vv. 1–2, possibly replacing the original account of Isaac's naming by his mother as explained in vv. 6–7 ("J").

III

Genesis 21:7 is the anchor point for the story of Hagar's final expulsion (vv. 8–21). In contrast to Genesis 16, it is not so much a story about Hagar as one about Ishmael and Isaac, seen first with Sarah's,

---

[23] The root ענה seems to be the special term for subordination, not for cruel treatment.

[24] A. Brenner, "Female Social Behaviour: Two Descriptive Patterns within the 'Birth of the Hero' Paradigm", VT 36 (1986), pp. 257–73 (p. 272). Brenner subsumes both chapters under the same type (1a) of the paradigm, i.e. she does not see a difference between them.

then with Abraham's, and finally with Hagar's eyes. To her the messenger delivers an oracle of assurance (v. 17b), but what follows
(v. 18) is not so much new information as new interpretation of 16:12
(combined with 12:2).

An important device to highlight the different perspectives is the
sequence of the three "Leitwort" terms: יֶלֶד ("born", "child": vv. 8
[based on v. 7], 14, 15, 16), בֵּן ("son", vv. 10, 11, 13), and נַעַר ("boy",
vv. 12, 17, 18, 19, 20).[25] For his mother, the child is above all a יֶלֶד, the
child she has borne and nursed. For his father he is the "son" (בֵּן) –
and Sarah tries in vain to loosen this connection between father and
son by referring to Ishmael as "her (the servant's) son". Finally, in a
more "objective" perspective he is, as long as he is not an independent
man or family father, a "boy" (נַעַר) in the widest sense of the word.

The narrator of Gen. 21:8–21 and his audience have read or heard
Genesis 16, but they are living in a world that has changed. Some
aspects of the Hagar story have to be rewritten, but not replaced. The
main focus (though not the topic itself) is now totally different. When
things are seen with the eyes of Sarah as Isaac's mother, it is Isaac's
position which is in danger, not Hagar's or Ishmael's. The moment to
realize this is Isaac's weaning.

Abraham is giving a party on this occasion.[26] He is the proud father
of a son of his old age who will now, at probably about three years
old, leave the narrow contact with his mother and gradually enter the
men's world under his father's control. It is a moment of transition,
comparable for instance to the occasion when formerly in Europe (in
the German countryside until about the twenties of the last century)
a little boy got his first trousers instead of a skirt. For his mother it
is a moment of farewell, of awareness that from now on he will no
longer be nursed and protected by herself.[27] This is exactly the point
at which she sees "the son of Hagar the Egyptian[28] whom she had

---

[25] It is I. Fischer, *Die Erzeltern Israels. Feministisch-theologische Studien zu Genesis
12–36* (BZAW 222; Berlin and New York, 1994), p. 307, who has drawn special attention to the relevance of the three terms and their relation to each other.

[26] Whether this is a common custom at the narrator's time can be left open here;
at least it seems not to be unusual to mark the transition by some rite of passage
(1 Sam. 1:22–28).

[27] Cf. 1 Sam. 1:22–28. Hannah brings little Samuel to Eli when she has weaned
him.

[28] That she is Sarah's handmaid is no longer mentioned.

borne to Abraham" making jokes.[29] There need not be anything disgraceful in what she observes: the elder brother is perhaps just teasing the younger one who until then has only been his mother's baby, as would be quite natural. But Sarah realizes that there will always be the problem that Ishmael is Abraham's firstborn son: "The son of this bondwoman shall not inherit with my son, with Isaac!" This is a very personal and emotional statement. Now it is perfectly clear that her handmaid's son is not hers. Nevertheless he is the firstborn of this father, and so there will be the danger for Isaac not to succeed his father in the *patria potestas* after Abraham's death.

N. Lohfink thinks that ירשׁ here means "to take the position of the head of the family",[30] but the argument might be circular, for it is supported only by 21:10 and Gen. 15:3–4. In general ירשׁ qal seems to describe a legal claim of ownership and the act of taking possession or actuating it (1 Kings 21:15, 19).[31] If v. 10 refers directly to Genesis 15, as may be supposed, it also contains a reference to the promise of the land.[32] In Genesis 15 ירשׁ qal is used as a keyword (vv. 3, 4, 7, 8).

The only way to get rid of Ishmael will be Abraham's "divorce" (גרשׁ, v. 10) from Hagar. Hagar is now seen as a legal co-wife of Abraham and as such she is the mother of a rival to Isaac. That the question of inheritance is brought up is surprising enough in the context of the Abraham Cycle, for Abraham is still a foreigner in the land. Only when we think of what is written in Gen. 15:3–4 can we understand the connection of Abraham's "seed" with his "heir" (v. 12). This is, indeed, a solid basis for assuming that Gen. 21 goes back to a writer identical with, or at least closely connected to, the author of Genesis 15* and also Genesis 20*.

The author of the second Hagar narrative lives in later times and in different social conditions from the author of Gen. 16. The old institution of surrogate mothership by a maid of the wife has disappeared;

---

[29] The meaning of צחק pi. has often and controversially been discussed; it is the same term that is used for David's dancing before the ark (2 Sam. 6). In both cases there need not be anything indecent in it, although the occasion or the special circumstances may seem unfitting.

[30] N. Lohfink, ירשׁ jāraš", *ThWAT* 3 (1982), pp. 953–85, esp. p. 967: "Es geht um Sukzession des Familienchefs". Prov. 30:23, שׁפחה כי־תירשׁ גברתה, is part of the proverbial description of a topsy-turvy world.

[31] Cf. H. Donner, *Gesenius*[18], 2, pp. 500–02.

[32] For the promises see Emerton, 1982 (cf. n. 5).

Sarah now calls Ishmael "the son of the woman-servant" in order to avoid calling him "your son". Yet his father sees him as his son. Hence Abraham needs a special revelation to hear that "after Isaac your seed shall be called" (v. 12).[33] In other words, the lineage of promised blessing will be continued by Isaac although Ishmael is Abraham's "seed", too, and will also be made a nation (v. 13). One might even detect here a hidden allusion in advance, a prolepsis, to the problem of primogeniture that will be so important for the later patriarchal period.

J. A. Emerton has shown that "the promises of a son to Abraham in…xviii 10, 14, and of the land in xii 7…are original" in their literary context J, and that "so too are the promises in xv 4–5, 18, but the chapter is late",[34] or, more precisely, that for the latter "affinities with Deuteronomy and other evidence point to a relatively late date", viz. to later pre-exilic times.[35]

I have argued that Genesis 21:8–21 is answering questions that may have arisen in the years between the time of "J" (which I would like to call the "Judaean Grundschicht") and that of the author of chapter 21. Both narratives are rooted in the same traditio-historical complex concerning Ishmael and Hagar, but Genesis 21 is a thorough re-reading of Genesis 16:1–2, 4–9, 11–15, caused by social and political changes. The focus of the story has changed: whereas in chapter 16 the position of the גבירה had been at stake, in chapter 21 it is that of the firstborn as opposed to another son of the same father.

It has been shown that in order fully to understand Gen. 21 one also has to know Genesis 15. A detailed comparison between chapters 15 and 21 would be rewarding, but it cannot be undertaken here. It would show that characters and their emotions are drawn individually in chapter 15 just as has been observed in chapter 21. In my opinion the most interesting observation is the fact that Genesis 16 "works" without any preceding promise of the son and is even more plausible then, as it is just another story of separation after the first one, regarding Lot, in chapter 13. Both are means of concentrating on Abraham's line of blessing.

---

[33] *Beth realisationis*, according to E. Jenni, *Die hebräischen Präpositionen. 1: Die Präposition Beth* (Stuttgart, Berlin and Köln, 1992), p. 168 (no. 1956).
[34] Emerton, 1982, p. 18.
[35] Emerton, 1982, p. 17 with n. 2 (bibl.).

Genesis 21 is, indeed, focused on the promised son Isaac and his role as the next "father" of Israel. In order to let the promise become true, Abraham has to follow God's command and dismiss his son Ishmael together with Hagar. Perhaps that is why, according to the same author,[36] in Genesis 22 he will have to show that he would not withhold his "unique son" Isaac either.

---

[36] I would not, in fact, call him an "editor" or a "redactor", because I presume that these chapters belong to a literary unit which may still – following the main ideas that were presented together with the term "Jehovist" by J. Wellhausen, *Prolegomena zur Geschichte Israels* (6th ed., 1905; repr. Berlin and Leipzig, 1927), p. 8, n. 2 – be entitled "JE". This abbreviation need not be decoded by the original (and problematic) "Jehovist"; rather, it can be interpreted as a symbol for a "JErusalem-oriented" history (of Israel's origins) that may have been composed in the late pre-exilic period, probably in connection with circles that were influenced by the precursors of Deuteronomy. For the character of Wellhausen's "JE" see R. Smend, *Die Entstehung des Alten Testaments* (ThW 1; Stuttgart, Berlin, Köln and Mainz, 1978), §11, esp. p. 64. It was the literary unit "JE" that the "P" writer(s) probably read and interpreted.

THE NABATAEAN "GOD OF THE FATHERS"

John F. Healey

In 1929 Albrecht Alt, in his ground-shifting essay on "Der Gott der Väter",[1] invoked the epigraphic evidence provided by the Nabataean inscriptions to support his argument that the Hebrew patriarchal narratives showed traces of earlier nomadic religious tradition. This approach combined the nineteenth/early twentieth-century interest in casting light from Arabia on the patriarchal narratives with the early twentieth-century form-critical effort to get back to the earliest forms and elements of the texts. Subsequent scholarship has thrown doubt on many of the basic theses and conclusions of Alt and his followers, such as the assumption that the family unit formed the basis of the origins of Israelite religion[2] and even his minimal confidence over the recovery of history from the texts.[3] The Ugaritic texts were published soon after Alt wrote his essay and patriarchal religion could then be seen in the new light of El-worship.[4] In the context of these developments the Nabataean evidence was marginalized on the grounds that it is very late in date. It receives scant attention in later discussions.

I cannot contribute usefully to the discussion of the nomadic or other origins of Israelite religion or the traditions of the Book of Genesis, but it is noteworthy that the patriarchs are *presented* in the Pentateuch as settling nomads, whether this is historically authentic information or not. This concept certainly became part of the Israelite self-understanding: "A wandering Aramaean was my father" (Deut. 26:5). Several of Alt's fundamental points remain valid: in the narratives available

---

[1] A. Alt, *Der Gott der Vater* (BWANT 3/12; Stuttgart, 1929), ET "The God of the Fathers", in *Essays on Old Testament History and Religion* (Oxford, 1966), pp. 1–77. I first read the Alt essay in 1970, soon after I met John Emerton and was attending his lectures in Cambridge. It is a pleasure to dedicate this short paper to him in recognition of all the help and encouragement he has given me over so many years.

[2] M. Köckert, *Vätergott und Väterverheißungen: Eine Auseinandersetzung mit Albrecht Alt und seinen Erben* (FRLANT 142; Göttingen, 1988), pp. 137–41.

[3] See the review in C. Westermann, *Genesis 12–36: A Commentary* (translated by J. J. Scullion from *Genesis 12–36* [BKAT; Neukirchen, 1981]; London, 1986), pp. 105–13.

[4] Westermann, *Genesis*, p. 106.

to us patriarchal religion includes the habit of referring to the divinity as "the God of my/your father", patriarchal religion is presented
as different from later Yahwism and the tradition claimed that the
self-revelation of God as Yahweh took place at a particular point after
the patriarchal age (Exod. 3 and 6): in theory his name was unknown
earlier. The undermining of Alt's wider conclusions does not necessarily render the Nabataean material irrelevant to the understanding
of what the biblical authors had in mind (even if that was only an
imagined tale of origins). What I propose to do here is to look again
at the Nabataean evidence, without implying anything about the real
nomadic or other origins of Israelite religion.

The phenomenon which drew Alt's attention was the habit, in the
Pentateuchal texts, of referring to the god of the patriarchs as the god
of a named individual. It is summed up by the phrase "the god of the
fathers", though it mainly occurs in the form "the god of my/your
father" (cf. Gen. 31:5, 29, 42; 49:25; 50:17) and in the separate titles
"the god of Abraham", "the god of Isaac", and "the god of Jacob" (Gen.
31:5, 29, 42; Exod. 3:6), as well as a number of associated epithets, such
as "the Fear of Isaac" and "the Mighty One of Jacob" (Gen. 31:42, 53).
We may note also Gen. 26:24; 28:13; 32:10; 46:1, 3.

There are two elements to this kind of usage. Firstly, the god being
referred to remains, at the moment the phrase in question is used,
anonymous. This anonymity need not in itself have any particular
significance. The title "Emeritus Regius Professor of Hebrew at Cambridge" is anonymous in itself, but in a particular context, as in this
volume, there is nothing mysterious about who is being referred
to! The title "the god of Abraham" is not of itself a circumlocution
or euphemism in which the divinity's true name is being avoided.
Clearly, in the biblical context, there is nothing taboo or secret about
which god is being referred to in the narratives in question and Alt
discussed the specific cases where the phrase is immediately explained
by the use of the tetragrammaton (Gen. 28:13) or by reference to El
Shadday (Gen. 49:25). Historiographically, on the JEDP analysis the
setting aside of the name Yahweh by the Elohist tradition until it was
revealed at Horeb/Sinai is a separate issue: it is a literary device, since
the reader knew all along which god was involved. The J author (if
he existed) had no inhibition about using the name Yahweh from the
start and does not hold the reader in imaginative suspense. It would
certainly be very speculative, and played no part in Alt's argument, to

see here any connection with the separate issue of the later traditional Jewish use of a substitute for the divine name.

The other, and more important, element in this usage is the associating of the deity in question with a particular ancestor or particular ancestors. The implication here might be that this kind of locution reflected the fact that the deity in question belonged to a particular type of personal or family or tribal deity. In principle this might be the case in either a monotheistic, henotheistic, or polytheistic context. In the case of the last two it might be conceded by a worshipper of the family god that other families or tribes had their own deities. Here we note Gen. 31:53: "May the god of Abraham and the god of Nahor judge between us". In Alt's discussion (unaffected by the discoveries which were about to take place at Ugarit) the gods of the fathers are contrasted with the local Els and Baals of pre-Yahwistic Palestine, the gods of the fathers coming to be closely integrated into the Yahwistic tradition. This is the perspective represented already in Exod. 6:2ff. On this analysis the family gods of Abraham and of Isaac and of Jacob (certainly of Nahor) might even have been originally separate deities who were retrospectively subsumed within a monotheistic historical perspective.

Another, slightly different, interpretation of "the god of Abraham" *et al.* might see here a reference to a *personal* god, of the kind known particularly from Mesopotamia and frequently referred to in works on Mesopotamian religion.[5] This aspect was fully explored by R. Albertz.[6]

Wyatt's attempt[7] to turn all the references to the God of the Fathers into references to El seems to me unconvincing, simply because of the number of adjustments to the texts and special pleadings which are involved. Albertz similarly doubts some of the eliminations of the

---

[5] T. Jacobsen, *The Treasures of Darkness: a History of Mesopotamian Religion* (New Haven and London, 1976), pp. 145–64; J. Black and A. Green, *Gods, Demons and Symbols of Ancient Mesopotamia: An Illustrated Dictionary* (London, 1982), p. 148; J. Bottéro, *Religion in Ancient Mesopotamia* (translated by T. L. Fagan, Chicago and London, 2001), pp. 91, 165; Westermann, *Genesis*, p. 108.

[6] R. Albertz, *Persönliche Frömmigkeit und offizielle Religion: religionsinterner Pluralismus in Israel und Babylon* (Calwer Theologische Monographien, Reihe A, Bibelwissenschaft, Bd. 9; Stuttgart, 1978).

[7] N. Wyatt, "The Problem of the 'God of the Fathers'", *ZAW* 90 (1978), pp. 101–4.

same kind advocated by M. Köckert.[8] Wyatt's final point (p. 104) that
the patriarchal texts are late and therefore we should not seek analogies
with the (nomadic) gods of the fathers of other traditions – if Alt was
in his mind, he must have meant the Nabataean tradition – overlooks
the fact that the Nabataeans were near contemporaries of the authors
of at least some of the patriarchal narratives (see further below).

Alt was quite careful in his use of comparison with the Nabataean
evidence (and the more restricted Palmyrene evidence) and despite
the fact that his conclusions are now regarded as outdated, the general
comparison is still instructive (assuming that comparison is a valid
activity, which some appear to doubt).

The Nabataean and Palmyrene religious traditions are remarkable
for a number of reasons, but most obviously because of the historical
and cultural context in which they were produced. The total number
of inscriptions in these two Aramaic dialects, dated to between about
100 B.C. and A.D. 350, is well over 8,000: the Nabataean inscriptions
in particular are very difficult to count, since they have never been
compiled in a single corpus, but with the Palmyrene we are in a more
satisfactory situation in that a single corpus, with minor omissions
and relatively few additions, contains over 2,800 items (some being
very short inscriptions on tokens).[9] Alt referred to the fact that the
Nabataean materials were difficult of access and eighty years on the
situation has got worse rather than better.

One of the most distinctive characteristics of these inscriptions
is the fact that they reflect both an emergence of new settlers from
north Arabia and a dramatic encounter with the settled populations of
Transjordan and Syria and then with the Seleucids and Romans. Thus
north Arabian deities like Dushara and al-'Uzzā, whose Arabian roots
are clearly reflected in early Islamic writings about pre-Islamic Arabia, were brought to the Levant by new migrants and became popular
even among the already settled populations.[10] In Roman contact they
came to be identified with Roman deities and were often worshipped

---

[8] R. Albertz, *A History of Israelite Religion in the Old Testament Period: From the
Exile to the Maccabees* (translated by J. Bowden from *Religionsgeschichte Israels in
alttestamentlicher Zeit* [ATD Ergänzungsreihe; Göttingen, 1992]; London, 1994), 1,
p. 250, n. 13.

[9] D. R. Hillers and E. Cussini, *Palmyrene Aramaic Texts* (Publications of the Comprehensive Aramaic Lexicon Project; Baltimore, 1996).

[10] J. F. Healey, *The Religion of the Nabataeans: a Conspectus* (Religions in the
Graeco-Roman World 136; Leiden, 2001), pp. 85–107, 114–19.

in sanctuaries which were at least superficially indistinguishable from Roman temples. Dushara, the most important Nabataean deity, came to be identified with Dionysus and Zeus and Helios, attracting Greek epithets like ἀνίκητος.[11] It is in this context that Alt saw an analogy with the settlement of the patriarchal groups and the domestication or sedentarization of their cults.

The specific group of inscriptions and deities with which Alt suggested an analogy appear in dozens of Nabataean inscriptions and a few Palmyrene ones. In this he was following a much earlier hint by Theodor Nöldeke.[12] I will not attempt to repeat the catalogue given by Alt, noting only that there are a few additions to be made resulting from more recent discoveries.

To summarize, the inscriptions in question, mostly in Nabataean Aramaic, but also Greek inscriptions from a Nabataean or related context, refer to dedications to "the god of so-and-so". The following are examples: *'lh w'lw* (*RES* §1434); *'lh ḥṭyšw* (*CIS* II, 354); *'lh m'ynw* (*RES* §2053); *'lh mtnw* (*RES* §2051); *'lh qṣyw* (*CIS* II, 174); *'lh š'ydw* (*CIS* II, 176), in all of which the construct of the noun *'lh'* is combined with a personal name. For the present purpose we may leave aside the Nabataean *'lh ṣ'bw*. The title in this case now seems likely to mean "the god Ṣa'bu", qualified in a Palmyrene inscription as *gd nbṭw*, the "Fortune (-deity) of the Nabataeans" (*CIS* II, 3991).[13]

A few cases are less clear because a place-name rather than a personal name may follow *'lh*. Thus *'lh mnbtw* in *RES* §1432. If such cases exist they would conceptually fall outside the present discussion, since one of the major points made by Alt in his original treatment was that the Nabataean gods of the fathers were remarkable for *not* being tied to a particular sanctuary, though one could well imagine that an individual ancestral god might in the course of time become so attached. The possibility that the personal name involved in particular titles was that of the first priest of the particular deity, the first worshipper, would fit with this (though there is a complication over what role such sanctuaries might have had in the nomadic context).

---

[11] Healey, *Religion*, p. 102.

[12] In J. Euting, *Nabatäische Inschriften aus Arabien* (Berlin, 1885), pp. 62–63.

[13] Healey, *Religion*, pp. 153–54; and note now, in the context of an inscription from Uraynibah, D. F. Graf and M. J. Zwettler, "The North Arabian 'Thamudic E' Inscription from Uraynibah West", *BASOR* 335 (2004), pp. 53–89.

There is also an instance of a *goddess* being identified in the same way, on an often-reproduced relief found in the Temple of the Winged Lions at Petra. The iconography of the relief suggests that the goddess is assimilated to Isis and she is called: *'lht ḥyn br nybt,* "the goddess of Ḥayyan son of Naybat".[14] In so far as the identification of the goddess with Isis is certain we may have here an interesting clue to the nature of the relationship between the individual and the deity. The cult of Isis became popular throughout the Roman world and was one of the cults to which individuals chose to connect themselves, in theory undergoing a kind of initiation process.[15] Another such cult attested among the Nabataeans is that of the goddess Atargatis.[16] These deities appear to be associated generally not with the major sanctuaries but with minor cult-locations in obscure places where the devotees of the deity could meet in seclusion. This would correspond with what we know of such elective, personal cults.[17]

Unfortunately the Nabataean inscriptions using the formula "the god of so-and-so" are mostly uninformative about the meaning of the titles or the cults involved. Westermann made particular point of the fact that the titles used in Genesis are also bereft of meaning until brought into association with the narratives which reveal aspects of the god concerned.[18] However, one of the Nabataean inscriptions, which happens to be one of the earliest of the series cited by Alt (c. A.D. 20), is the inscription in a rock-cut sanctuary at Petra, in which a deity, Dutara (obscure, but perhaps a variant of the divine name Dushara),[19] is described as the god of Ḥotayshu (*dwtr' 'lh ḥtyšw*) (*CIS* II, 354: 2 – the readings are not certain).[20] This sanctuary is also located at an

---

[14] P. C. Hammond, "Ein nabatäisches Weiherelief aus Petra", in G. Hellenkemper Salies (ed.), *Die Nabatäer: Erträge einer Ausstellung im Rheinischen Landesmuseum Bonn* (= *Bonner Jahrbücher* 180 [1980]; Cologne, 1981), pp. 137–41.

[15] Healey, *Religion*, pp. 137–40; and in a wider context, W. Burkert, *Ancient Mystery Cults* (Cambridge, MA and London, 1987); L. H. Martin, *Hellenistic Religions. An Introduction* (New York and Oxford, 1987), pp. 72–81.

[16] Healey, *Religion*, pp. 140–41.

[17] An individual's choice to worship a particular deity would, of course, create a family cult through being passed on to his or her descendants. We cannot tell whether Ḥayyan passed on his devotion to Isis.

[18] Westermann, *Genesis*, p. 108.

[19] See R. Wenning, "Bemerkungen zur Gesellschaft und Religion der Nabatäer", in R. Albertz (ed.), *Religion und Gesellschaft. Studien zu ihrer Wechselbeziehung in den Kulturen des Antiken Vorderen Orients* (AOAT 248; Münster, 1997), p. 190.

[20] Healey, *Religion,* p. 152; *The Nabataean Tomb Inscriptions of Mada'in Salih* (JSSSup 1; Oxford, 1993), p. 141.

inaccessible spot and appears to have been principally dedicated to the cult of the god 'Obodat.[21]

What is notable from our point of view is the fact that in this inscription referring to the god of Ḥotayshu the name Ḥotayshu also appears as the name of the *father* of the dedicators of the inscription. While it remains uncertain whether the two Ḥotayshus are the same person, i.e. the father of the dedicants and the individual with whom the cult or its origin is associated (since an earlier ancestor may have given his name to the god), it is overwhelmingly likely that the name refers to two individuals within the same family. Thus the implication seems to be that we are dealing with the family god of those concerned.

As is the case in the patriarchal narratives, it is not uncommon for the deity's proper name to be cited alongside the title associating him with a particular individual. Apart from the slightly uncertain Dutara above, another deity, named only once in a Nabataean source, is Ashar (or Ashad), "the god of Muʿaynu" in *RES* §2053 dated A.D. 124. He had a temple (*bt 'šrw*) at Deir el-Meshqūq in the Ḥawrān and the same god is found at Palmyra.[22] The titles *'lh mtnw* and *'lh š'ydw* (above) clearly refer in fact to Baalshamin, while *'lh w'lw* is qualified as "the great god" in *RES* §1434. In all these cases there is an implication that the family god (if that is the correct interpretation of origin) was identified with one of the "high" gods, gods worshipped in temples in fixed locations. In another case, an inscription from Simj in the Ḥawrān, the god in question is linked with a larger unit, a tribe, *'l qsyw*, and identified as Baalshamin: *dnh 'bd 'l [q]syw l'lhhm b'l[šmn]* (*RES* §2042). Here we appear to be at a point of transition from individual/family religion towards the religion of a socially constructed "political" entity, the tribe and ultimately the nation.

There is also evidence in Nabataean inscriptions and iconography of the protective deity of particular cities (τύχη). In the Ḥawrān *š'y'w* is the local deity of Sīʿ (*RES* §1092),[23] while the city of Bosra is personified

---

[21] Healey, *Religion*, pp. 147–51.

[22] Healey, *Religion*, pp. 141–2, with further references.

[23] D. Sourdel, *Les cultes du Hauran à l'époque romaine* (Paris, 1952), pp. 49–52; Ch. Augé, "Sur la figure de Tyché en Nabatène et dans La Province d'Arabie", in F. Zayadine (ed.), *Petra and the Caravan Cities* (Amman, 1990), pp. 131–46; R. Wenning and H. Merklein, "Die Götter in der Welt der Nabatäer", in T. Weber and R. Wenning (eds.), *Petra. Antike Felsstadt zwischen arabischer Tradition und griechischer Norm* (Mainz, 1997), pp. 106–7.

in an inscription from Petra.[24] Allāt may also have been regarded as the Tyche of Bosra.[25]

Evidence of "the god of so-and-so" is also found in Greek inscriptions, mostly from the Ḥawrān: θεὸς Ἀμέρου, θεὸς Ἀρκεσιλάαου, θεὸς Αὔμου etc.[26] Sometimes we find the accompanying Greek phrase θεὸς πατρῷος. In Safaitic and Palmyrene inscriptions *gd*, "Fortune(-deity), Tyche", sometimes takes the place of *'lh* (as we have seen in the case of the Ṣaʿbu inscription above). The identification with one of the high gods, as seen in the Nabataean cases above, is also evident in Greek examples: θεὸς Αὔμου is qualified with the title ἀνίκητος, "unconquered", normally reserved for Helios, and used in Roman times of Dushara (see above).

A final aspect of the Nabataean evidence adds another structural layer: there are family god titles ("the god of so-and-so") in which the person named is a Nabataean king. Here we appear to have evidence of a transition in which the family god originally associated with the king or royal family is identified as the *national* god. The formulae vary. Most general (and vague) is *'lh mr'n'*, "the god of our lord", followed by the name of a king, sometimes Aretas,[27] sometimes Rabel (*RES* §§83; 2036). There were, according to the standard counting, several Nabataean kings with these names (four Aretases and two Rabels). Variants include direct reference to "the god of Rabel"[28] and "the god of Maliku"[29] (there were two Malikus), which make an even closer link with the "family god" tradition. Occasionally no king is named to clarify *'lh mr'n'* (*CIS* II, 350).

As in the patriarchal texts, the name of the deity is sometimes added and often implicit. The main Nabataean god, who is particularly associated with the royal family, is Dushara and he is explicitly identified

---

[24] J. T. Milik, "Nouvelles inscriptions nabatéennes", *Syria* 35 (1958), pp. 248–49 (no. 7); "Quatre inscriptions nabatéennes. Une visite épigraphique à Pétra", *Le Monde de la Bible* 14 (1980), p. 15.

[25] Sourdel, *Les cultes*, p. 50.

[26] Alt, "The God of the Fathers", pp. 71–76.

[27] Healey, *Nabataean Tomb Inscriptions*, p. 134 (inscriptions H 11:6; 28:6; 36:8).

[28] *CIS* II, 218; Milik, "Nouvelles inscriptions", pp. 231–35; K. Dijkstra, *Life and Loyalty. A Study in the Socio-Religious Culture of Syria and Mesopotamia in the Graeco-Roman Period Based on Epigraphical Evidence* (Religions in the Graeco-Roman World 128; Leiden, 1995), pp. 312–13.

[29] N. I. Khairy (with an additional note by J. T. Milik), "A New Dedicatory Nabataean Inscription from Wadi Musa", *PEQ* 113 (1981), pp. 19–26.

as the deity several times.[30] In others the title *'lh rb'l* (*CIS* II, 218)[31] may allude to A'ra, the god of Bosra.[32] We know that this deity was identified with Dushara.[33] The title "the god of Maliku" (see above) appears to refer to Baalshamin.[34]

This evidence implies a dynastic state cult, not personal or family religion, though it is easy to see how the cult favoured by the royal family or by individual kings might be elevated to a national status. Dushara and Dushara-A'ra enjoyed this status. Dushara is even invoked on coins.[35] Finally we may have a hint of systematic religious reform involving incorporation of deities not traditionally connected with the royal house. Thus an inscription in Wadi Ramm lists the Nabataean gods and describes them all as *'lhy mr'n'*, "gods of our lord (the king)".[36]

In the Nabataean evidence, therefore, we seem to find indications of a gradation of religious activity which stretches from

(i)   the cult of the personal god, to
(ii) the inherited cults of families whose memorable ancestor was associated (perhaps in thanksgiving for deliverance of some kind) with the family god, to
(iii) cults associated with whole tribes through perceived common ancestry.

These different forms of religious devotion, none of which is by definition tied to a particular territory, could then undergo further transformations on to a level – I hesitate to call it a higher level, since this would imply a value judgment which we are not in this context

---

[30] *CIS* II, 350 with no king mentioned; J. Starcky, "Les Inscriptions nabatéennes et l'histoire de la Syrie méridionale et du nord de la Jordanie", in J.-M. Dentzer (ed.), *Hauran I. Recherches archéologiques sur la Syrie du sud à l'époque hellénistique et romaine* (Paris, 1985), p. 181.

[31] Milik, "Nouvelles inscriptions", pp. 231–35; Starcky, "Les inscriptions nabatéennes", p. 181.

[32] Dijkstra, *Life and Loyalty*, pp. 310–14.

[33] Healey, *Religion*, pp. 97–100.

[34] J. T. Milik in Khairy, "A New Dedicatory…", p. 25; Dijkstra, *Life and Loyalty*, pp. 55–57.

[35] K. Schmitt-Korte, "Nabataean Coinage – Part II. New Coin Types and Variants", *NumC* 150 (1990), p. 110.

[36] R. Savignac, "Le sanctuaire d'Allat à Iram (suite) [III]", *RB* 43 (1934), pp. 576–77: no. 19.

entitled to make – in which the familial dimension of the cult was replaced by a focus on

  (a) elective personal devotion to a cult which does not have familial or geographical boundaries (Isis, Atargatis, etc.);
  (b) city cults (evidence mostly from areas of Greek and Roman influence: Bosra, Sīʿ – one is tempted to compare city deities such as Athena); and
  (c) national cult of the deity proclaimed to be the god of the king.

This is no more than an attempt to bring order into the chaos of the Nabataean evidence of the god of the fathers which contains many uncertainties. It is, however, suggestive of analogies with some aspects of ancient Israelite religion and thus not irrelevant.

Mention may be made of some other aspects of Nabataean religion and culture which find echoes in Jewish tradition (though not always specifically identifiable as of the Old Testament period). I mention them only in summary form. Some have been explored elsewhere:

  (i) Nabataean aniconism;[37]
  (ii) Nabataean "Rechabitism";[38]
  (iii) Nabataean secondary burial;[39]
  (iv) (a tendency to) monotheism.[40]

Again there are uncertainties and the temptation to overload slight evidence is great. The conclusion that there was opposition to drinking wine on the part of some elements in Nabataean society (ii) involves extrapolating from a single inscription dedicated to an Arabian deity who apparently has a programmatic objection to wine (like Allah, the main god of the Kaʿaba in Mekka), but there are other aspects of the

---

[37] Healey, *Religion*, pp. 185–89; T. N. D. Mettinger, *No Graven Image? Israelite Aniconism in its Ancient Near Eastern Context* (Coniectanea Biblica, OT Series 42; Stockholm, 1995), pp. 57–68; K. van der Toorn (ed.), *The Image and the Book: iconic cults, aniconism, and the rise of book religion in Israel and the Ancient Near East* (CBET 21; Leuven, 1997).

[38] Healey, *Religion*, pp. 143–47.

[39] Healey, *Religion*, pp. 169–70.

[40] Healey, *Religion*, pp. 189–91; "Towards the Fall of Idols: Emergent Monotheism in the Pre-Islamic Near East", in D. F. Graf and S. G. Schmid (eds.), *Fawzi Zayadine Festschrift* (= ADAJSup 1) [forthcoming].

Rechabite lifestyle presented in Jer. 35, such as the refusal to build houses and plant vineyards, which are also reported as Nabataean characteristics by Diodorus Siculus (after Hieronymus of Cardia).[41] Aniconism (i) and the custom of secondary burial (iii) are indisputable Nabataean features and aniconism may be regarded as characteristic of the whole cultural area of north-west Arabia, including Jordan-Palestine.

The tendency to monotheism (iv) is much more difficult to assess. A plausible case can be made for the view that the Aramaeans and Arabs of the Levant and Arabia were, in the last centuries B.C. and the early centuries A.D., already participating in a drift (not programmatic or prophet-inspired) towards a more monotheistic viewpoint. In the epigraphy there is evidence of the growing predominance of certain "high" gods, like Baalshamin. Local gods like the Nabataean Dushara begin, it seems, to dominate the older pantheon, to the extent that the minor gods are fading. In some areas it is not impossible that Jewish influence had a role, as it did in the Mediterranean. This is plausibly argued to be the case in South Arabia, where the cult of the Merciful One began to replace the older worship of the many deities.[42] On the other hand some of the monotheizing tendencies may be found already in ancient Mesopotamia without any likelihood of Jewish impact.[43] In Palmyra, we have evidence of an element of abstraction entering the divine epithets, notably the focus on the god called "Blessed-be-his-Name-Forever".[44] It would be wrong to conclude that a strict monotheism had been reached here, but monotheistic ideas seem to have been in the air.

Returning to Alt, general comparisons of the kind he employed are associated with a particular phase in Old Testament study under the influence of luminaries like William Robertson Smith and Julius

---

[41] Diodorus Siculus XIX, 94.2–3. The comparison of the Rechabites with the Nabataeans is reviewed, perhaps with overly negative conclusions, by C. H. Knights, "The Nabataeans and the Rechabites", *JSS* 38 (1993), pp. 227–33.

[42] See Ch. Robin, "Du paganisme au monothéisme", in Ch. Robin (ed.), *L'Arabie antique de Karib'îl à Mahomet* (Aix-en-Provence, 1992), pp. 139–55; and most recently "Le Judaïsme de Ḥimyar", *Arabia* 1 (2003), pp. 97–172; "Ḥimyar et Israël", *CRAIBL* 2004/2, pp. 831–908.

[43] S. Parpola, "Monotheism in Ancient Assyria", in B. N. Porter (ed.), *One God or Many? Concepts of Divinity in the Ancient World* (Transactions of the Casco Bay Assyriological Institute 1; Casco Bay, 2000), pp. 165–209.

[44] See conveniently G. A. Cooke, *A Text-book of North-Semitic Inscriptions* (Oxford, 1903), pp. 297–300 (nos. 135, 137, 138).

Wellhausen, both of whom relied much on the nineteenth-century discovery of Arabia. These influences had a profound impact on the History of Religions approach to the Old Testament which flourished under authors such as Ivan Engnell. This openness to comparativism is still characteristic of some Scandinavian scholarship (e.g., that of T. N. D. Mettinger).

The effect of the *ex Arabia lux* movement was, however, doubly unfortunate. It tended to force the biblical record into a predetermined mould, underestimating indicators to the contrary. It also treated Arabia Antiqua as a convenient archaeological spoil-heap (as in philological exploitation of the Classical Arabic dictionaries, often underestimating the uncertainties). Even now, after 150 years of scholarly research based on epigraphic evidence, it is very difficult to be clear about most aspects of pre-Islamic Arabian religion in general and Nabataean religion in particular: the Nabataean god of the ancestors is just not well enough understood to be used as a key to pre-Yahwistic Israelite religion.

However, the modern scholarly approach to the patriarchal narratives does have a positive consequence for anyone wishing to advocate the relevance of evidence such as that provided by the Nabataean inscriptions: the time distance between the Nabataeans and the biblical texts in question is now much shorter. Few scholars now see in the patriarchal narratives a reflection of the early to mid-second millennium B.C. In this respect Wyatt[45] was missing the point that the authors of the patriarchal narratives attempted to *represent* the earlier period by emphasizing nomadism and family religion.[46] And it is reasonable to assume that their attempt to create a religious history of the age of the patriarchs is based on an awareness of nomadic religion in their own time. It is important to note, therefore, that the Nabataeans are known to have been present in Transjordan at least from the fourth century B.C. and possibly earlier.

The narratives attempt to portray nomad (pre-settlement) religion by focusing on family gods and tribal ancestors. The authors were partly aware of sedentarizing groups of nomads like the Nabataeans and "the god of the fathers" may have been part of the patriarchal

---

[45] Wyatt, "The Problem...", p. 104.
[46] This is effectively the position of Albertz, *History of Israelite Religion*, pp. 27–29.

world they imagined because such concepts were known from contemporary nomads from northern Arabia. The evidence provided by the Nabataean texts does not prove that the god of the fathers was part of the conceptual or social world of the "historical" Abraham, Isaac, and Jacob, or that they lived a nomadic lifestyle, but it may be relevant to the question of how the Israelites later understood themselves. The Israelites and Nabataeans may thus be connected after all.

THE TRANSITION FROM GENESIS TO EXODUS

Graham Davies

Early in 1999 I read a paper on "The First Word of the Book of Exodus – 'And'" to the Cambridge Old Testament Seminar, over which John Emerton presided for many years. It marked the beginning, appropriately, of my serious writing for the *International Critical Commentary* on Exodus which John Emerton had, as the Old Testament Editor of the series, invited me to write. My purpose was to argue that the book of Exodus should not be seen as a new beginning but as a continuation of Genesis, and in particular that the end of Genesis provided the explicit theological key which was missing from the early chapters of Exodus themselves (until 2:23–25). The paper was written just before the publication of Konrad Schmid's *Erzväter und Exodus* gave fresh impetus to questions about the antiquity of the connection between the material included in the two books, questions which had first been raised by Rolf Rendtorff and others in the 1970s.[1] These questions were directed especially at the existence of the Yahwist source of the Pentateuch as an early, pre-exilic, account of Israel's origins (and indeed those of humankind as a whole). The patriarchal promises attributed to that source and its date were the subject of two important essays by John Emerton.[2] There are therefore several reasons why this is an appropriate essay for me to contribute to a volume in celebration of John Emerton's eightieth birthday and I do so as an expression of my deep gratitude for his inspiration and friendship, which now extend back over forty years.

---

[1] K. Schmid, *Erzväter und Exodus: Untersuchungen zur doppelten Begründung der Ursprünge Israels innerhalb der Geschichtsbücher des Alten Testaments* (WMANT 81; Neukirchen, 1999). For references to other recent discussion of these questions see below, esp. nn. 18–20.

[2] J. A. Emerton, "The Origin of the Promises to the Patriarchs in the Older Sources of the Book of Genesis", *VT* 32 (1982), pp. 14–32; "The Date of the Yahwist", in J. Day (ed.), *In Search of Pre-Exilic Israel* (JSOTSup 406; London and New York, 2004), pp. 107–29.

The earliest physical evidence for the join between Genesis and Exodus is found in some scrolls from the Judaean desert which certainly or probably contained both books. In general it seems that these books were written on separate scrolls, but in the case of 4QGen-Exod[a] (formerly regarded as two separate manuscripts), 4QpalGen-Exod[l], and probably 4QExod[b] and Mur1, there is good reason to think that both books appeared on the same scroll.[3] But even here, in the two cases where the join between Genesis and Exodus survives (the second and third mentioned above), there is a larger gap between the end of Genesis and the beginning of Exodus than is found between successive sections of the same book (three blank lines in 4QpalGen-Exod[l], at least two lines in 4QExod[b]), so that the break is clearly recognised.[4] One could also refer to the manuscripts of 4QReworkedPentateuch (4Q158, 364–367), though only one of them (4Q364) has surviving fragments which contain passages of both Genesis and Exodus in their biblical order.[5]

The textual criticism of Exodus points to a tighter link between the two books. In both the Masoretic Text and the Samaritan Pentateuch a *waw* appears at the beginning of Exodus 1:1 (ואלה שמות בני ישראל),[6] just as at the beginning of Leviticus and Numbers, but not at the beginning of Genesis, which really is the beginning, and also not at the beginning of Deuteronomy. This supports in a rather superficial way the view that Genesis to Numbers were compiled to form a continuous literary work – the so-called "Tetrateuch", while Deuteronomy is

---

[3] For the two latter instances see *DJD* XIV, pp. 79–80, and *DJD* II, p. 75, which is also confident that this early second century A.D. MS included one of the Numbers fragments (7); if so Mur1 might be a whole Torah.

[4] Rabbinic rulings required four lines: *b. Baba Bathra* 13b; for other references see *DJD* IX, p. 18.

[5] 4Q158 as we have it most probably contains entirely a sequence from Exodus, with comparable passages from Genesis and Deuteronomy interleaved at what were thought to be appropriate points. The Book of Jubilees also contains a continuous narrative from Genesis to Exodus, with many elaborations, and the transition occurs in ch. 46, in a form that diverges in some interesting ways from the biblical narrative. 4QParaphrase of Genesis and Exodus (4Q422), as its name implies, evidently gave a summary of both books, but the text in Exodus at least is even further removed from the Pentateuchal form of the text. For further evidence of the Pentateuch as a single unit from the second century B.C. and later see Schmid, 1999, pp. 316–52, to which the references to the Greek translation of "the law" in the *Letter of Aristeas* could be added.

[6] Von Gall's edition of the Samaritan Pentateuch prints the *waw* and he gives no variants. Both Sadaqa's and Tal's editions and Cambridge Add. 1846 (the "Burnt Codex" of the 12th century) also read ואלה.

separate, and even the beginning of another major literary work, the Deuteronomistic History.[7] It is true that there is no equivalent to this *waw* in the Septuagint (except for a couple of miniscules) or in the Vulgate. But this can be put down simply to the translators' freedom in rendering their original, especially after the division of the Pentateuch into separate "books" became established. There is some possible evidence that a text without the *waw* was found also in Hebrew manuscripts. The only Judaean Desert MS. to include the beginning of Exodus 1:1, 4QpalGen-Exod[l], begins a line with אלה and no *waw*. But the edition notes: "It is possible that the scribe wrote a large , isolated *waw* as the first letter of this word... in the otherwise blank line 4 to signal the beginning of Exodus, as the scribe of 4QpalGen-Exod[m] did routinely for large paragraph-divisions within Exodus [e.g. at 10:1 – pl. X, small fr.]. No other such case has been preserved in this scroll, but the scribe may have treated the major division between Genesis and Exodus differently from paragraph-divisions."[8] Secondly, there is a little evidence that transliterations of the Hebrew text into Greek and Latin did not always represent the *waw*, and presumably this would be because they were sometimes made from Hebrew MSS which did not include it.[9] But even if there was a reading without *waw* in Hebrew manuscripts, the reading with *waw* is surely to be preferred as the more difficult reading, as it is much easier to see why someone would have removed a *waw* at the beginning of the book than to envisage one being added secondarily. The commentator on Exodus is therefore obliged to turn back to Genesis when studying its opening chapters, and *vice versa*. On doing so, it is clear that the two books are linked in several more substantial ways.

---

[7] The next six books of the Hebrew canon all begin with *waw*, which is at least a *prima facie* indication that they form a continuous literary work with Deuteronomy. It must be admitted, however, that the (apparently) independent books of Ezekiel, Jonah, Ruth and Esther also begin with *waw* (ויהי to be precise): are these to be regarded as "pseudo-continuations"?

[8] *DJD* IX, p. 26.

[9] The LXX MS 551 (13th cent.) has the title of Exodus as επισιμωθ (presumably for ελισιμωθ), while MS 56 (11th cent.) does represent the waw by a *beta* (see Wevers' edition of Exodus, ad loc., lower apparatus); and in the Vulgate the majority reading of the title is: *incipit liber ellesmoth id est exodus* (it is only the Clementine edition of the late 16th century which has *liber exodus hebraice ueelle semoth* according to Weber's editio minor). This corresponds closely to Jerome's version of the Hebrew title (*ele smoth*) as given in *Ep.* 32.1.2 (CSEL 76, 2nd ed. [1996], p. 252).

First it is necessary to do some source-criticism, and for the
moment of a rather simple and uncontroversial kind. The basic distinction between Priestly and non-Priestly material has remained
largely unchanged here, and elsewhere in the Pentateuch, since the
mid-nineteenth century and even in recent years, when the chronological and literary relationship between the two narrative strands has
often been thought of in new ways (of which more later).

There has been a substantial consensus about the origin of Exodus
1:1–6. Verses 1–5 come from the Priestly source and v. 6 from a non-
Priestly source, generally identified as J. A separation between these
two units is already suggested by the formal differences between them
(a list with an introduction contrasting with a narrative element), and
the vocabulary and style of vv. 1–5 are strongly Priestly, whereas such
features are lacking in v. 6.[10] Moreover, the Joseph-centred focus of
v. 6 fits much better with the main Joseph-narrative in Genesis and
with v. 8 than with the rather meagre account of P which generally
treats the descendants of Jacob as a single unit. Verse 7 is also regularly
attributed to the Priestly source.[11] In the remainder of Exodus 1 and
the following chapters it is not difficult to detect two parallel strands
of narrative which to a large extent duplicate one another. On the one
hand 1:13–14 and 2:23b–25 present a Priestly account of the oppression of the Israelites and God's response to their cry for help, which
leads smoothly into the commissioning of Moses and Aaron in 6:2–7:7
(note especially the explicit references to the covenant between God
and the ancestors which he "remembers" in 2:24 and 6:4–5). These
verses are embedded in a fuller non-Priestly account of the same events
(and the first confrontation of Moses and Aaron with Pharaoh), which
includes the commissioning of Moses and Aaron in 3:1–4:17. Similarly, at the end of Genesis there has been general agreement that the
Priestly strand consists of 46:6–27; most of 47:5–11, 27b–28; 48:3–6(7);
49:1a, 28b–33; 50:12–13. These passages describe the coming of Jacob

---

[10] See the standard critical commentaries and, on v. 1, M. Paran, *Forms of the
Priestly Style in the Pentateuch. Patterns, Linguistic Usages, Syntactic Structures* (Heb.;
Jerusalem, 1989), pp. 47–97; cf. S. McEvenue, *The Narrative Style of the Priestly Writer*
(Rome, 1971), who speaks of a "short-circuit inclusion" (e.g. pp. 43, 51–52) and cites
the very close parallel in Gen. 7:16 (p. 67).

[11] The combination of פרה, שׁרץ and רבה is found elsewhere only in the P Flood
Story and its sequel (Gen. 8:17, 9:7) and the use of שרץ to refer to humans rather than
animals only in the latter passage. The emphatic במאד מאד is found only in P (Gen.
17:2, 6, 20) and Ezekiel (9:9, 16:13).

and his family to Egypt and their flourishing there. It is clear from 47:5–11 that Joseph had come to Egypt before the rest of the family and achieved a position of high honour there (cf. 42:45b–46a = P), but the recognisably Priestly sections give no explanation of how all this came about, in contrast to the lengthy and detailed Joseph-story in the non-Priestly text, which concludes with his death at the end of Genesis 50. In each of these strands there are a number of indications, explicit and implicit, that Genesis and Exodus are meant to be read as a single story. For the present study I shall confine myself mainly to passages between Genesis 46 and Exodus 7.

Genesis and Exodus in the Priestly Source

In the Priestly strand we have already observed that God's covenant with Abraham, Isaac and Jacob (Gen. 17; 35:9–13 = P) is "remembered" by him as he contemplates the situation of their descendants in Egypt (Exod. 2:24; 6:4–5). In fact there is a strong implication that it is because of that covenant that he is moved to do something about it (6:5–6). This grounding of the Exodus deliverance in the covenant with the ancestors is a largely distinctive feature of the Priestly theology (Deut. 7:8 provides one precedent elsewhere), the more common association being between the ancestral promise/covenant and the entry into the land of Canaan. A link between Genesis and Exodus is also made by the Priestly verses at the beginning of Exodus 1, first explicitly and then implicitly. The opening list of names reproduces information that has already appeared both in Gen. 46:8–27 (with more detail) and further back in 35:22b–26. It could be suggested that this latter passage and Exodus 1:1–5 were designed to form an *inclusio* around the second part of the Priestly story of Jacob. Three details in Exodus 1:1–5 make further connections with the later chapters of Genesis. The description of Jacob's sons as "sons of Israel", while also probably aimed at smoothing the transition to what follows by employing P's regular expression for the people as a whole (cf. 1:7, 13; 2:23, 25; 6:5 etc.), gains its legitimacy from the renaming of Jacob as Israel in Gen. 35:10, the Priestly parallel to 32:28 in the non-Priestly material. The reference to those who "came down to Egypt" recalls what has been said in Gen. 46:6–8; and the mention of Joseph's earlier arrival coincides with what is also assumed in Gen. 47:5–11. Verse 7 also looks back to Genesis, though implicitly, as Walter Brueggemann and others have observed: most of the verbs used occur in key Priestly passages in Genesis 1–9, of mankind in general, and in the promises to Abraham and Jacob that their offspring will be numerous (Gen. 1:28; 8:17; 9:1, 7; 17:2, 6; 28:3; 35:11: cf. 48:4). Indeed the fulfilment of these promises has already been noted in Gen. 47:27(P).[12]

If we turn back to the end of Genesis and look for links forward to Exodus in the Priestly sections, we are at first sight disappointed, as clear references to a departure from Egypt are lacking. Nevertheless the careful reader of the Priestly strand of Genesis would certainly recall that the promises to Abraham and Jacob included not only an increase in numbers but eventual possession of the land of Canaan, which could only come about by leaving Egypt (cf. Gen. 17:8; 28:4; 35:12; 48:4). Moreover the mention of the "inheritance" (נחלה) of Ephraim and Manasseh in Gen. 48:6 evidently has in view the territory which Jacob's descendants were to possess in Canaan, as it does very often elsewhere both in P and in Deuteronomy;[13] and the Priestly account of Jacob's burial at Machpelah (49:29–33; 50:12–13) explicitly recalls Abraham's purchase of the field and cave there as a foothold in the land which had been promised to him (Gen. 23 = P).

Genesis and Exodus in the non-Priestly texts

In the non-Priestly strand there are also explicit cross-references between the end of Genesis and the beginning of Exodus, and this time in both books. We may begin with the vision which Jacob receives at Beersheba, on his way to see his son Joseph in power in Egypt. After the introductory dialogue, God reassures Jacob as follows: "Do not be afraid to go down to Egypt, for I will make of you a great nation there" – the fulfilment of the promise first made to Abraham in Genesis 12:2 – "I myself will go down with you, and I will also bring you up again; and Joseph's own hand shall close your eyes" (Gen. 46:3–4). "I will bring you up again" sounds as if Jacob will return alive to Canaan, with Joseph beside him when he dies there. The visit to Egypt is only for a

---

[12] This could be the reason for the inverted (S-P) word-order in Exod. 1:7, implying that the increase in numbers was seen as already an established fact, not a fresh development. For the general point see W. Brueggemann, "The Kerygma of the Priestly Writers", *ZAW* 84 (1972), pp. 397–413, reprinted in W. Brueggemann and H. W. Wolff, *The Vitality of Old Testament Traditions* (Atlanta, 1975), pp. 101–13.

[13] See BDB, p. 635; *ThWAT* 5 (1986), pp. 352–55.

temporary stay. But as the story develops, this hope is transferred to Jacob's descendants (48:21), and Jacob assigns to Joseph "one shoulder", שְׁכֶם אַחַד, the territory of Shechem (by a play on words) in the central hills of Canaan (v. 22).[14] Jacob himself is, by his own request, to be buried in Canaan with his ancestors, so in a sense "brought up again" (48:29–31; 50:1–11). Indeed Joseph and his family, except for the children, form part of the funeral cortege, and the verb "go up" is used of them in 50:7, quite naturally from a geographical point of view, but evocatively too perhaps, in the light of both the original assurance to Jacob in 46:4 and its later use in relation to the Exodus. Yet any idea that this might be the decisive return to Canaan is repeatedly excluded: Joseph seeks leave from Pharaoh to go, and promises to return (50:5), the family members are accompanied by Egyptian officials (50:7, 9), the children and livestock are left behind in Egypt (50:8), the Canaanites describe the whole party as "Egyptians" (50:11). And so Joseph and his brothers, along with the rest, return to Egypt (50:14) and the closing scenes of reconciliation and Joseph's death are evidently played out there, in the place where Joseph still holds power (cf. 50:22). But before he dies, Joseph looks forward to the time when Jacob's descendants will be "visited" by God and be "brought up" out of Egypt to the land promised to their ancestors (50:24) and makes them swear to take his bones with them, presumably for reburial in Canaan (v. 25). There is then a constant focus on the expectation of a return to Canaan, albeit deftly and imaginatively handled.

In the opening verses, indeed chapters, of Exodus there is, conversely, a pronounced looking back to Genesis. The references to the death of Joseph and his brothers "and that whole generation" and to a Pharaoh who "did not know Joseph" (Exod. 1:6, 8) serve to introduce and explain what is to follow as a change, and indeed a change for the worse, from the situation of honour and prosperity described at the end of Genesis. The surprising fear of the new Pharaoh that the Israelites will "go up from the land" also makes much more sense in the

---

[14] The reference appears to be to a variant of the tradition in Gen. 33:19 and ch. 34: cf. H. Gunkel, *Genesis*, 3rd ed. (HKAT; Göttingen, 1910), pp. 474–75; G. von Rad, *Das erste Buch Mose. Genesis* (ATD; Göttingen, 1953), p. 366 (ET, revd. ed., 1963, pp. 413–14); C. Westermann, *Genesis 37–50*, (BKAT; Neukirchen, 1982), pp. 216–17, with ref. to R. de Vaux, *Histoire Ancienne d'Israël* (Paris, 1971), pp. 584–86 (ET, pp. 637–39); D. M. Carr, *Reading the Fractures of Genesis* (Louisville, 1996), pp. 210–11 (adaptation of the Joseph-story to the wider promise theme, using "an older element": p. 211, n. 69).

light of the recurrent appearances of this verb there. As his measures
to curtail their growth in numbers repeatedly fail, the verbs "multiply"
(רבה) and "become strong" (עצם) become a *Leitmotif* of ch. 1 (vv. 9,
10, 12, 20), and they recall both the general sense of Gen. 46:3 and the
frequent occurrences of the verb רבה in the non-Priestly promises to
the ancestors all through Genesis, which culminate in Joseph's words
to his brothers about God's plan to preserve "a numerous people" (עם
רב), "as he is doing today" (50:20).[15] Further on, in chapters 3–4, there
are several references back to the ancestors by name (3:6, 15, 16; 4:5;
compare also the general expression "ancestors" in 3:13, 15, 16; 4:5),
and in chapter 3 both the verb "bring up" (3:8, 17) with reference to
a return to Canaan, and the curious expression "visit" (פקד, with the
infinitive absolute again, as in Gen. 50:24–25: see 3:16) reappear. There
is therefore a concentration of allusions to Genesis, at least in chapters
1, 3 and 4 of Exodus.

More than this, there are also several indications of the theological basis for Yahweh's intervention in Exodus in the non-Priestly
material. In the commissioning of Moses Yahweh twice refers to the
Israelites as already "my people" (3:7, 10), a status and relationship
which is only explained, but very adequately explained, by the fact
that he introduces himself to Moses as "the God of" Abraham, Isaac
and Jacob, or more generally "of your ancestors" (see the references
above). It is evidently as the descendants of those whose stories are
told in Genesis that the Israelites are said to have a claim on Yahweh's
attention. Another phrase, "the God of the Hebrews", is used in 3:18
(and also several times later on, in 5:3; 7:16; 9:1, 13; 10:3), and this too
provides a narrative connection to the later chapters of Genesis, since
the family of Jacob are several times referred to there as "the Hebrews"
(Gen. 39:14, 17; 40:15; 41:12, 43:32), as well as in the early chapters of
Exodus (1:16, 19; 2:6–7, 11, 13). It is true that there is nothing in the
non-Priestly Exodus narrative that corresponds to the allusions in P
to the "covenant" with the ancestors, but this of course matches the
almost total absence of such language from the non-Priestly narratives
in Genesis (15:18 is the only case).

---

[15] The expression עם רב is sometimes taken to include (Westermann) or to mean
(Ruppert [n. 39]: cf. the use of חיה hiphil in 47:25) the Egyptians. But in the context
of Joseph's words to his brothers this is less likely (cf. Gunkel, von Rad), and taken as
a reference to Jacob's family the phrase recalls the similar words in 45:7.

It would be possible to add further instances of what might be called "narrative continuity" between Genesis and Exodus (for example, the location of the Israelites in "[the land of] Goshen" in both books [Gen. 45:10; 46:28–29, 34; 47:1, 4, 6b, 27a; 50:8; Exod. 8:18; 9:26]; and see further below). But those that I have examined are sufficient to show that both the Priestly and the non-Priestly strands have bridged the "generation gap" between the patriarchal age in Genesis and the Exodus story in a number of ways.

The Meaning and Origin of the Links between Genesis and Exodus

The reasons for spending so long on establishing this are twofold. One is theological. If one examines Genesis on the one hand and Exodus on the other from the point of view of the history of religion or history more generally, there is a lot to suggest that they represent communities and religious behaviour of quite different kinds at the beginnings of Israel's history, even if Albrecht Alt, the scholar who gave classic expression to the differences, also felt bound to add that there was a "basic similarity" there.[16] It is entirely possible, and even likely, that behind the respective complexes of tradition there were once quite separate groups of people, who originally had no connection with one another.[17] But the biblical narrators have gone out of their way to link them together and in particular to insist that the God of the Exodus, whose name is revealed there as Yahweh, is personally identical with the God of the ancestors in Genesis (or even their *gods*, in the plural). The very use of the name Yahweh at many points in Genesis is the strongest indication of this. The theological implications of this "join" are enormous, not least for Christian theology from the New Testament onwards.

But, important as this is, it is especially because of recent discussion of literary history that I have wanted to describe the textual evidence

---

[16] A. Alt, *Der Gott der Vater* (BWANT 3/12; Stuttgart, 1929), pp. 66–68 (ET, *Essays on Old Testament History and Religion* [Oxford, 1966], pp. 60–62). See further, e.g., R. W. L. Moberly, *The Old Testament of the Old Testament* (Minneapolis, 1992), and nn. 52–53.

[17] But not quite certain: the status of Jacob/Israel as the eponymous ancestor of all the tribes could point to some kind of prior relationship between the "Exodus group" and (some of) the other groups that later combined to form the Israelite tribal league.

at such length. Earlier critical scholarship held that, while the Priestly narrative was from the fifth or sixth century B.C., the non-Priestly narrative was based on one, two or even three source-documents of pre-exilic origin. But since the turn of the twenty-first century there has been a strong, and growing, current of opinion which holds that the narrative link which we have been considering was only established at a comparatively late stage of the composition of the Old Testament. The suggestion has been made that a continuous narrative extending from Genesis to Exodus (and probably to somewhere beyond) was first put together by the author(s) of the Priestly source or layer in the Pentateuch. Not everyone is saying this by any means – John Van Seters and Christoph Levin still speak of a Yahwist (J) source prior to P (though not by much), in Germany a number of scholars still hold to the view that there was one or even two full-length narrative sources before the Exile (e.g. A. Graupner, L. Ruppert, L. Schmidt and W. H. Schmidt), as do John Emerton and Ernest Nicholson in England, and David Carr in the United States has recently presented a case for what he prefers to call a "pre-Priestly proto-Pentateuch" in the context of a discussion with adherents of the newer view. But a vocal body of younger German and Swiss scholars has made the latter, to say no more, a serious option which needs to be evaluated. In fact the foundations for it were already laid in Rolf Rendtorff's monograph of 1977 and even earlier,[18] but it has received wider attention through the monographs of K. Schmid (see note 1) and J. C. Gertz and the contributions of these and other scholars to two composite volumes published in 2002 and 2006.[19]

---

[18] R. Rendtorff, *Das überlieferungsgeschichtliche Problem des Pentateuch* (BZAW 147; Berlin and New York, 1977: ET 1990): see already his "Der 'Yahwist' als Theologe. Zum Dilemma der Pentateuchkritik", *Edinburgh Congress Volume* (VTSup 28; Leiden, 1975), pp. 158–66 (ET in JSOT 3 [1977], pp. 2–10); and R. Kessler "Die Querverweise im Pentateuch. Überlieferungsgeschichtliche Untersuchung der explizite Querverbindungen innerhalb des vorpriesterlichen Pentateuchs" (unpublished diss., Heidelberg, 1972).

[19] J. C. Gertz, *Tradition und Redaktion in der Exoduserzählung: Untersuchungen zur Endredaktion des Pentateuch* (FRLANT 190; Göttingen, 2000); J. C. Gertz, K. Schmid and M. Witte (eds.), *Abschied vom Jahwisten: Die Komposition des Hexateuch in der jüngsten Diskussion* (BZAW 315; Berlin and New York, 2002); T. B. Dozeman and K. Schmid (eds.), *A Farewell to the Yahwist?* (SBLSympS 34; Atlanta, 2006); see also for partly similar views R. G. Kratz, *Die Komposition der erzählenden Bücher des Alten Testament* (Göttingen, 2000: ET 2005).

The remainder of this paper will consider the treatment of the non-Priestly narrative strand by these writers, to see whether they have made a convincing case against the view that it represents an older connection between the stories now contained in the books of Genesis and Exodus. I shall concentrate on chapters 1 and 3 of Exodus and chapter 50 of Genesis. The issues have already been examined by others (such as T. B. Dozeman, J. Van Seters, C. Levin and D. M. Carr) and in earlier (mainly unpublished) studies of my own,[20] and I shall draw on these earlier discussions where appropriate.

(i) *Exodus 1*

Konrad Schmid has argued that the whole of Exodus 1, apart from the Priestly verses 7 and 13–14, is post-Priestly in origin, so that the older, independent Exodus-story began with the account of Moses' birth in Exod. 2:1–10.[21] Even here one might ask whether the references to "Levi" in 2:1 do not need some preparation and explanation such as they now find in the Genesis narratives. But we shall focus here on the two mentions of Joseph in 1:6 and 1:8: why does Schmid attribute them to a post-Priestly redactor? He sees the reference to the new Pharaoh in 1:8, reasonably enough, as the beginning of the episode which continues in vv. 9–12 and he claims that the starting-point of Pharaoh's reasoning, the statement that "the Israelite people are more numerous and more powerful (רב ועצום) than we" (v. 9), refers back to and presupposes the Priestly account of the Israelites' growth in numbers in v. 7, and so it (and the section to which it belongs, including v. 8) must be later than P.[22] But is this convincing? It can be and has been argued that v. 9 makes good sense by itself, and that Pharaoh's words were used by the original narrator to introduce the fact that the Israelites were now a large community, not just a family.[23]

---

[20] See the essays of the scholars named in Dozeman and Schmid (eds.), 2006; also C. Levin, "Abschied vom Jahwisten?", *ThR* 69 (2004), pp. 329–44, and "The Yahwist: The Earliest Editor in the Pentateuch", *JBL* 126 (2007), pp. 209–30; M. Gerhards, *Die Aussetzungsgeschichte des Mose* (WMANT 109; Neukirchen, 2006), pp. 60–70 (cf. 118–21); and my reviews of Gertz, 2000, in *JTS* N.S. 53 (2002), pp. 571–75, and of Gertz, Schmid and Witte (eds.) in *BiOr* 62 (2005), cols. 315–17.

[21] Schmid, 1999, pp. 69–73.

[22] Schmid, 1999, p. 71.

[23] Kratz, 2000, p. 287; Blum, "Die literarische Verbindung von Erzvätern und Exodus. Ein Gespräch mit neueren Endredaktionshypothesen", in Gertz, Schmid and Witte (eds.), pp. 119–56 (145); D. M. Carr, "What is Required to Identify Pre-Priestly

But 1:9 may also refer back to a non-Priestly statement of the growth of the Israelite people. Although most of the language of 1:7 reflects that of Priestly passages in Genesis, the verb עצם, "grew strong", there does not, and it has often been suggested that it came from a parallel account in the full non-Priestly narrative, where the verb עצם is used several times (Gen. 26:16 [cf. 18:18]; Num. 14:12; 22:16; as well as Exod. 1:9 and 20). Exod. 1:9 may therefore have been based on this non-Priestly account rather than on the wording of P. John Van Seters, who takes this view, has also noted that Gen. 50:20 refers to the keeping alive of "a numerous people" (עם רב), which is very close to the wording of Exod. 1:9.[24]

What about the reference to Joseph's death in 1:6? Schmid notes that it resumes what has already been said in Gen. 50:26. That verse, according to him, is part of a very late redactional layer. But supposing for a moment that this is the case, does it not leave entirely open the possibility that Exod. 1:6 is part of a continuous narrative source or layer that is older than the redactional layer in question? Erhard Blum, in his earlier work, had seen 1:6 as the continuation of Gen. 50:24, the verse which also looks forward in its doubled use of פקד and its use of עלה hiphil to Exod. 3:16–17.[25] But in a more recent essay he abandons this view and agrees with Gertz that there is nothing earlier than P in Exod. 1:1–10.[26] Why? Partly because he now finds, with Gertz, that the transition from Gen. 50:24 to Exod. 1:6 is awkward from a narrative point of view: he seems impressed by Gertz's claim that it is somewhat "tragicomic" to follow the promise that "God…will bring you up" to the land of Canaan with the report of the brothers' death still in Egypt.[27] Perhaps this is to read the "you" in Gen. 50:24 too rigidly and to overlook the successive deferments at the end of Genesis of Jacob's family's return to Canaan, which may be a deliberate feature of the story-teller's maintenance of suspense. Blum's other reason for his change of mind is that he now sees Gen. 50:24 as closely associated with 50:25–26, which are for him part of one of the latest,

---

Narrative Connections between Genesis and Exodus? Some General Reflections and Specific Cases", in Dozeman and Schmid (eds.), pp. 159–80 (172).

[24] J. Van Seters, "The Report of the Yahwist's Demise Has Been Greatly Exaggerated!", in Dozeman and Schmid (eds.), pp. 143–57 (152–53).

[25] E. Blum, *Studien zur Komposition des Pentateuch* (BZAW 189; Berlin and New York, 1990), pp. 102–03.

[26] Blum, 2002, pp. 145–46.

[27] Gertz, 2000, p. 360; cf. Blum, 2002, p. 149.

"hexateuchal", layers in the composition of the Pentateuch (cf. Josh 24:32).[28] Whatever one makes of that view of vv. 25–26 (see below), it is not at all clear that they are the original continuation of v. 24 and therefore they need not be relevant to determining its origin. In any case, as Blum acknowledges, it is perfectly possible (and even likely) that Exod. 1:6 (and v. 8) could be the continuation (or rather conclusion) of a version of the Joseph-story even if the latter did not have an explicit anticipation of the Exodus such as we find in Gen. 50:24.[29] There is really no solid reason for supposing that Exod. 1:6 is a very late addition to the Pentateuch and for discounting it as part of an early non-Priestly "bridge" between Genesis and Exodus.

Gertz's treatment of Exodus 1 is less far-reaching than Schmid's in that he does recognise (most of) verses 11–22 as part of the old independent Exodus-story: as he sees, something like its account of Egyptian oppression is needed to set the scene for what is recounted in chapter 2.[30] But in relation to verses 6 and 8 (and 9–10) he follows much the same line of argument as Schmid, and the combination of this with his view of verses 11–22 actually produces a new problem, as he recognises: from a purely grammatical point of view v. 11 could not be the beginning of an independent narrative, since it lacks an explicit subject for its first main verb, and in addition the imposition of hard labour is entirely unmotivated. Gertz concludes that the original beginning of the episode has been lost, or removed.[31] But is it not simpler to see it in the verses which, with Schmid, he has himself assigned to a later redactional layer? In other words, the process of reasoning on which Gertz has set out points most probably to verses 6 and 8–10 being the introduction to the non-Priestly Exodus-story (עַמּוֹ in v. 9 then provides the unexpressed subject for v. 11), complete with their references back to the preceding story of Joseph and his brothers.[32]

---

[28] Blum, 2002, pp. 150–51.
[29] Blum, 2002, p. 148 n. 137.
[30] Gertz, 2000, pp. 370–79.
[31] Gertz, 2000, pp. 358–70, 381–82. Gertz's suggestion (p. 359) that Exod. 1:8 may be the original continuation of Gen. 50:26 (the other account of Joseph's death) rather than Exod. 1:6 makes no real difference, as there is nothing in Gen. 50:26 itself which requires a late date (only, if anything, in 50:25, but that connection may not be original). See further Gerhards, pp. 63–66.
[32] Kratz's argument and conclusion (2000, pp. 287–88) differ somewhat from those of Schmid and Gertz, but are no more persuasive.

(ii) *Exodus 3*

It was in the absence of any reference to the patriarchal promises in Exodus 3 that Rendtorff first saw a problem for the idea of a continuous Yahwist source with a high theological profile extending from Genesis into Exodus.[33] Blum duly attributed it (and 4:1–18) to a separate stage of composition, his "D-Komposition", a somewhat surprising decision in view of the frequency of the references to the ancestral promises in Deuteronomy itself.[34] According to Konrad Schmid 3:1–4:18 is even further removed from an early account of the Exodus, since he concludes that it is entirely post-Priestly in origin, being modelled on the somewhat similar Priestly account of the commissioning of Moses and Aaron in Exod. 6:2–7:7(13).[35] This at a stroke eliminates several plausible examples of a pre-Priestly linkage between the patriarchal and Exodus narratives (see above for the detailed references). But, not surprisingly, such a drastic revision of literary history has met with considerable opposition, even from those who agree with Schmid on other matters, or have come to do so, such as Gertz and Blum.[36] The latter accept Schmid's argument in relation to 4:1–17, but find a substantial pre-Priestly strand in chapter 3. Of course it is still possible for them to find reasons for regarding allusions to Genesis as being of a later origin, but the arguments may then seem more like special pleading, at least in some cases. Even more critical responses to Schmid's position have been made, with good reason, by Dozeman (especially), Van Seters and Carr, whose comparisons with Gen. 46:1–5 are especially significant.[37] In fact the account of Moses' encounter with God in 3:1–4:17 is in many respects quite different from the Priestly version in 6:2–7:7 and the differences (especially the Midianite setting) favour the view that it was earlier than P (and D) rather than later. Moreover, the rather restrained references to the patriarchal figures (including the absence of explicit references to the promise of the land of Canaan to them) are, if anything, most compatible with a quite early version of

---

[33] Rendtorff, 1977, pp. 65–70 (ET, pp. 84–89).
[34] Blum, 1990, pp. 32–35.
[35] Schmid, 1999, pp. 186–209.
[36] Gertz, 2000, pp. 261–305; Blum, 2002, pp. 124–30.
[37] T. B. Dozeman, "The Commission of Moses and the Book of Genesis", in Dozeman and Schmid (eds.), pp. 107–29; Van Seters, 2006, pp. 155–56; Carr, 2006, pp. 166–67, 175–79.

the patriarchal narratives in which the promise theme may not have been as dominant as it is now.

(iii) *Genesis 50*

Passages which link the Exodus story to the patriarchal narratives are found at the end of Genesis as well as the beginning of Exodus, and so discussion has also focused on the affinities and dating of Genesis 50. In older Pentateuchal criticism there was something of a consensus that most of the account of Jacob's burial in 50:1–14 was from J, verses 12–13 being from P, and the concluding section leading up to Joseph's death (vv. 15–26) was all from E.[38] A minority have found evidence of J as well as E in verses 15–26.[39] A change began with Rendtorff's observation that 50:24 incorporated the so-called "oath-formula" in Joseph's assurance that God would take his brothers to the land of Canaan and with his more general view that the occurrences of this formula from Genesis to Numbers were part of a late redactional layer which helped to unify the originally separate sections of the Pentateuchal narrative.[40] Rendtorff also expressed surprise that earlier scholars had been so ready to attribute the age-formulae in 50:22b and 50:26a ("Joseph was 110 years old" at the time of his death) to one of the older sources, although his own review of examples showed that these verses did not in fact conform to the regular Priestly expression used frequently elsewhere in Genesis.[41] On the basis of this and his own more detailed studies Blum initially concluded that v. 24 with most of the rest of vv. 22–26 was part of his exilic *D-Komposition*, while 50:22b and 50:26a were later additions to it.[42] This still left, in verses 24 and 25, two strands of a forward-looking link to the books which follow in a layer earlier than P, since the reference to Joseph's bones being taken back to Canaan in v. 25 also implied a future departure from Egypt. Not surprisingly Konrad Schmid devoted special attention to these verses and his conclusion was that they can be shown to be dependent on

[38] So still A. Graupner, *Der Elohist. Gegenwart und Wirksamkeit des transzendenten Gottes in der Geschichte* (WMANT 97; Neukirchen, 2002), pp. 364–77.

[39] So, e.g., O. Eissfeldt, *Hexateuch-Synopse* (Leipzig, 1922), pp. 105–06*; recently L. Ruppert, *Genesis: ein kritischer und theologischer Kommentar*, 4 (Würzburg, 2008), pp. 538–41.

[40] Rendtorff, 1977, pp. 75–79 (ET, pp. 94–100).

[41] Rendtorff, 1977, pp. 135–36 (ET, pp. 162–63), esp. p. 136 n. 10 (ET, p. 163 n. 1).

[42] Blum, 1990, pp. 255–59.

and later than P.[43] This at first sight remarkable conclusion has been followed not only by Gertz but by Blum, in a significant revision of his earlier views.[44] The arguments are based, characteristically, not so much on the contents of these verses themselves but on the larger redactional layers of which they are said to be a part. In the case of vv. 25–26 this means for Schmid Genesis 15, Exodus 3–4 and Joshua 24, all three of them passages which he holds to be dependent on the Priestly source (respectively Gen. 17, Exod. 6–7 and Exod. 14 – cf. Josh. 24:6–7) and held together by a series of common characteristics. The details of his argument need fuller treatment than is possible here, but it is not at all clear that the longer passages mentioned are in their entirety dependent on P.[45] At most isolated verses can be explained in this way, but that says nothing about the remainder of the passages and therefore nothing about Gen. 50:25–26. Verse 24, as already noted, belongs to a long sequence of passages in which the oath-formula occurs, beginning with Gen. 24:6. Schmid's case for its post-Priestly origin appears to be based on three arguments: a claim that the theology expressed in the formula combines elements from Dtr and P (an argument already made by Thomas Römer), its presence in a bridge-passage (Gen. 50:22–26) which has "already been shown to be post-Priestly", and the late, in some cases post-Priestly, dating of other passages in which the oath-formula appears.[46] None of these arguments is decisive: the first overlooks the possibility that reference is made to the land-promise in the non-Priestly material; the second is based (at most) on the claims made about verses 25–26, when v. 24 may well be more originally associated with verses 22–23 and/or verses 15–21; and the third assumes that the oath-formula was only used in one, very late, layer of the Pentateuch, when there is better reason to see it as a motif which appeared in a succession of stages of composition, possibly beginning even before Deuteronomy.[47]

---

[43] Schmid, 1999, pp. 230–33, 242–50 on vv. 25–26; and pp. 294–99 on v. 24.

[44] Gertz, "The Transition between the Books of Genesis and Exodus", in Dozeman and Schmid (eds.), pp. 73–87 (79–82; cf. id., 2000, pp. 361–65); Blum, 2002, pp. 148–51, 153.

[45] For some critique see Carr in Dozeman and Schmid (eds.), pp. 169–72, esp. p. 172 on Josh 24:6–7.

[46] Schmid, 1999, pp. 298–99.

[47] Cf. G. I. Davies, "Covenant, Oath and the Composition of the Pentateuch", in A. D. H. Mayes and R. B. Salters (eds.), *Covenant as Context: Essays in Honour of E. W. Nicholson* (Oxford, 2003), pp. 71–89.

In a more recent essay Schmid has sought to widen the gap between the end of the non-Priestly Joseph-story and the Exodus-story, by building on his earlier claim that the Joseph-story in effect ends in Canaan.[48] If Gen. 50:22–26 are regarded as very late, the verse which stands in the way of such an impression is 50:14, which reports Joseph's return from Canaan with his entourage after the burial of Jacob. Schmid now argues that this verse is not part of the original non-Priestly Joseph story, so that the dialogue between Joseph and his brothers in the following verses is set in Canaan, not Egypt.[49] Gertz has taken this up and sees 50:14a as part of P, continuing what is generally recognised to be the Priestly version of Jacob's burial in vv. 12–13 and providing the otherwise missing "bridge" between that and the Priestly Exodus-story.[50] This looks rather like robbing Peter to pay Paul! In fact the "stolen property" is very evidently such. Whereas the Priestly account of Jacob's burial gives Joseph no special place (it is "his sons" who bury him in vv. 12–13, in accordance with the Priestly version of Jacob's instructions in 49:29–33), 50:14 recognises Joseph as their leader, as he had been both earlier in chapter 50 and in the non-Priestly account of Jacob's instructions in 48:29–31.[51] Moreover it is hard to imagine Joseph's brothers expressing such anxiety about their future as they do in 50:15–18 if they were now in Canaan, rather than still in Egypt where Joseph's power was unchallengeable. Like it or not, therefore, the non-Priestly Joseph-story ends in Egypt, and with it the non-Priestly story of Genesis as a whole, and as such it needs (and looks forward to) a continuation of the story in which a permanent return to Canaan has yet to be described.

Thus at all three points that we have considered (Exodus 1 and 3; Genesis 50) there is a strong link between Genesis and Exodus in the non-Priestly material, which there is no good reason to see as post-Priestly. The case for such a link being first introduced by P has not been made.

---

[48] Schmid, 1999, pp. 59–60.

[49] K. Schmid, "Die Josephsgeschichte im Pentateuch", in Gertz, Schmid and Witte (eds.), pp. 83–118 (103–04); cf. id., "The So-Called Yahwist and the Literary Gap between Genesis and Exodus", in Dozeman and Schmid (eds.), pp. 29–50 (32–33).

[50] Gertz, in Dozeman and Schmid (eds.), pp. 77–79. where he also ascribes v. 22a to the *Endredaktion*.

[51] See already Carr in Dozeman and Schmid (eds.), pp. 168–69.

Conclusion

I will end with three concluding remarks. First, possible literary links between the non-Priestly sections of Genesis and Exodus are not limited to the clear cross-references noted earlier. Robert Alter recently identified an impressive series of linguistic and thematic correspondences which balanced his initial impression of a striking change at the beginning of Exodus, as "the narrative moves from the domestic, moral and psychological realism of the Patriarchal Tales to a more stylised, sometimes deliberately schematic, mode of storytelling that in a number of respects, especially in the early chapters of the book [of Exodus], has the feel of a folktale".[52] In addition to some features which have already been mentioned he notes the following: the Egyptians as people who kill foreigners (1:22; cf. Gen. 12:12); the echo of the Flood story in the story of Moses' birth, highlighted by the use of the same word תֵּבָה for the water craft in each case; the parallel between the story of Moses meeting his future wife by a well (2:16) and the similar stories about Isaac and Jacob in Genesis 24 and 29; the "plundering of the Egyptians" in 3:22 as a recapitulation of the wealth with which Abraham leaves Egypt in Gen. 12 (cf. 20 and 26); the fear of the snake formed from Moses' staff in 4:3 as an echo of Gen. 3:15a; Moses' concern about his kinsmen in Egypt in 4:18, which is expressed in very similar words to Joseph's question about his father in Gen. 45:3; and the parallel between Yahweh's enigmatic assault on Moses in 4:24–26 and Jacob's encounter with God in Gen. 32 as "a mysterious stranger", both corresponding to "the folktale pattern of a perilous rite of passage that the hero must undergo before embarking on his mission proper".[53] It did not take a modern folklorist to spot this parallel: it was already picked up in one of the texts of 4QReworkedPentateuch (4Q158, fr. 1–2).[54]

And Alter's examples could be added to: in the story of the burning bush God addresses Moses (3:4) in terms that are closely remi-

---

[52] R. Alter, *The Five Books of Moses* (New York and London, 2004), p. 300; cf. pp. 299 and 301.

[53] Ibid., pp. 311–12, 315, 324–25, 329–31.

[54] *DJD* V, pp. 1–2. This and the well-story, together with the surrounding journey-motif, are the key elements in R. S. Hendel's case for an extended parallel between the whole Jacob-story and the early chapters of Exodus in his *The Epic of the Patriarch: The Jacob Cycle and the Narrative Traditions of Canaan and Israel* (Harvard Semitic Monographs 42; Atlanta, 1987).

niscent of his words to Abraham and Jacob (Gen. 22:1, 11; 46:2), and the phrase "I am the God of your father" (3:6) is typical of the theophanies to the patriarchs (e.g. Gen. 46:3). The extent of these and the other connections of style, vocabulary, motif and theme is much greater than might have been expected. One may or may not accept all these claimed "echoes" or "foreshadowings", but I suspect that there is enough there to add some further weight to the argument for narrative continuity between Genesis and Exodus in the non-Priestly material. To attribute all of them to a late post-Priestly redactor would leave rather little for an early independent Exodus narrative, and in any case what would be the justification for the separation of these elements from their contexts?

Secondly, I should like to go one step beyond others who have been critical of Schmid and Gertz and refer to the non-Priestly narrative as JE. It seems to me that, despite what is becoming the common view, there are enough indications of a double strand in the non-Priestly material, both in Genesis and in Exodus, to justify a form of the older view that it includes extracts from what were once two separate versions of the story of Israel's origins, which used to be called J and E with good reason. Within Genesis 50 and Exodus 1 it is notable, for example, that there are two statements of Joseph's death (Gen. 50:26; Exod. 1:6), neither of which is obviously redactional or late. But parallel accounts have often not been preserved (and they may not always have existed), and it is also likely that the redactor or author who made use of J and E contributed additional material of his own, which it is not always easy to distinguish convincingly from the underlying source-material. Some recent commentators continue to attempt this (e.g. L. Ruppert on Genesis (completed in 2008) and W. H. Schmidt on Exodus (ongoing)), but the arguments are in my view often inconclusive. When I speak of JE, therefore, I do not mean simply the contributions of the redactor/author traditionally known as R[JE] but the whole of the non-Priestly material, which it may often not be possible to subdivide further convincingly. Since Wellhausen in his pioneering works often used the siglum in this way, there is a good precedent.[55]

---

[55] Among recent scholars I think this brings me closest to Erich Zenger and his reconstruction of a "Jerusalemer Geschichtswerk" from the early to mid-seventh century (see his *Einleitung in das Alte Testament*, 2nd ed.[Stuttgart, 1996], pp. 108–23).

Thirdly and finally, there is the question of dating. One of the few things on which the contributors to *A Farewell to the Yahwist?* all agree is their rejection of von Rad's Yahwist dated to the early monarchy. Levin and Van Seters are quite clear that their "J" sources are from the exilic period, and Carr only tentatively suggests that his "pre-Priestly proto-Pentateuch" may go back to the late monarchy period.[56] Many, perhaps all, of the various arguments for such a late date are far from conclusive.[57] At most they give a date for the completion of JE (the "non-Priestly account") as a whole, but the underlying material from the sources, some of which retains its original profile quite clearly, must be considerably older – not perhaps as early as von Rad and his many followers thought, but from the ninth or the eighth century B.C. – and that very likely already included the join between what became Genesis and Exodus.

---

[56] In Dozeman and Schmid (eds.), p. 160.

[57] See Emerton, 1982 and 2004; E. W. Nicholson, *The Pentateuch in the Twentieth Century: The Legacy of Julius Wellhausen* (Oxford, 1998), pp. 132–60; G. I. Davies, in J. Barton and J. Muddiman (eds.), *The Oxford Bible Commentary* (Oxford, 2001), pp. 34–35.

NOVELISTS AS INTERPRETERS OF GENESIS

Bertil Albrektson

Hermann Hesse, the writer, had a cook, a cultivated lady who was a refugee from Vienna. She sometimes also read aloud to him as Hesse had poor eyesight. Once she read the chapter about Tamar and Judah from Thomas Mann's *Joseph und seine Brüder*. She reported that afterwards Hesse made the slightly enigmatic remark: "Manchmal sieht man doch, daß die Dichter nicht ganz überflüssig sind" ("Sometimes it is evident that the writers are not entirely superfluous").[1]

Hesse's claim is a rather modest one, but others have been more bold. Some have argued that authors of fiction who rewrite and supplement biblical stories can play an important part in the interpretation of the original texts and make significant contributions to a better understanding of their meaning and message. Modern fiction is, however, not normally listed among the exegetical tools of biblical scholars, and I must confess that I had not, until fairly recently, reflected much on novelists as interpreters of Genesis or any other biblical book. But a doctoral dissertation which was presented in January 2007 in the Faculty of Theology at the University of Uppsala[2] made me aware of the subject, and I have since discovered that the young scholar at Uppsala is not the only one to pay attention to this question. There is, for instance, an interesting and instructive book by Terry R. Wright, *The Genesis of Fiction: Modern Novelists as Biblical Interpreters*, published in 2007 (obviously my title for this paper is inspired by Wright's subtitle).[3]

All the works discussed by Professor Wright are "novels which take stories from the Book of Genesis as their starting point", rewriting them and "attempting to make sense of them in the twentieth

---

[1] T. Fein, "Als Köchin bei Hermann Hesse", in V. Michels (ed.), *Hermann Hesse in Augenzeugenberichten* (Frankfurt am Main, 1991), p. 239. Cf. D. A. Prater, *Thomas Mann: a Life* (Oxford, 1995), p. 348.

[2] L. Sjöberg, *Genesis och Jernet. Ett möte mellan Sara Lidmans Jernbaneepos och bibelns berättelser* (Stockholm, 2006).

[3] T. R. Wright, *The Genesis of Fiction: Modern Novelists as Biblical Interpreters* (London, 2007).

century".[4] But this is done in very different ways; several types of retelling can be discerned. Some narrators retain both the historical setting and the main course of events of the original story and confine themselves to embellishing and expanding it. A famous example of this kind of retelling is of course the work that Hermann Hesse was listening to: Thomas Mann's *Joseph und seine Brüder*, which expands the 20 or so biblical pages into a mammoth work running to 1355 pages in the single-volume edition. Other writers, while keeping the original characters and the biblical setting, use them above all to express their own personal views, sometimes as a protest against the biblical version, as in Mark Twain's ironical "Autobiography of Eve" and other similar works of his. Here the protagonists still bear their biblical names: Adam and Eve, Cain and Abel, Noah, and so on, though these individuals are sometimes strikingly different from their scriptural models. A further step away from the original is taken in stories which are transferred to modern surroundings – or at least contain so many anachronisms that we feel the characters are our contemporaries, even if they are called Noah and Shem and Ham, as in Jeanette Winterson's comic parody of the Flood story, *Boating for Beginners*. Still further away from the outward form of the biblical tale and from the kind of retelling represented by Thomas Mann is John Steinbeck's well-known novel *East of Eden*. It is about settlers in the Salinas Valley in Northern California in the late nineteenth and early twentieth century, but the title discloses its basis in Genesis 4, as do also passages in which some of the characters discuss different translations of verse 7 of the biblical chapter. Professor Wright argues, not without reason, that the novel provides "both a commentary upon Genesis 4 and a supplementary narrative based upon it".[5]

Compared with these different retellings of episodes in Genesis, the Swedish epic which is analysed in the Uppsala thesis mentioned a moment ago represents yet another type. The story, as in Steinbeck's *East of Eden*, takes place in the late nineteenth century and in an environment that is manifestly different from the biblical setting. But whereas the American novel may still be described as a kind of retelling of at least the essence of a narrative from Genesis, the relation to the Bible is here much more fragmentary. The Swedish epic, though

---

[4] Wright, *The Genesis of Fiction*, p. ix.
[5] Wright, *The Genesis of Fiction*, p. 51.

full of allusions and references to biblical texts, is no retelling, however disguised, of a continuous narrative sequence.

The author of this Swedish dissertation is called Lina Sjöberg, and the title of her book is *Genesis och Jernet. Ett möte mellan Sara Lidmans Jernbaneepos och bibelns berättelser,* which means "Genesis and the Iron. A meeting between Sara Lidman's Railway Epic and the biblical narratives". The presence of the word "iron" should perhaps be explained to an English-speaking audience. The Swedish word for "railway" is literally "iron way" (just like German "Eisenbahn"), and the theme of the five volumes, written during the nineteen-seventies and -eighties, is the building of a railway through inland northern Sweden at the end of the nineteenth century. They depict the rise and fall of the male protagonist, a local farmer and politician who is the driving force of the whole enterprise, and they portray his family relations, especially with his wife and other women. The characters are country people from northern Sweden, not biblical figures at home in Palestine. But there are many references to the Bible, and one of the principal female characters is in fact called Hagar. One important purpose of this dissertation is to uncover such references and to analyse them. Two chapters in Genesis are particularly interesting in this connection, chapters 16 and 21, about Abraham, Sarah and Hagar.

According to the author, her purpose is not only to interpret these modern Swedish novels in the light of their references to biblical texts but also "to interpret the story in Genesis in the light of the modern literary texts".[6] She attempts, as she herself expresses it in her brief English summary, "to follow the path of intertextuality in two directions".[7] My spontaneous reaction was that the first direction is entirely natural and scholarly: to investigate the character and functions and effects of the allusions to biblical stories and biblical figures in a modern work of fiction seems a worthwhile task.

The second direction, however, from the modern novels to the narratives in Genesis, looked to me rather hazardous, and I was rather curious how the author would justify this backward movement. The attempt to read Genesis 16 and 21 in the light of an epic from our own time rather reminds one of the young scholar Persse McGarrigle in

---

[6] Sjöberg, *Genesis och Jernet,* p. 325.
[7] Sjöberg, *Genesis och Jernet,* p. 325.

David Lodge's entertaining novel *Small World*. This promising young man had written a thesis "about the influence of T. S. Eliot on Shakespeare".[8] Is this second part of Sjöberg's dissertation just another postmodernist puzzle or might some real insights be gained this way? After all, not even the fictitious thesis on Eliot's influence on the Bard of Avon is quite as silly as it sounds: it turns out to be not about what the somewhat misleading title makes us believe but about a much more plausible problem: the question of the influence of our familiarity with *Prufrock* or *The Waste Land* on our reading of Shakespeare, which is obviously a different matter. So there is reason to look closely and carefully at what Sjöberg is trying to do.

In the English summary of the thesis the author writes:

> In the second part of the dissertation I read the biblical texts of Genesis 16 and 21 in the light of the modern epic, *Jernbaneeposet*, in order to deal with the following questions: 'How could/should the biblical scholar proceed in order to transfer the intuitive knowledge, expressed through hints, allusions and poetic style in modern fiction, to the field of biblical scholarship? Can art be used as a means of interpretation in biblical scholarship?'
>
> The background to these questions is the observation that personal relationships, a common theme in the Genesis stories, cannot be, or are not, easily accessible with the help of traditional biblical scholarship. Having tried to understand the relationships between Abraham, Sarah and Hagar in Genesis, and having voiced a number of questions due to textual silence or gaps in the texts, I turn to the works of a number of well-known biblical scholars, representing a range of 'methods'. These scholars sometimes present answers to my questions concerning human relationships and emotions in Genesis [...]. But none of them give satisfactory answers to all or even most of the questions.
>
> Therefore, I return to *Jernbaneeposet* and engage in a close reading of those parts that contain frequent references to the biblical story. This reading inspires two models of explanation, which I bring back to the Hebrew text, and the models offer solutions to my questions.[9]

---

[8] Cf. also F. C. Black and J. C. Exum, "Semiotics in Stained Glass: Edward Burne-Jones's Song of Songs", in J. C. Exum and S. D. Moore (eds.), *Biblical Studies/Cultural Studies: the Third Sheffield Colloquium* (Sheffield, 1998), p. 316, n. 6, where this fictitious postmodern dissertation is mentioned. Black and Exum's approach is very similar to that of Sjöberg: they "want to establish influence in both directions. Whereas biblical studies might conceivably ask how the Bible has influenced Burne-Jones, cultural studies invites us to invert the question and ask how Burne-Jones's window might influence the Song of Songs, that is, our interpretation of it" (p. 316). Sjöberg, *Genesis och Jernet*, refers to Black and Exum on p. 21, n. 18.

[9] Sjöberg, *Genesis och Jernet*, pp. 326f.

There are, in the modern epic by Sara Lidman, three principal characters which show certain similarities with characters in Genesis: a man called Didrik, his wife called Anna-Stava, and a wet-nurse called Hagar. Through a number of references and allusions in the text some correspondences between these persons and the biblical Abraham, Sarah, and Hagar are established. The question now is in which way the modern text can serve as an exegetical instrument.

It is important to remember that Sjöberg is above all interested in the personal relationships between the principal characters in Genesis 16 and 21 and the feelings expressed in the Hebrew text. And this preoccupation with the emotional aspects of the story immediately raises the problem whether her interest is actually matched by the original text itself. Does the biblical text really answer the questions that Sjöberg puts to it?

Many years ago a Cambridge literary historian called L. C. Knights wrote a famous essay with the title "How Many Children Had Lady Macbeth?".[10] He criticized the idea that the main business of writers is to create characters, and that the best narrators are able to invent and describe imaginary persons who take on a life of their own and who – as one Shakespeare critic expressed it – "remain as real to us as our familiar friends".[11] Knights reminds us that all we have are "the words on the page, which it is the main business of the critic to examine".[12] We cannot treat literary characters as if they were real people; it leads to futile "inquiries into 'latent motives'" and "into pseudo-critical investigations that are only slightly parodied by the title of this essay"[13] (i.e. How Many Children Had Lady Macbeth?). A Swedish literary scholar, Professor Lars-Åke Skalin, has developed Knights's idea, and the title of his inaugural lecture is a kind of Swedish version of Knights's provocative wording; it is called "Vad gör Medea på fritiden?"[14] ("What does Medea do in her spare time?"). Skalin argues that instead of regarding Medea as a real person and judging her thoughts

---

[10] L. C. Knights, "How Many Children Had Lady Macbeth?", in idem, 'Hamlet' and other Shakespearean Essays (Cambridge, 1979), pp. 270–306. The essay was first published in 1933.

[11] L. P. Smith, On Reading Shakespeare (London, 1933), as quoted by Knights, "How Many Children", p. 272.

[12] Knights, "How Many Children", p. 275.

[13] Knights, "How Many Children", p. 306.

[14] L.-Å. Skalin, "Vad gör Medea på fritiden?", Installationsföreläsningar 1995/96, http://www.info.uu.se/publ/fp1996/19.html, accessed 29.01.08.

and actions in a realist perspective, the literary scholar must treat all characters as fiction and analyse how this fiction is constructed.

It seems to me that one of the problematic aspects of Sjöberg's thesis is precisely that she wants to answer questions for which the Hebrew texts do not supply the answers. The personal relations between Sarah, Hagar and Abraham and the emotional aspects of their life together are not really the focus of attention for the biblical narrators in Genesis 16 and 21. Not that they are entirely indifferent to these aspects: they are good storytellers and definitely capable of depicting these characters with psychological sensitivity. But they do not dwell on this topic: their main interest is concentrated on the ongoing story of the divine promise of a son and heir to Abraham and the threat to its fulfilment. The glimpses of a family drama are more of an embellishment. That Sara Lidman and Sjöberg are interested in emotional relations between the protagonists does not guarantee that the biblical authors are.

I just quoted a passage from Sjöberg's summary where she mentions "two models of explanation" which she extracts from her reading of the novels and brings back to the Hebrew text. The main problem, according to her, is that most exegetes have failed to pay sufficient attention to the personal relationships and emotions in the domestic triangle drama between Abraham, Sarah and Hagar. And her two models are said to answer questions that previous interpreters have neglected. Her first model is based on an analysis of the wife's desire/disgust in a context which resembles chapter 16 in Genesis, and the second model is linked to the husband's accentuated interest in Hagar, which appears in a situation suggestive of chapter 21.

Sjöberg's analysis of the character of Anna-Stava, the wife in the novels, results in a double view: Anna-Stava both feels attracted to Hagar, the wet-nurse, an attraction that has a clear sexual tinge, and she is at the same time filled with intense disgust. This "first model of explanation" is, for Sjöberg, a pattern to be applied to the relationship between Sarah and Hagar in Genesis 16.

Chapter 16 begins in the following way: "Sarai, Abram's wife, had not borne him any children. She had an Egyptian slave-girl named Hagar." This introductory verse, which to my mind seems quite straightforward and innocent, is taken to imply that there is an emotional relationship between Sarah and Hagar.

Inspired by the novel's depiction of Anna-Stava, Sarah's counterpart in the epic, Sjöberg interprets the subsequent verses in the following way: the relationship with Sarah becomes unimportant to Hagar when she discovers that she is pregnant. This makes Sarah jealous of Abraham: she sees him as a rival who has taken her place in Hagar's world. In v. 5 Sarah says to Abraham: "The wrong done to me is your fault! I gave my slave-girl to your embrace, and when she saw that she was pregnant, she looked down on me". This is seen as an outburst of jealousy and despair; Sarah feels slighted and even abandoned by Hagar.

The interpretation inspired by Lidman's epic seems strange and far-fetched. Surely the reason why Sarah turns to Abraham and complains to him is not that she is jealous of Abraham and regards him as a rival for Hagar's attachment but simply that in the setting of the patriarchal narratives the husband is responsible for safeguarding justice in accordance with the legal system and the customs of the time. When Sarah feels offended it is to her husband that she must appeal.

The reason why Sjöberg's idea of a lesbian bond between Sarah and Hagar seems far-fetched is not only that it has no support whatsoever in the Hebrew text: the narrative also originated in a moral and religious environment where such a portraiture seems extremely unlikely, to say the least.

The second model of explanation which Sjöberg extracts from her reading of the Northern epic has to do with Didrik's, the husband's, increasing interest in Hagar, and it is applied to the story in Genesis 21. In v. 14 we hear about the expulsion of Hagar. Abraham provides her with bread and water, puts Ishmael on her back and sends her away. The whole scene is depicted with utmost restraint: not a word too much, no mention of Abraham's or Hagar's emotions at the parting, only a bare account of the basic actions. What Abraham thought, what Hagar felt remains a secret. It is a telling example of the biblical style that Erich Auerbach has described in the famous first chapter of *Mimesis*: "the elaboration of only so much of the phenomena as is necessary for the purpose of the narrative, all else left in obscurity; the decisive points of the narrative alone are emphasized, what lies between is nonexistent; [...] thoughts and feelings remain unexpressed, are only suggested by the silence and the fragmentary speeches".[15] But

---

[15] E. Auerbach, *Mimesis: the Representation of Reality in Western Literature*, transl. from the German by W. R. Trask (Princeton, [1953]1974), p. 11. In order to get closer to the German I have substituted "elaboration" for Trask's "externalization" and "feelings" for his "feeling". The original runs: "...wird nur dasjenige an den Erscheinungen herausgearbeitet, was für das Ziel der Handlung wichtig ist, der Rest bleibt im Dunkel; die entscheidenden Höhepunkte der Handlung werden allein betont, das Dazwischenliegende ist wesenlos; [...] die Gedanken und Gefühle bleiben

Sjöberg is not content to respect the reticence of the Hebrew narrator. Verse 14, she avers, "describes a painful separation".[16] She speculates, inspired by the characters resembling Abraham and Hagar as they are portrayed in the Northern epic. She sees Abraham as emotionally engaged, as he links up with Hagar after what happened in chapter 16. She states that "Abraham stands for the tender emotions in the parting scene",[17] and she speaks about "the expressions of Abraham's emotional and existential experiences".[18] Well, we can all guess what Medea does in her spare time, we are all free to supplement the author's narrative with our own poetic imagination, and so, of course, is Sjöberg. Only it is essential not to mistake such activities for scholarly exegesis.

There is a kind of ambiguity in the way Sjöberg presents her methods and results. On the one hand she makes considerable pretensions: by using modern novels she claims to be able to solve problems which traditional exegetical methods cannot cope with. This concrete aim is coupled with a theoretical claim: to present a method for the use of modern fiction in the interpretation of biblical narratives, a method that is applicable also to texts other than the particular stories treated in her thesis.[19] On the other hand she seems to realize that the actual results are very uncertain; she admits that she cannot, with her exegetical honour intact (her own phrase, p. 308), assert that Hagar is lesbian or that Abraham and Hagar had a close emotional relationship. To quote her own concession: "I do not claim that my interpretation is [...] inherent in the Hebrew text, but I do claim that the modern literary work of art promoted the understanding of relationships and emotions in the Hebrew text in a particular biblical scholar – myself".[20] But such a private and subjective interpretation is not enough: the minimum demand on the intersubjectivity of a scientific statement must be upheld in the humanities as well as in the natural sciences.[21] What

---

unausgesprochen, sie werden nur aus dem Schweigen und fragmentarischen Reden suggeriert" (E. Auerbach, *Mimesis: dargestellte Wirklichkeit in der abendländischen Literatur* [Bern, 1946], p. 16).

[16] Sjöberg, *Genesis och Jernet*, p. 307: "skildrar en smärtsam separation".

[17] Sjöberg, *Genesis och Jernet*, p. 307: "De ömsinta känslorna i avskedsscenen står Abraham för".

[18] Sjöberg, *Genesis och Jernet*, p. 307: "uttrycken för Abrahams emotionella och existentiella upplevelser".

[19] Sjöberg, *Genesis och Jernet*, e.g. pp. 24ff., 311ff., 327.

[20] Sjöberg, *Genesis och Jernet*, p. 327.

[21] Cf. E. D. Hirsch, Jr., *Validity in Interpretation* (New Haven and London, [1967] 1976), pp. viii–ix: "The theoretical aim of a genuine discipline, scientific or humanistic,

remains of her grand ambitions is imaginative fiction, not scholarly results that can be said to contribute to a reliable and demonstrable interpretation of the biblical stories. The application of fiction breeds fiction. And as the results are so scanty and speculative, the method she advocates does not have much to speak for it; nor does she ever present it in a detailed and systematic way.

I would like to emphasize once more that these critical comments do not affect the part of Sjöberg's thesis in which she investigates the way biblical stories and figures have been used in the Railway Epic. That section seems to me to contain useful contributions to our understanding of an important Swedish literary work, not least the analysis of the three levels of "markers", "means" and "effects" of the biblical influences.[22] But if her interpretation of "modern literary texts in the light of their references to the biblical material" is a creditable piece of research, I do not think this can be said of her attempt "to interpret the story in Genesis in the light of the modern literary texts".

Novelists as interpreters of Genesis – of course the author of the Railway Epic never claims to interpret Genesis: the connection is an indirect one,[23] and it is Sjöberg who declares that she has found a key to the interpretation of Genesis 16 and 21 in this modern epic. But there are other novelists who relate directly to the biblical characters, using them as protagonists in their own narratives in a creative and imaginative response to the stories and figures in Genesis, sometimes preserving their time and setting, sometimes transferring them to modern surroundings. Can they promote better interpretations of the biblical texts? Well, it partly depends on what we mean by "interpretation" – a word which has several shades of meaning.

James Barr once made a distinction between two kinds of interpretation, "which are so different as hardly to deserve to be called by the same name",[24] and a Swedish philosopher, Göran Hermerén, in an instructive essay distinguishes between no less than eleven types

---

is the attainment of truth, and its practical aim is agreement that truth has probably been achieved. Thus the practical goal of every genuine discipline is consensus – the winning of firmly grounded agreement that one set of conclusions is more probable than others – and this is precisely the goal of valid interpretation."

[22] Sjöberg, *Genesis och Jernet*, chapter 3 (pp. 61ff.), and chapter 6 (pp. 154ff.).

[23] This is acknowledged by Sjöberg, *Genesis och Jernet*: see p. 182.

[24] J. Barr, *The Typology of Literalism in ancient biblical translations* (MSU X; Göttingen, 1979), p. 290 [16].

of interpretation.[25] Even without making a careful philosophical division it is nevertheless possible to distinguish between some main categories. The first meaning specified for the verb "interpret" in the *Oxford English Dictionary*[26] is "to expound the meaning of (something abstruse or mysterious)". This use of the term can easily be exemplified in the Book of Genesis itself, where Joseph first interprets the dreams of Pharaoh's cupbearer and baker and then those of Pharaoh himself. A related shade of meaning is the more general "to render (words, writings, an author, etc.) clear or explicit; to elucidate, to explain", which seems a reasonable definition of the task of an exegete. But the word "interpret" can also be used about a rather different kind of activity. To quote again the *OED*: "To bring out the meaning of (a dramatic or musical composition, a landscape, etc.) by artistic representation or performance; to give one's own interpretation of; to render". Typical examples of this would be, say, Lawrence Olivier's version of Hamlet or Hilary Hahn's rendering of Sibelius's violin concerto. Many artists of course wish to be faithful to what they understand to be the author's or composer's intention, but it is also possible to treat the text of a drama or the notes of a concerto as merely a kind of raw material for one's own particular artistic concern – there have lately been many examples of this on the stage.

No doubt this last definition best fits the work of novelists rewriting biblical stories. Their retellings may reflect the modern author's understanding of the initial story and of the characters, their actions and motives. But it is also quite possible that the picture painted of a biblical figure in a new setting may not be intended as a faithful expression of the author's understanding of the prototype but rather as a free creation of the author's own imaginative power, something that goes beyond the biblical model and may even be fashioned as a parody or as a protest against the scriptural character and what it stands for. The editors of *The Bible According to Mark Twain* point out that his "many attempts to rewrite and supplement the biblical account of creation and its aftermath [...] range from farce to fantasy to biting satire".[27]

---

[25] G. Hermerén, "Tolkningstyper och tolkningskriterier", *Tolkning och tolknings-teorier: Föredrag och diskussionsinlägg vid Vitterhetsakademiens symposium 17–19 november 1981* (Stockholm, 1982), pp. 269–292, esp. pp. 273ff.

[26] *The Oxford English Dictionary*, Second Edition, prepared by J. A. Simpson and E. S. C. Weiner, vol. VII (Oxford, 1989), s.v.

[27] *The Bible According to Mark Twain: Writings on Heaven, Eden, and the Flood,*

The retelling of biblical stories may have very little to do with the original narrative and its message: what we have is instead a vehicle for the modern author's own ideas and concerns. Harold Fisch in his *New Stories for Old: Biblical Patterns in the Novel* speaks of a "point where interpretation becomes something more like a reinventing of the story, a creative extension of its possibilities".[28] It seems consistent with ordinary linguistic usage to apply the term "interpretation" to such artistic activities, but it is important to remember that they are nevertheless utterly different from scholarly attempts to uncover the original or plain sense of a text.[29]

In *The Genesis of Fiction* Wright also tries to reveal the extent to which the authors he considers "succeed in shedding new light on some aspects of the biblical text",[30] a purpose which seems perhaps not entirely different from Sjöberg's ambitions. Though his main attention is engaged with other questions – such as the various authors' dependence on midrashic material and their ideological attitudes – it is of interest to establish whether he is also able to present some exegetical results of these artistic interpretations of the biblical originals. As far as I can see, however, the strictly exegetical outcome, as with Sjöberg, is negligible.[31] His demonstration of these authors' awareness of midrashic traditions is thorough and instructive, and he also points out that they are able to foster personal and existential insights through their imaginative rewriting. But Wright has little to say about purely exegetical conclusions that could be drawn from these artistic treatments of the biblical material. The modern authors do not help us to get a clearer view of the ancient Hebrew texts, their form and content or better to understand their original message – the

---

H. G. Baetzhold and J. B. McCullough (eds.), (Athens, GA and London, 1995), p. xvi.

[28] H. Fisch, *New Stories for Old: Biblical Patterns in the Novel* (Basingstoke and New York, 1998), p. 17.

[29] For an instructive and persuasive defence of the use of the contested term "plain sense" see J. Barton, *The Nature of Biblical Criticism* (Louisville and London, 2007), pp. 69ff., esp. pp. 101ff.

[30] Wright, *The Genesis of Fiction*, p. 169.

[31] The same is true of Black and Exum's study of Burne-Jones and the Song of Songs (see above, n. 8): it is a profitable investigation of the stained-glass window and the artist's use of the biblical text, but in the other part of the study, which is supposed to answer the question "how Burne-Jones's window might influence the Song of Songs, that is our interpretation of it", no distinct exegetical results are in the end reached.

questions the novelists raise and the light they shed are ideological, not exegetical. This is not a defect in Wright's valuable investigation, but an interesting indication of the fragility of Sjöberg's principal thesis.

Mark Twain's many provocative rewritings of the early chapters of Genesis give evidence of the blasphemous intensity of the author's anger against Old Testament religion. They are interesting as expressions of his passionate views on traditional piety, and it is easy to agree with Wright that Twain's writings "force readers to confront the many questions which the biblical narrative raises",[32] but these are not really the type of questions that a biblical scholar tries to answer.

The same may be said of Steinbeck's *East of Eden*, which is treated by Wright in an interesting and informative way. Again the problems are more of a moral than of a scholarly nature, they are problems of application and attitude rather than of objective knowledge.

Real exegetical results are conspicuous by their absence also in Wright's analysis of Jeanette Winterson's farcical adaptation of the Flood story, *Boating for Beginners*. He uncovers "a serious purpose to this 'comic book'", but this is found in Winterson's own views of "the limits of religious language"[33] and in her indignation at aspects of the biblical text which seem morally revolting to a modern reader. Wright's studies are certainly instructive and important, but they do not result in a clearer understanding of the original texts. Winterson's rewritings cannot serve as a tool-box for biblical scholars interested in the meaning and message of the Pentateuchal stories themselves.

Wright also discusses two novels by Jenny Diski dwelling on episodes from Genesis, especially on the sacrifice of Isaac: their titles are *Only Human* and *After These Things*. Like Winterson, Diski uses her versions of the biblical stories as mouthpieces of her own human and psychological understanding of the course of events, without the supernatural explanations of the original authors and redactors. However interesting and artistically profitable this may be, it naturally does not provide keys to a better comprehension of the narratives as they are found in the Hebrew Bible. The same may be said about Anita Diamant's *The Red Tent*, a tendentious reworking of Genesis 34, using midrash as a literary model: it is not really an interpretation of the

---

[32] Wright, *The Genesis of Fiction*, p. 50.
[33] Wright, *The Genesis of Fiction*, p. 82.

original stories but rather a rival narrative, inspired by modern ideologies, especially a feminist one.

Thomas Mann's mighty work *Joseph and His Brothers* is characterized by Wright as "the most impressive of all the novels considered"[34] in his book *The Genesis of Fiction*, and I am tempted to describe Wright's chapter on Thomas Mann with the same words: it strikes me as the most impressive of all his sections. His demonstration of Mann's dependence on his midrashic sources is most instructive; he is both critical – as in his statement that Mann's technique "at times comes perilously close to what in other circumstances might be termed plagiarism"[35] – and also sensitive to the artistic qualities of Mann's use of this material: ironic, subtle, humorous, profound. He also paints a vivid picture of Mann, like his rabbinic sources, "probing and probing at the details of the text until some answers begin to emerge".[36] And even if Mann's readers will not always agree with these answers, Wright is convinced that "his questions […] nearly always go to the heart of the biblical story".[37] To my mind Mann's midrashic method of filling up the gaps and silences of the Hebrew narrator at times comes a little too close to wondering how many children Lady Macbeth had, as when Mann asks how many years Joseph spent in Potiphar's house and how many in the prison – a question which is answered after several pages of somewhat laborious reasoning: ten years and three years respectively.

In many cases, of course, the questions do in a sense "go to the heart of the biblical story". These questions are questions of evaluation and application, they elicit personal and subjective reactions to moral and religious issues. Again we may establish that novelists as interpreters of Genesis do not, as a rule, provide us with exegetical tools: the problems they try to solve are not those that can be given objective and demonstrably correct or probable solutions, they are questions of personal attitude and existential choice.

Those are problems that priests and preachers must face and biblical scholars cannot solve. Their task is to try to understand what the biblical texts mean,[38] using all philological and historical and literary

---

[34] Wright, *The Genesis of Fiction*, p. 167.
[35] Wright, *The Genesis of Fiction*, p. 147.
[36] Wright, *The Genesis of Fiction*, p. 167.
[37] Wright, *The Genesis of Fiction*, p. 167.
[38] I write "mean" rather than "meant", following Barton, pp. 80–86.

evidence available, applying strict rules of logic. It is also an important task to investigate how these biblical texts have been understood and applied in the past. Here the ideological readings have their place as *objects* of research, not as presuppositions or controls. We must make the basic distinction "between discovering what texts mean and evaluating or using them", as John Barton has so simply and aptly expressed it in his excellent *The Nature of Biblical Criticism*.[39] Novelists inspired by Genesis use, apply and attack the biblical texts, biblical scholars attempt to understand them, regardless of their own ideological convictions. That is why genuine exegetical lessons cannot as a rule be learnt from novelists.

*   *   *

"To try to understand what the biblical texts mean, using all philological and historical and literary evidence available, applying strict rules of logic" – the words I just used to describe the core of a biblical scholar's task also seem to me to sum up John Emerton's achievement. What we, his colleagues, may attempt, he has accomplished. In the present climate of relativistic absurdities and ideological influences he has continued, unperturbed, his learned, lucid and logical investigations, faithful to the scholarly ideals that alone can justify the acceptance of our subject in a scientific university. I would be tempted to summarize this in the watchword "Back to John Emerton!", were it not for the fact that he is an example and a leading figure, which makes it perhaps more appropriate to exclaim "Forward to John Emerton!".

---

[39] Barton, p. 188. See also Barton's reference to Umberto Eco's distinction between interpreting a text and using it, p. 85, n. 28.

PART B

ISAIAH

ISAIAH AS A PROPHET TO SAMARIA AND HIS MEMOIRS*

Menahem Haran

I

Chapter 6 in the book of Isaiah is the vision of the prophet's call. Speaking in the first person, the prophet portrays what befell him "in the year that King Uzziah died", implying that it was committed to writing only after this year and after the events depicted here, probably not before the time of Jotham or Ahaz. Against the background of the sights in the Temple and one of the seraphs touching his lips with a live coal, the prophet hears the Lord's voice sending him to "this people": "Hear, indeed, *šim'û šāmô'a*, but do not understand, and see, indeed, *ûr'û rā'ô*, but do not know" (6:9). That is to say, you are neither ready nor capable of understanding what you hear, nor of knowing what you see, and therefore the decree has been issued. The heavenly voice continues: "This people's heart fattens, and its ears become heavy, and its eyes shut", because "this people" fears that if it were to see and hear and understand, then it would "turn and be healed". The three verbs in the *hiph'il* conjugation, *hašmēn, hakbēd* and *hāša'*, were interpreted and rendered by many scholars as imperatives. In order to explain the wonder that such divine orders are given to a prophet, it was argued that the difficulties "created by this startling, and even harsh, statement…are partly due to the tendency of Scripture writers to refer all things immediately to the will of God".[1] It is inconceivable, however, that God would command the prophet to "make heavy" the ears of

---

* It is a pleasure to dedicate these observations to Professor John A. Emerton, a friend of long standing. The following commentaries on the book of Isaiah are referred to only by the name of the author: J. Blenkinsopp, *Isaiah 1–39* (AB; New York, 2000); G. B. Gray, *Isaiah I–XXVII* (ICC; Edinburgh, 1912, 1956); A. Dillmann, *Der Prophet Jesaia⁵* (KeHAT; Leipzig, 1890); B. Duhm, *Das Buch Jesaia⁴* (HKAT; Göttingen, 1922); O. Kaiser, *Isaiah 1–12*, 2nd edn (OTL; London, 1983); S. Krauss, *The Book of Isaiah* (Warsaw, 1904; Jerusalem, 1969 [Heb.]); S. D. Luzzatto, *The Commentary of R. S. D. Luzzatto on the Book of Isaiah* (Tel-Aviv, 1970 [Heb.]); J. Skinner, *Isaiah I–XXXIX*, rev. ed. (CBSC; Cambridge, 1915 [1954]); O. Procksch, *Jesaia I* (KAT; Leipzig, 1930); H. Wildberger, *Jesaia I²* (BKAT; Neukirchen, 1980).

[1] Skinner, p. 50. Cf. also, e.g., Wildberger, p. 256.

"this people" and "fatten" its heart. Rashi correctly understood the three verbs as describing a worsening situation. As he puts it: "Their heart is increasingly fattening and their ears are increasingly stopped from hearing". That is, the three verbs are not used in the imperative, but in the uninflected infinitive. Indeed, the *hiph'il* infinitive form can "express the obtaining or receiving of a concrete or abstract quality" or of "the entering into a certain condition".[2] Consequently, due to the unwillingness and inability of "this people" to see, to hear and to understand, the decree cannot be abolished. This is what God further continues, by stating (vv. 11–12) that this condition of blindness and deafness will go on "till towns lie waste, *šā'û* [for the verb cf. 2 Kgs 19:25; Isa. 37:26], without inhabitants, and houses without men, and the ground is utterly desolate". In short, the land will be emptied of its inhabitants.

Who is "this people" whom Isaiah designates for annihilation, and whose land will lie desolate? Many assumed as self-evident that the reference is to the kingdom of Judah. If, indeed, it is Judah that the prophet earmarks for ruin, with its cities being "without inhabitants", one is tempted to connect the appointed destruction with the historical contact between the kingdom of Judah and the Babylonian empire. From here it is only a single, small step to assume that the reference is to the destruction of Judah by the Babylonians, with the accompanying – and in fact strange – conclusion that this prophecy was subsequent to 586 B.C.E.[3] The correct explanation, however, is that the destruction in chapter 6 refers to the kingdom of Ephraim. It should be realized that this vision is directed to the Northern Kingdom, whose inhabitants (and not the Judaeans) he calls "this people", even if we admit that this expression has a somewhat deprecatory tone, as many a scholar has

---

[2] Many exegetes and scholars, from Ibn Ezra to Luzzatto and the most recent writers, interpreted the three verbs as "hardening the heart", "Verstockungsbefehl" in the words of Wildberger (p. 255). Rashi was followed by Isaac Abrabanel in understanding them to be unchangeable infinitives. The quotation above is from GK §53d, e. The three verbs in Isa. 6:10 are used in an intransitive sense (without the accusative). The verb *hāša'* (*hiph'il* infinitive, not the past tense, which is *hēša'*) comes from the root *š'*, which, as an intransitive verb, means "coated, sealed". For this root cf. Isa. 29:9.

[3] Thus especially Kaiser, pp. 118–23, 132–33. In his introduction to the English edition he writes (p. viii) that he would prefer that his commentary on Isa. 6–8 be read first. There are those who claim that vv. 12–13 were added after the destruction of Jerusalem. Blenkinsopp does not refute this view, but argues that the depiction of the destruction could also be suitable for the results of Sennacherib's invasion in 701 B.C.E.

observed (while assuming that the reference is to Judah). It is not suggested that this phrase, wherever it appears, speaks of Ephraim. Yet, in
Isaiah's prophecies, where this phrase is more conspicuous than usual,
it is said in reference to Ephraim only. This is not the only indication
of reference to the Northern Kingdom in this prophecy or in other
prophetical units or fragments in Isaiah's writings. Actually, wherever
this sign appears in Isaiah it joins together with other and at times
more explicit signs, with which it goes well together.[4] Thus, Isaiah
prophesied not only to Judah and Jerusalem, but also to Samaria. The
fact that this is not stated outright in the book's heading is not proof
to the contrary (the heading of a prophetic book and what is reflected
in its contents do not always completely correspond).

Chapter 6 is written in the first person, unlike chapter 7, and the
claim that a change of person took place in chapter 7, from Isaiah in
the first person to speech about him, has not been sufficiently proven.[5]
The change from first to the third person suggests that chapter 7 is
not a direct continuation of chapter 6. As a matter of fact, chapter
7 contains no report of execution of the divine command given to
Isaiah in chapter 6, according to which the prophet was sent to "this
people" to inform them that the Israelite kingdom will be depleted of
its inhabitants. Instead of this, chapter 7 speaks of Isaiah's coming to
Ahaz with the tidings that he should not fear "those two smouldering

---

[4] Several scholars (most notably B. Duhm and, before him, A. Dillmann) already
noted that the expression "this people" in Isaiah refers to the kingdom of Ephraim,
but took care to add: also, or mainly, to Judah. More than a century ago there was one
who assumed that the reference is solely to Ephraim: see H. Hackmann, *Die Zuku-
nftserwartung des Jesaia* (Gottingen, 1893), pp. 52–54, 70–76. Following him, some
agreed with him, and this was Jerome's opinion in his time (J.-P. Migne, *Patrologia
Latina*, 24 [Paris, 1845], p. 229), which appears to be correct. Gray (p. 110) maintains
that there cannot be a total distinction between "this people" in v. 9 and "a people of
unclean lips" in v. 5, that must be Judah. This argument misses the point. Isaiah lived
"among a people of unclean lips", but in the vision of his call he is sent to "this people", as the text has it: "Go, say to this people" (v. 9). Alternatively, we would contend
that there is a germ of truth in Ibn Ezra on 6:5: "The meaning of 'a man of unclean
lips', in my opinion, is that the prophet grew up among Israel [Ephraim], who were
impure in deed and speech and he learned from their speech; comp. 'and warned me
not to walk in the way of this people' [8:11]. He therefore says, I dwell in the midst of
a people of unclean lips." Indeed, for at least some time the prophet must have really
stayed in the kingdom of Ephraim. See also below, n. 10.

[5] This claim is Duhm's (pp. 71, 74), who maintains that in 7:3 *wayyō'mer YHWH
'ēlay* was replaced by *wayyō'mer YHWH 'el yeša'yāhû* (this is not impossible though
not supported by LXX), and in v. 10 *wā'ōsip* was replaced by *wayyôsep YHWH* (which
is not probable). Other scholars followed Duhm's opinion.

stumps of firebrands" (7:4), Rezin of Aram and Pekah of Israel, who desired to invade the Judean kingdom. The two kings will not realize their goal, and Ahaz's people may, nay, must, put their trust in God (7:9: "If you will not believe, surely *lō' tēʾāmēnû*, you shall not endure"). Isaiah also gives a sign, *'ôt*, of the anticipated destruction of Aram and Ephraim: the "young woman", *'almāh*, whoever that may be, according to any of the current interpretations (cf. below, sect. II), is about to give birth to a son, whom she shall name Immanuel, that is, God is with us, with the kingdom of Judah. The prophet could not have surmised, of his own, whether the young woman would give birth to a son or a daughter, nor the name that the newborn would be given. This announcement, which is the sign, is given to Ahaz as God's word, and according to the biblical practice, the sign is given in order to prove that the prophecy itself will come to pass.[6] The sign is a sort of guarantee of the fulfillment of the prophecy, which itself is delivered afterwards: "Before the child learns to reject the bad and choose the good", that is, before he will be weaned, the ground "whose two kings you dread" shall be abandoned (7: 14–16).[7] That is, Aram and Ephraim will be exiled, and, as a result, the destruction of Ephraim threatened in chapter 6 will come about anyhow. Nevertheless, this is not a direct continuation of the preceding chapter, because the destruction here is intended for both Ephraim and Aram, and in connection with the

---

[6] Ibn Ezra states in the name of R. Saadiah Gaon "that the sign is that he will be a male", which appears to be the plain meaning. The import of the Immanuel prophecy, and the sign it contains, have led to no end of scholarly indecision. E. J. Kraeling, "The Immanuel Prophecy", *JBL* 50 (1931), pp. 277–92, fruitfully surveyed and classified the different views and possibilities, but many other publications have appeared in the meantime (after his survey, Kraeling voiced his own opinion, on pp. 292–97, which is quite strange; he maintains, *inter alia*, that Isa. 7:7–17 was removed from 2 Kgs 16).

[7] The *l* in *lᵉdaʿtô* ("by the time he learns", v. 15) denotes the time. "To reject the bad and choose the good" indicates the end of his nursing period (cf. Deut. 1:39), which in the Ancient Near East lasted for three years or more. The eating of curds and honey (Isa. 7:15, 22) should be a sign of prosperity, but here it is linked to the appearance of the Assyrian army. Many scholars experienced difficulties in resolving this question, since saying that this consumption is a sign of distress (as does Blenkinsopp, p. 235) seems wholly forced. Some lost no time in declaring v. 15 to be an addition, and some expanded this suspicion to include v. 22 (see Wildberger, pp. 295–96, 306). The truth is that these verses promise the eating of curds and honey to the Judaeans, since the pressure exerted against them by Aram and Israel will cease after the latter's land "shall be abandoned". The stumbling block here lies in understanding "this people" as applied to Judah. If we understand the emptying of the land of its inhabitants in chapter 6 as referring to Ephraim, while chapter 7 (v. 16) explicitly states that the land of the "two kings.... shall be abandoned", not that of Judah (as in the erroneous interpretation of Procksch, p. 123), the obstacle is removed.

rescue of Judah from both. Furthermore, Isaiah is accompanied to the
meeting with Ahaz by his son Shear-jashub, who is no longer an infant
and walks by himself. Since the son bears a symbolic name (cf. 10:
21–22) and was undoubtedly born to Isaiah after the prophetic call,
several years had to elapse between what is related in each of the two
chapters. The ruin of Aram and Ephraim will be performed by Assyria,
whose appearance is mentioned in v. 17, concluding the unit 7:1–17.
Note the wording of this verse: "The Lord will cause to come upon you
and your people...the king of Assyria". No mention is made of the
abandonment of the land of Judah.[8] The unit 7:1–17 is followed by an
assemblage of passages that speak of the appearance of the Assyrians
in the land (7:18–25).

II

Chapter 8 returns us to Isaiah's first-person address. If it were not
for the explicit fact that Isaiah already has children, all of whom have
been given symbolic names, suggesting that they were born after his
call, the chapter could have been viewed as the continuation of chapter
6. However, chapter 8 as well is not really the execution report of the
order given to the prophet in chapter 6. The major part of the chapter is the unit vv. 1–18, which is formulated entirely in the first person and is divided into several stanzas. In the first stanza (1–4), God
commands Isaiah to write on "a large sheet" (of papyrus) the words
"For Maher-shalal-hash-baz" (literally: pillage hastens, looting speeds),
which also serves the prophet as a name for the son born to him. The
written words, with the name given to his son, serve for the prophet as
a sign of the fulfillment of the prophetic affirmation that the Assyrian

---

[8] LXX on v. 17 reads: "But, Ἀλλὰ, the Lord will cause to come upon you and your
people", which might be the correct version, since the word "but" connects and con-
trasts the verse to the one preceding it: the land of the two kings "shall be abandoned" – but the Lord will bring the Assyrian monarch upon you and your people.
Verses 19–20 create the impression that the Assyrians will spread throughout all
parts of the land. One of the Tiglath-pileser inscriptions mentions Ahaz ("Jehoa-
haz") among the twenty kings who offered tribute to him (D. D. Luckenbill, *Ancient
Records of Assyria and Babylonia*, I (Chicago, 1926), §801; A. L. Oppenheim, in *ANET*,
p. 282a); cf. 2 Kgs 16:7–8. It has not been determined whether Isaiah's portrayal of the
appearance of Assyria in Judah is a prophecy that was not realized exactly as written.
Possibly, several of the monarchs who paid tribute to Tiglath-pileser were allied with
Aram and Israel.

monarch would shortly conquer Damascus and Samaria and loot them. In the second stanza (5–10) God further says to Isaiah that, since "this people", which is Ephraim, "has spurned the gently flowing waters of Siloam", that symbolize the Davidic dynasty, and rejoices with the son of Remaliah, God will bring on Ephraim "the mighty, massive waters of the Euphrates, the king of Assyria", that shall "flow over all its channels, and overflow and pass [even] through Judah reaching up to the neck" – reach only – and "his outspread wings will fill the breadth of your land", but nothing is said of destroying Judah.[9] After this the prophet addresses the peoples and "far countries" – that is, not only Aram and Israel, but also the peoples who were allied with them (and who, in the circumstances of the time, sought to stand against Assyria): "Gird yourselves [for war] – you shall be broken". All your plotting shall be frustrated, for God is with us, the people of Judah. The details of the intent of the third stanza (11–15) are vague. Basically, it begins with the address by God, who cautions Isaiah "not to walk in the way of this people" (v. 11), and then shifts to the second person speech, apparently directed to Isaiah's disciples. The prophet demands that they not fall prey to "what this people says", and to hold in awe only "the Lord of Hosts" (v. 13; cf. v. 18, with the addition of "who dwells on Mount Zion").[10] In the concluding verses (16–18)

---

[9] 8:6: *ûmᵉśôś 'et rᵉṣîn* – "an infinitive with [the letter] *mem*, as in the Aramaic language, like *ûmispār 'et rōbaʿ yiśrā'ēl* [number the dust-cloud of Israel]" (Num 23:10) and "the infinitive occasionally entails the time and person mentioned before it" (Luzzatto). Critical scholars attempt to emend the text, without success. Many interpreted the "wings" at the end of v. 8 ("whose wings are spread as wide as your land is broad") as referring, as Luzzatto put it, "to the spread of the river's water". "But the outstretched wings far more naturally imply protection" (Gray, p. 148, with references to many biblical passages). Gray adds: "if that is implied here also, the point of the figure is that the entire land of Judah will dwell in safety…undisturbed by any futile raging of the nations" (with a reference to v. 9). He also observes (p. 150) that the end of v. 8 could have been written: ב ארץ [*kî* in defective spelling, as in Phoenician inscriptions] עמנו אל. If so, then the ends of vv. 8 and 10 resemble each other. This is not confirmed by LXX (though such confirmation is not indispensable).

[10] V. 11: Read *wayyissrēnî* ("and he warned me") instead of *wᵉyyissrēnî* ("and he will warn me"). Ibn Ezra: "Behold, *wᵉyyissrēnî* [i.e., the verse beginning with this word] shows the truth of my explanation of the expression 'unclean lips'" (see above, n. 4). V. 14: "He [the Lord of Hosts] shall be for a sanctuary, *lᵉmiqdāš*" – many accepted Duhm's emendation: *lᵉmôqēš*, for a snare. "And a stone of offence and a rock of stumbling for both houses of Israel" – for God will bring Assyria upon them ("both houses of Israel" is a unique phrase). "A trap and a snare for the inhabitants of Jerusalem" – this does not speak as yet of the destruction of the city. V. 15: "And many shall stumble" – "many of them…many of the people of Ephraim shall be sent into exile by the king of Assyria" (Luzzatto).

of the unit the prophet speaks of the preservation of the testimony and the sealing of the "teaching", *tôrāh*, among his disciples, with an expectation until the Lord fulfills this prophecy (with the Assyrians coming), up to which time he and his children will be "as signs and portents in Israel" (= Ephraim).

The explanation of the expression "this people" as referring to Judah not only led scholarly research to strange conclusions (that the destruction of which chapter 6 speaks refers, as it were, to Jerusalem), but also compelled scholars to impose on the text – in chapters 6 and 8, and every other place in the book of Isaiah in which "this people" occurs – a patently forced interpretation. They were forced to argue that the statement concerning "this people" spurning "the gently flowing waters of Siloam" while "delighting in Rezin and the son of Remaliah" (8:6), is an oblique reference to the wish of a part of the people to separate from the house of David and rely upon Rezin and Pekah[11] – as if Isaiah had to defend the Davidic dynasty against its subjects. In fact, the relation of certain prophecies of Isaiah to Ephraim need not be determined solely on the basis of the meaning of "this people". Alongside this expression, we have, as noted above, additional signs, explicit enough, of the relation of those prophecies to Ephraim. Moreover, some of the indicators of the northern background of Isaiah's prophecies appear without the "this people" wording, and even so they decide the issue.[12] In the unit 8:1–18 these indicators are "who is hiding his face from the house of Jacob" (an appellation for Israel), and

---

[11] As Krauss puts it in his commentary. This view is also held by the Rabbis (B. San. 94a; Tg. Jonathan on Isa. 8:6), and commented by Rashi (with a midrashic vein), Kimḥi, Ibn Ezra (on Isa. 8:7: "against them – against the men of Judah who conspired against Ahaz"), Abrabanel, Luzzatto, as well as A. Kuenen (*Historisch-kritische Einleitung in die Bücher des AT*, II [Leipzig, 1892], p. 42) and many modern scholars. See, e.g., the twisted explanations offered many years ago by K. Fullerton ("The Interpretation of Isaiah 8:5–10", *JBL* 43 [1924], pp. 254–72) and later by Gray (p. 146), Skinner (p. 73), Wildberger (p. 323), and Blenkinsopp (p. 240). These scholars also indicated the contradiction between the rejoicing of the people of Judah in Rezin and the son of Remaliah according to 8:6 (on the assumption that "this people" refers to Judah) and the fear of these two according to 7:2–4. For an additional example of the confusion created by not distinguishing between "this people", referring to Ephraim, whose destruction is promised, and Judah, who is assured of withstanding the Assyrian pressure, see recently: G. C. I. Wong, "Is 'God with Us' in Isaiah VIII?", *VT* 49 (1999), pp. 426–32.

[12] The additional units or fragments of Isaiah addressed to Samaria are: 8:23; 9:7–10:4 continued(!) in 5:25–30; 10:20–23; 28:1–22 (v. 14: the two words *'ašer bîrûšālāim* are an interpolation; see Duhm). On these, cf. for the present the remarks in M. Haran, *The Biblical Collection*, III (Jerusalem, 2008), pp. 137–40, 143–44, 210–15 (Heb.).

"as signs and portents in Israel" (which is Ephraim, as we observed). Here they are added to "this people" (that according to the express statement in v. 6 "spurned" the kingdom of Judah and in whose way, according to v. 11, the prophet was warned not to follow).

The unit 8:1–18 both resembles and is dissimilar to the unit 7:1–17. It resembles the unit in chapter 7 because of the proximity of the two units in both content and form. Each sets forth a parallel narrative, in which the central role is assigned to the prophet's wife (it transpires that the "young woman" of 7:14, as well, has a sexual relationship with Isaiah).[13] She bears him a son and the son is given a symbolic name that expresses Isaiah's prophetic expectation. In each of the units, two divine messages are delivered, with the recurring headline in the beginning of the second pronouncement: "Again the Lord spoke to...saying, *wayyôsep YHWH dabbēr 'el...lēʾmōr*" (7:10; 8:5), which does not appear elsewhere. Likewise, the divine announcements in both units have very similar content: in chapter 7 God promises that the scheme of Aram and Ephraim to breach Jerusalem will not come to pass, because their land shall be abandoned due to the appearance of Assyria. In chapter 8 God declares that, since "this people", Ephraim, spurned the Judaean monarchy and allied itself with Rezin and the son of Remaliah, the Assyrian monarch will lay waste Damascus and Samaria. To some degree, there are also verbal points of contact between the two units.[14] In contrast, however, the two units are dissimilar, first of all because in 7:1–17 Isaiah does not speak in the first person, and attributing any autobiographical nature to this unit would be forced. Chapter 7 speaks of a nameless "young woman" who gives birth to Immanuel, while chapter 8 mentions the "prophetess", the prophet's wife, who, too, is nameless, but gives birth to Maher-shalal-hash-baz. The name Immanuel is given by the young woman, and is a sign of the fulfillment of Isaiah's prophecy (7:14), while the

---

[13] Thus Rashi, Ibn Ezra, and many others. Luzzatto (p. 78) correctly stated that "*ʿalmāh* is the term for a healthy and energetic girl, whether or not a virgin". This does not rule out the possibility of her being in matrimonial relations with the prophet.

[14] Compare 7:5: *yāʿaṣ...rāʿāh* with 8:10: *ʿuṣû ʿēṣāh*, "it shall be foiled"; 7 7: "it shall not stand, it shall not come to pass" with 8:10: "speak a word – it shall not stand"; 7:14–16: "shall conceive and bear a son, and shall call his name...for before the child knows" with 8:3–4: "and she conceived and bore a son...call his name...for before the child knows". Cf. also 7:5: "because, *yaʿan kî*, Aram has devised" with 8:6: "because, *yaʿan kî*, this people have spurned" (and also 29:13: "because, *yaʿan kî*, this people have approached"). The phrase *yaʿan kî* appears four times in Isaiah (also in 3:16), and three further times in all the rest of the Hebrew Bible.

name Maher-shalal-hash-baz is divinely authorized (8:3), and it, too, is a type of sign – as a proof for what God had proclaimed in advance. The difference between the two units is illustrated by the fact that in chapter 7 "Immanuel" is the name of the son born to Isaiah (which, according to many versions, is written as a single word and this is correct), while in chapter 8 (v. 10), it is a clause incorporated in the prophet's speech and written as two words: *'immānû 'ēl.*

The difference between 7:1–17 and 8:1–18 and the separation between the two clearly show that the attempts to force 7:1–17 into Isaiah's "memoirs", in order to create a continuity from the beginning of chapter 6 to 8:18, are groundless. There is even less of a basis for the notion that after the memoir passages Isaiah, or one of the redactors, completed everything stated until the end of chapter 8, or until 9:6.[15] Isaiah's "memoirs" might very well have begun in chapter 6, as many assume, but no more than two broken fragments of them reached the compilers. We must assume a historical gap (which, in the case of Isaiah, lasted longer than for other prophets) between the writing and the collection phases. It is definitely possible that these two "memoir" fragments are the earliest texts from Isaiah's writings. They should not, however, be imagined as the initial "nucleus" that grew until it encompassed the entire extant book. The memoir fragments were among the other materials that reached the compilers, as morsels left from the prophet's table and from everything connected with him and his activity. The book we possess was composed from the remains.

---

[15] See Kaiser, p. 114. Even if we accept Duhm's emendations to 7:3, 10 (above, n. 4), we are still left with the assemblage of passages 7:18–25, which cannot be turned into first-person speech. The first to define the entire division 6:1–9:6 as "memoirs", *Denkschrift*, was K. Budde, *Jesajas Erleben – Eine Gemeinverständliche Auslegung der Denkschrift des Propheten (Kap. 6.1–9.6)* (Gotha, 1928).

"TAKE A LARGE WRITING TABLET AND WRITE ON IT": ISAIAH – A WRITING PROPHET?

Alan Millard

Oral tradition has been widely credited with a major role in the creation and presentation of ancient Hebrew literature throughout the twentieth century, with writing having little place until late in the process. This position was crystallized in Eduard Nielsen's book *Oral Tradition*[1] and modified by Susan Niditch in her *Oral Word and Written Word*, subtitled *Orality and Literacy in Ancient Israel*, who saw written forms existing beside oral.[2] Nielsen cited Ivan Engnell's dictum "reduction to writing is linked with a general crisis of confidence"[3] and enlarged it: "The change from oral to written literature does not take place because cultural summits have been reached, nor because the ability to read and write has become common property, but because the culture itself is felt to be threatened – from within by syncretism, and from without by political events."[4] The idea is expressed in a similar way by H. Vorländer,[5] according to John Emerton's summary, "the spread of the Aramaic language constituted a threat to the traditions both of the Israelites and of the Assyrians and Babylonians...Since the old myths and epics in Sumerian and Akkadian were transmitted largely in oral form, their existence was threatened, and there was a need to commit them to writing...For the Jews there were the further problems of the loss of the archives in Jerusalem, and the deportation of the upper crust of society threatened the continued existence of the nation and its culture. The exiles were unable to carry much with them to Babylonia and there was a need to collect and write down the traditions that were remembered. Vorländer does not exclude the

---

[1] E. Nielsen, *Oral Tradition* (London, 1954).
[2] S. Niditch, *Oral Word and Written Word: Orality and Literacy in Ancient Israel* (Library of Ancient Israel; Louisville, 1996, London, 1997).
[3] Nielsen, *Oral Tradition*, p. 33, citing I. Engnell, *Gamla Testamentet: en traditionshistorisk inledning* (Stockholm, 1945), p. 42.
[4] Nielsen, *Oral Tradition*, p. 60.
[5] H. Vorländer, *Die Entstehungszeit des jehowistischen Geschichtswerkes* (Europäischen Hochschulschriften 23.109; Frankfurt, 1978) pp. 347–49.

possibility that some pre-exilic documents had been preserved, but he thinks that committing the traditions to writing on a broader basis began only with the exile."[6] J. A. Soggin in his often used *Introduction to the Old Testament* expressed this simply: "The need to put down traditional material in writing usually arises in moments of crisis; for Israel in the time of the exile of 587 or a little earlier..."[7] Without wanting to make a caricature, the picture these authors create seems far-fetched: enemies advancing, or already present, would destroy any existing records together with many of those who maintained memories of the past, so scribes sat furiously committing all they could gather to a limited number of tablets or scrolls which they could store carefully or carry with them into exile. This picture is to be rejected not because it is unlikely, but rather because it is out of harmony with the evidence from the ancient world. The Lachish Letters were the principal Hebrew documents Nielsen could use from outside the Bible and it is true they were apparently written as the Babylonians were overrunning Judah; some of the ostraca found more recently at Arad and at other sites belong to those final years, too. They, of course, are mundane remnants from daily life, messages and accounts, not literary records gathering memories, or chronicles of the kingdom's history, which would have been written on scrolls of leather or papyrus. They happen to survive because they lay in the debris of destroyed towns, the archaeological levels which yield the majority of material remains. People of the past, like their present descendants, normally discarded old, irrelevant papers, so that only the most recent writings may remain in the ruins of their buildings. If a place was violently destroyed, whole archives of some citizens or officials might be buried, as in the cases of the Old Assyrian merchant quarter at Kanesh in Anatolia, or the Late Bronze Age city of Ugarit. If the place was abandoned for other reasons – an epidemic, loss of water-supply, political change – current documents would be removed with other possessions, only the unwanted ones might be left behind to delight a modern archaeologist, as at the "heretic pharaoh" Akhenaten's short-lived capital, Akhetaten, El-Amarna. The process is demonstrable at many sites and proved by dated cuneiform tablets from Babylonia and Assyria, where few may

---

[6] J. A. Emerton, "The Date of the Yahwist", in J. Day (ed.), *In Search of Pre-Exilic Israel* (JSOTSup 406; London, 2004), pp. 107–129, see p. 120.

[7] J. A. Soggin, *Introduction to the Old Testament* (London, 1976), p. 59.

survive from two or three centuries of life at a place, then scores from the final century.[8] Vorländer is quite wrong in stating that Babylonian and Assyrian literature was put into writing because of the encroachment of Aramaic; no appreciable increase in the quantity of literary tablets can be attributed to that reason; there are numerous examples from various periods unrelated to the arrival of Aramaeans or any other foreigners, hostile or not. Therefore the concept of scribes busily writing texts as the consequence of a threat should be abandoned.

The role of writing in the creation of the biblical books of prophecy has attracted more attention lately. As the scribes were the ones who produced most early Hebrew writing, they were responsible for collecting and editing prophetic oracles, according to Karel van der Toorn. He claims the occasions when a prophet himself would write are rare. He accepts three biblical references, Hab. 2:2; Isa. 8:1 and Jer. 29:1, and adds Lachish Letter 3. (Isa. 30:8 is excluded as a later addition.) Each of these is a short message. When pre-exilic prophets wrote, "They resorted to the written word when they judged an oral delivery less apt to reach their intended audience. Not a single time, though, did they write in view of preserving their words for future generations."[9] Observing how Assyrian officials sent written reports of oracles spoken by different individuals to Nineveh where some were collected on large tablets, van der Toorn suggests temple scribes in Jerusalem recorded prophecies given there by men like Jeremiah, under the authority of the high priest, the texts then being deposited in the temple's archives. Yet the books of the prophets we read today may not contain those oracles, for the oracles in the books "seem often too general to have been of interest to the temple officials; many of them are artful and literary, and not very specific in content. Nothing in the Book of Amos, for example, is as particular and specific as the prophecy Amaziah reports to the king."[10] However, van der Toorn's expectations should not control his conclusions. The three references

---

[8] A. Millard, "Observations on the Eponym Lists", in S. Parpola, R. M. Whiting (eds), *Assyria 1995* (Helsinki, 1997), pp. 207–15, and "Why do we have the Texts we do? Survival of the Latest?", in P. Bienkowski, C. B. Mee and E. A. Slater (eds), *Writing and Ancient Near Eastern Society, Papers in Honour of Alan R. Millard* (JSOTSup 426; London, 2005), pp. 301–19.

[9] Karel van der Toorn, *Scribal Culture and the Making of the Hebrew Bible* (Cambridge, MA, 2007), pp. 178–82.

[10] Van der Toorn, *Scribal Culture,* p. 183.

to prophets writing do not require us to suppose that they wrote no other texts. Biblical writers may have seen no need to report normal activities, although modern scholars often seem to expect that, so prophets or their disciples writing down their oracles may have been commonplace (see further below). Van der Toorn's position is founded on the sort of absence of evidence for which John Emerton criticized Vorländer, commenting that while a modern reader might have expected the books of Kings to mention the "writing prophets", "it seems that...the ancient historian thought otherwise".[11]

Although the prophecy tablets found at Mari and Nineveh were stored in palace archives, while two from Eshnunna in Babylonia may have lain in a temple archive,[12] and no others have been found as independent documents, that does not mean there were no others. The oracles kept at Mari and Nineveh all relate to the kings and are almost wholly positive in their attitude to them. Given the nature of those monarchies, it may be doubted that hostile oracles would have been accepted or kept. Oracles delivered to ordinary individuals may not have been written, or if they were, not have been kept once they had been fulfilled, or shown to be false, just as the consultation of omens conducted for those outside the court was rarely recorded. Van der Toorn argues that the Hebrew prophets were at home in the temple where there were priestly scribes, literacy being a tool of the priests' trade, who may have made records of the prophecies. The temple in Jerusalem, he maintains, "was as much a center of literacy as the royal palace" and, after citing instances of the Torah related to the temple, he continues, "The temple was the center, too, of written prophecy".[13] Further, he says, "In light of the comparative evidence of the Neo-

---

[11] Emerton, "The Date of the Yahwist", p. 111.

[12] M. Nissinen, *Prophets and Prophecy in the Ancient Near East* (P. Machinist (ed.), Writings from the Ancient World 12; Atlanta, 2003) conveniently collects all the cuneiform texts. Note that the two tablets containing oracles for an Old Babylonian king of Eshnunna (pp. 93–93) are the only "prophecy" texts that may have been placed in a temple, but as the tablets were acquired on the antiquities market, that is uncertain; they could equally well have lain in a palace archive.

[13] Van der Toorn, *Scribal Culture*, pp. 86–87. As "an instructive aside", he cites the Ugaritic colophon of the scribe Ilimalku, giving him the title "Secretary of Niqmaddu", but readers should be aware that "secretary" is not a universally accepted rendering of Ugaritic ṯ'y. D. Pardee, for example, gives simply "ṯā'iy-official" in "Canonical Compositions (West Semitic), 1. Ugaritic Myths. The Ba'lu Myth (1.86)", in *COS*, 1, pp. 241–74, see p. 273, n. 281. Ilimalku was a scribe and a chief priest, but not certainly a royal secretary as well.

Assyrian oracles, it is possible that the archives of the Jerusalem temple kept records of the oracles delivered in the precincts of the sanctuary", later admitting that "the existence of a file of oracle records in the archives of the temple…remains a matter of informed speculation".[14] In fact, the delivery of many of the Neo-Assyrian oracles was associated with the temple of Ishtar at Arbela, but they were despatched in writing to Nineveh and the tablets, or their copies, stored in the palace there, not in a temple.

Despite making a case for priestly records of prophets' words, van der Toorn considers it unlikely that those who collected oracles and stories of a prophet would have used temple records, relying instead on memory.[15] In doing so he has to be assuming that, although oracles were written down, sometimes at least, no records were ever kept elsewhere, something that cannot be proved or disproved. The productive points of comparison between cuneiform and Hebrew prophecies should not result in an assumption of similarity in every respect, as the difference in range and content of the Hebrew books sufficiently shows. Therefore there is no compelling reason to expect that copies of a Hebrew prophet's words would be kept in a palace or temple archive, or only there. Cuneiform tablets containing literary compositions have been excavated in private houses scattered through Babylonian and Assyrian towns and in Ugarit.[16] Before turning to epigraphic evidence from Judah, information from Egypt should be brought into play, for his focus on cuneiform texts in discussing the writing of prophecies has led van der Toorn to ignore some relevant discoveries made there. Egyptian temples certainly had libraries and scriptoria, "the house of Life", with books in them. Unhappily, most of the temples stood on damp ground near the Nile, so any books left lying in them will have perished. While many of the major surviving literary papyri have lost their provenances through accidents of discovery, several belong in groups which can be ascribed to tombs, so had been the property of the individual owners whom they accompanied, and a few fragmentary ones were excavated from houses in Lahun where, presumably,

---

[14] Van der Toorn, *Scribal Culture*, p. 183.
[15] Van der Toorn, *Scribal Culture*, p. 184.
[16] See further, A. Millard, "Books in Ancient Israel", in C. Roche (ed.), *D'Ougarit à Jérusalem. Receuil d'études épigraphiques et archéologiques offert à Pierre Bordreuil* (Orient et Mediterranée 2; Paris, 2008), pp. 255–64.

they also belonged to individuals.[17] Besides them, hundreds of ostraca from Deir el-Medina, the village of craftsmen constructing and decorating royal tombs in the 18th to 20th Dynasties, illuminate their lives, revealing that they frequently copied extracts from literary works, some of which were found in their houses.

Writing was current across the kingdoms of Israel and Judah in the eighth and seventh centuries B.C., as Graham Davies's map locating provenances of ostraca and graffiti reveals.[18] However, the map can only mark the places of discovery of texts inscribed upon durable surfaces, stone, potsherds and metal. The number of sites, the quantity of ephemeral texts and the multitude of seals and impressions bearing owners' names should dispel any notion that writing was rare in the kingdom of Judah. The majority of writing was done on papyrus, leather, or wax-coated wooden tablets which have perished. The recovery of numerous clay bullae, which once sealed papyrus documents, attests their former existence.[19] Even if few people could read or write, many more knew about writing and its uses throughout the kingdom. If scribes were employed on legal and administrative duties, making accounts and lists, setting out legal deeds and writing letters, it is reasonable to expect some to have spent time writing other texts, as in Mesopotamia and Egypt, and the few examples of "literary" compositions among the Hebrew ostraca and graffiti prove that they did so. Those products are, by nature, quite brief, yet they are instructive. In Judah, one ostracon found (on the surface) at 'Arad probably bears part of a literary text (no. 88) as does another, from the fort at Ḥorvat 'Uza, the latter possibly of a "prophetic" nature.[20] There are lines of

---

[17] See S. G. Quirke, "Archive", in A. Loprieno (ed.), *Ancient Egyptian Literature* (Leiden, 1996), pp. 379–401.

[18] G. I. Davies, *Ancient Hebrew Inscriptions: Corpus and Concordance* (Cambridge, 1991), p. xxvi; for additional sites see vol. 2 (2004), pp. xviii–xix.

[19] See R. Deutsch, *Messages from the Past. Hebrew Bullae from the Time of Isaiah through the Destruction of the First Temple. Shlomo Moussaieff Collection and an Up to Date Corpus* (Tel Aviv, 1997 Heb.; 1999 English) and *Biblical Period Hebrew Bullae. The Josef Chaim Kaufman Collection* (Tel Aviv, 2003); contra S. Warner, "The Alphabet: An Innovation and Its Diffusion", *VT* 39 (1980), pp. 81–90, who argued that there was little writing other than on ostraca.

[20] F. M. Cross, "An Ostracon in Literary Hebrew from Ḥorvat 'Uza", in L. E. Stager, J. A. Greene, M. D. Coogan (eds), *The Archaeology of Jordan and Beyond. Essays in Honor of James A. Sauer* (Winona Lake, IN, 2000), pp. 111–13, reprinted in *Leaves from an Epigrapher's Notebook. Collected Papers in Hebrew and West Semitic Palaeography and Epigraphy* (Harvard Semitic Studies 51; Winona Lake, IN, 2003), pp. 135–37.

verse painted on wall plaster at Kuntillet 'Ajrud, early in the eighth century. One section may be translated, "And when God shines forth in the [heights...] the mountains will melt, the hills will crush [...] earth. The Holy One over the gods [...] prepare to [b]less Baal on the day of wa[r...to bless]the name of El on the day of wa[r...]". Other lines were scratched on a tomb wall at Khirbet Beit Lei some two centuries later. All of these indicate a readiness to write such texts and display them where they might be accessible to others to read.[21] These discoveries allow the possibility of literary works, including prophecies, being kept in the homes of prophets or their followers.

Egypt supplies more evidence in the form of a number of "prophetic" compositions: four are presented under the heading "Prophecy" in the anthology *Context of Scripture*. One of them, significantly, has a narrative introduction, set in the distant past, in which the king "stretched out his arm to a writing case and then he took for him a papyrus roll and a palette and put in writing" the words of the "author", Neferti, as he spoke about the future.[22] That the oldest copy dates from the 18th Dynasty long after the 4th Dynasty setting of the story, does not detract from the evident expectation that a "prophecy" might be put into writing immediately after it was spoken, as were other speeches.[23]

Could Hebrew prophets record their own oracles? Opinions vary widely from those who consider they did not, van der Toorn being a recent representative, through exegetes who follow Hermann Gunkel in perceiving a series of stages, beginning with a prophet or his immediate circle writing a few short passages which were eventually incorporated into a much expanded collection of traditions, to a few who credit a whole book to the named prophet, notably Shalom Paul in his commentary on Amos.[24] A "sheep-shearer, herdsman or fig-gatherer" like Amos (1:1; 7:14, REB), may not have been able to write, but there may well have been someone in Tekoa who could; it is also possible that Amaziah sent his message from Bethel to Jeroboam in

---

[21] For these texts see S. Aḥituv, *Echoes from the Past. Hebrew and Cognate Inscriptions from the Biblical Period* (Jerusalem, 2008), pp. 152–53, 173–77, 322–29, 233–35.

[22] N. Shupak, "The Prophecies of Neferti" in "Canonical Compositions (Egyptian), 2. 'Prophecy'", *COS*, 1, pp. 106–10.

[23] Shupak, "The Prophecies of Nerferti", p. 107, n. 6, refers to "The Eloquent Peasant".

[24] H. Gunkel, "Propheten II.B.", in *RGG*², 4, pp. 1538–54; translated by R. A. Wilson in J. Pelikan (ed.), *Twentieth Century Theology in the Making* (London and New York, 1969), pp. 48–75: see pp. 62–67. S. M. Paul, *Amos: A Commentary on the Book of Amos* (Minneapolis, 1991).

writing (Am 7:10). If any prophet or his followers thought it appropriate to write down his oracles, the distribution of surviving ancient
Hebrew epigraphs suggests it would not have been difficult to find a
scribe to do so. Inevitably, most scribes were trained to perform legal
and administrative tasks, following common patterns and using set
formulae,[25] but there is nothing to suggest that ordinary scribes could
not write at a prophet's dictation, just as they might write letters such as
the complaint about a worker's stolen cloak from Mesad Hashavyahu.[26]
Oral delivery can presume careful preparation, attention to form and
rhythm, as much as written composition. A prophet might utter his
words in a literary style, or he might ask his scribe to improve them.

The length of the Hebrew prophetic books leads to questions of prac-
ticality. The Babylonian and Assyrian "prophecies" are quite short, one
as short as two lines: " 'I (Ishtar of Arbela) rejoice over Esarhaddon,
my king! Arbela rejoices!' (By the mouth of the woman NN from PN
in the mountains)".[27] Short oracles, as Gunkel's disciples commonly
propose, were remembered, possibly written and later collected and
enlarged to make books. The pattern is logical. The assumption that
there were lengthy intervals between each stage is less sustainable,
unless there are clear historical or linguistic indications. Why may not
a prophet have kept records of his words over several years, during
which the content and his style may have changed, added to them,
arranged and re-arranged them, quoted from them in later utterances
and eventually created his own collection a decade or more later? The
impression often received of a prophet delivering his message then
disappearing from the scene, showing no more concern for his utterances, is misleading!

Information about the availability of scrolls in ancient Judah is lacking; Egypt, on the other hand, offers examples of scrolls of varying
size, those for administrative use being slightly larger. Ancient scrolls
were not huge, averaging perhaps 24 cms or 10 inches in height and
thus not so bulky to store or to transport as the scrolls commonly seen
in synagogues today. The familiar Egyptian *Wisdom of Amenemope* is
preserved on a papyrus roll about 1.70 metres or 5 feet 6 inches long

---

[25] For standardized education, see C. A. Rollston, "Scribal Education in Ancient
Israel: The Old Hebrew Epigraphic Evidence", *BASOR* 344 (2006), pp. 47–74.
[26] Aḥituv, *Echoes from the Past*, pp. 156–63.
[27] Nissinen, *Prophets and Prophecy*, p. 104.

in twenty-eight columns with about 475 lines overall. That is a small roll, others are longer, often three to six metres, roughly 10 to 20 feet, the standard being 3–3.5 metres or 9 to 12 feet. In the second century A.D. 6 metres or 20 feet, could contain two books of Homer's *Iliad*.[28] Longer still is the roll of Customs Accounts for 475 B.C. found in ruins of houses at Elephantine. It was originally about 13.5 metres or 44 feet, long, being made up of forty-six sheets. Written over the partly erased accounts is the Aramaic text of the *Words of Ahiqar*, with part of the text written again on the back of the scroll, duplicating some of the narrative. Ahiqar itself only occupied twenty-one columns or so, needing about 5.6 metres, which is over 18 feet. This is the oldest example of a West Semitic book scroll.[29] For comparison, the present book of Amos has about 300 lines of varying length as printed on twelve pages of *BHS*, and so would occupy only a short scroll. The whole book of Isaiah fills 104 pages of *BHS* and that, at Qumran, required a scroll of about 7.3 metres or 24 feet long, well beyond the standard. Leather rolls seem to have followed similar dimensions to the papyrus ones. Although three centuries may separate the Persian period papyri from the days of Isaiah, it is clear from the Egyptian papyri that the form of book current in the fifth century was no different from the forms current earlier, of which no examples survive in the West Semitic alphabetic script.

The book of Isaiah, like those of other prophets, has occasional references to political history, mentioning kings and events, and in Jeremiah they become most extensive. In arguing that prophecy is a "literary phenomenon", Philip Davies thought the presence of those references in sources which a later composer of prophetic books used could cause him to link an unrelated "prophetic scroll and an eponymous prophet" in his mind. He accepted the possibility of Judaean archives surviving into the Persian period to provide "minimal details of the reigns and activities of Judean and Israelite kings" for the writers of Kings.[30] That could be so. Yet the awareness of political situations and the circumstantial historical details in some of the prophetic

---

[28] F. G. Kenyon, *Books and Readers in Ancient Greece and Rome* (2nd edn., Oxford, 1951), pp. 50, 54.

[29] B. Porten and A. Yardeni, *Textbook of Aramaic Documents from Ancient Egypt 3. Literature, Accounts, Lists* (Jerusalem; Winona Lake IN, 1986), pp. 25–35.

[30] P. R. Davies "'Pen of iron, point of diamond' (Jer. 17:10): Prophecy as Writing", in E. Ben Zvi and M. H. Floyd (eds), *Writing and Speech in Israelite and Ancient Near Eastern Prophecy* (SBLSympS 10; Atlanta, 2000), pp. 69, 74, n. 18.

books are remarkably accurate. Most noteworthy is the preservation of the Assyrian dialect form of the name of king Sargon (Isa. 20:1) in contrast to the Babylonian form, implying that a contemporary, or nearly contemporary, record was made, for later writers and editors might have been expected to replace the Assyrian forms by the Babylonian (i.e. *šrkn* instead of *srgn*). (Here attention may be drawn to the presence of Tiglath-pileser's byname Pul, written *p'l*, four times in the contemporary Phoenician inscription of the Incirli Stele.[31] This confirms the accuracy of the later cuneiform Babylonian King-List A, of Berossus and Josephus, the Ptolemaic Canon and the Bible (2 Kgs 15:19; 1 Chr 5:26) in preserving the name. That accuracy could already be inferred from the evidence of tablets from the reign of Shalmaneser V, Tiglath-pileser's son, naming him as Ululayu, his name also present on the Ashur Ostracon from the mid-seventh century.[32] Accuracy is apparent, too, in the titles of Babylonian royal officials which are correctly given in Jer. 39:3 and 13 (*samgar, rab-sārîs, rab-mag, rab-ṭabbāḥîm*), all but one differing from the correct titles of Assyrian officers in 2 Kgs 18:17, cf. Isa. 36:2 (*tartān, rab-sārîs, rab-šāqeh*).[33]

Could Isaiah have written his prophecies? The examples of brief literary compositions provided by Hebrew epigraphy, noted above, prove the possibility of the short written sayings that Gunkel described. That people in the kingdoms of Israel and Judah could write prophetic words at greater length is suggested by the Tell Deir 'Alla Balaam text, dated near the beginning of the eighth century B.C. The text did not necessarily originate at Deir 'Alla and may have been considerably older (André Lemaire seeking its source in Damascus in the ninth or even the tenth century B.C.)[34] The *spr [b]l'm* was laid out as if copied from a scroll in a column of writing almost a metre high on the wall of a shrine. In the opinion of Manfred Weippert, it "gives evidence of

[31] S. A. Kaufman, "The Phoenician Inscription of the Incirli Trilingual: A Tentative Reconstruction and Translation", *Maarav* 14.2 (2007), pp. 7–26, see p. 18.

[32] References given in J. A. Brinkman, *A Political History of Post-Kassite Babylonia 1158–722 B.C.* (AnOr 43; Rome, 1968), pp. 61–62, 240, n. 1544, 243, n. 1560; see now K. Radner, "Salmanassar V. in den Nimrud Letters", *AfO* 50 (2003–04), pp. 95–104.

[33] A. R. Millard, "The Value and Limitations of the Bible and Archaeology for Understanding the history of Israel – Some Examples", in D. I. Block (ed.), *Israel. Ancient Kingdom or Late Invention?* (Nashville, 2008), pp. 9–24, see pp. 21–22.

[34] A. Lemaire, "Les inscriptions sur plâtre de Deir 'Alla et leur signification historique et culturelle", in J. Hoftijzer and G. van der Kooij (eds), *The Balaam Text from Deir 'Alla Re-evaluated* (Leiden, 1991), pp. 33–57, see p. 50, but note J. A. Hackett's dissent, "Response to…André Lemaire", ibid., pp. 79–84.

a scribal art which transcends the qualifications necessary for everyday writing. It presupposes a tradition of professional scribes which can ultimately be traced back to Second Millennium Egypt" and calls into question the hypothesis that literary activities did not arise in Israel and Judah prior to the middle of the eighth century.[35]

Babylonian and Assyrian officials wrote down the oracles that they heard, often in the Mari tablets as soon as they heard them, in order to send them to their kings because they were at a distance from them. When the speaker was at hand there was no need to write them for transmission. However, on occasion a prophecy might be recorded as part of an historical narrative. When Ashurbanipal sought the favour of Ishtar of Arbela in his cause against the rebel kings, she responded directly to him with an assurance, "Fear not!" and by a vision given to a dream-interpreter that night which he related to the king next day. The account was included in the king's "annals" which were buried in the foundations of buildings at Nineveh so that future generations could read of the king's prowess and piety.[36] Jeremiah had his words written to be read to king Jehioakim because he could not speak to the ruler himself, then had them re-written, clearly to stand as evidence against the king. Prophets used writing for the purpose that it was invented, to communicate. Their oral delivery may have preceded or followed the writing. Once inscribed, the prophets' words could be circulated far beyond their homes, just as the ostraca show that letters were sent from one place to another, taking their message to sympathetic ears. Once inscribed, the words would remain for posterity, unless a Jehoiakim intervened. For van der Toorn immediate publication was the only function: the prophets' "purpose in writing was confined to communicating a message to their contemporaries".[37] Certainly that was their primary purpose yet the message they conveyed often referred to future events and no-one could know how long they would live, whether they might experience them or not. When Isaiah wrote on the "large writing tablet" the name of his son who was not yet conceived, the forecast of Assyria's conquest of Damascus and Samaria was looking at least a year ahead (Isa. 8:1–4). In the light of the Ketef Hinnom amulets, the "large writing tablet", *gillāyôn gādôl*,

---

[35] M. Weippert, "The Balaam Text from Deir ʿAlla and the Study of the Old Testament", in Hoftijzer and van der Kooij, *The Balaam Text*, pp. 151–84, see pp. 176–77.

[36] Nissinen, *Prophets and Prophecy*, pp. 146–50, cf. pp. 137–44.

[37] Van der Toorn, *Scribal Culture*, p. 182.

may denote a sheet of metal, assuming the *gilyōnîm* of 3:23 are "mirrors", on which letters would need to be written by incision with a graving tool (*ḥereṭ*).

Preservation of prophecies that were soon fulfilled would vindicate their authors and give weight to later ones for which they might claim divine inspiration. The various Assyrian oracles directed to Esarhaddon may have been put in sequence on larger tablets for that reason. Passages in the king's inscriptions have close parallels with certain of the prophecies.[38] Had the clerks, or priests, kept those oracles to await their fulfilment and so check the authenticity of their speakers, in the spirit of Deut. 18:21, 22? The written texts would be witnesses to the prophets' words, whether or not they were alive, witnesses more precise than the memories of the most devoted disciples, just as texts of treaties testified to pledges made, themselves invoking as perpetual witnesses heaven and earth, as well as deities (cf. Isa. 1:2). Whether unfulfilled prophecies were stored for long in Nineveh is unknown. However, one prophetess of Kalah told Esarhaddon in Ishtar's name that she would "cut off the heel of Mugallu", the hostile ruler of Melid.[39] Esarhaddon did advance against Melid, but the outcome is not recorded, the prophecy may have appeared to fail. It was, his successor, Ashurbanipal, who could boast of the submission of Mugallu, who had behaved treacherously toward previous Assyrian kings.[40] The brief entry in Ashurbanipal's "annals" does not refer to any prophecy. Where unfulfilled Hebrew prophecies continue to exist (e.g. about the restoration of the Davidic dynasty) they either display hope that they would come about, or respect for the men whose names are attached to them, perhaps because other oracles of theirs had proved to be correct. To treat Isa. 7, for example, as a *vaticinium ex eventu* would be no more justifiable than treating the Assyrian forecasts in the same way. Presumably oracles that events refuted were discarded and their authors discredited.

Was Isaiah a "writing prophet"? His access to Ahaz and Hezekiah may imply he was a man of some standing in Jerusalem and so could

---

[38] Nissinen, *Prophets and Prophecy*, pp. 101, 133–34.
[39] Nissinen, *Prophets and Prophecy*, pp. 114–15.
[40] For Esarhaddon see Babylonian Chronicle iv.10 and Esarhaddon Chronicle 15 in J.-J. Glassner, *Mesopotamian Chronicles* (Writings from the Ancient World 19; Atlanta, 2004), pp. 200–01, 208–09; for Ashurbanipal see R. Borger, *Beiträge zum Inschriftenwerk Assurbanipals* (Wiesbaden, 1996), pp. 29 and 216.

have had training in scribal skills, not necessarily working as a professional scribe. If he did not write his own words, a secretary could act for him. The Hebrew epigraphic corpus illustrates the availability of writing, the Deir 'Alla and Egyptian texts the possibility of lengthier compositions than the oracles in cuneiform. The Mari letters certainly exhibit a readiness to write the prophetic words as soon as they were heard. It is easy to discount ancient statements and replace them with hypothetical reconstructions but they appear and disappear over the decades while the ancient texts remain. The book of Isaiah testifies to the work of a prophet whose words were fulfilled, at least in part, and so deserved preservation.

It is a pleasure to join many colleagues in congratulating John Emerton, longstanding friend and esteemed scholar.

THE SUFFERING SERVANT OF DEUTERO-ISAIAH:
JEREMIAH REVISITED

Katharine J. Dell

There has been a long tradition of connecting Jeremiah with the "servant" in Deutero-Isaiah, both in Jewish and Christian tradition. C. R. North[1] (1956) mentions that Saadyah Gaon (a Jewish writer who died in 942) favoured links with Jeremiah and that Ibn Ezra found Gaon's interpretation attractive. Judah ben Balaam (c. 1080) stated that the description of the Servant is "quite consistent with such an interpretation".[2] In Christian tradition North cites E. W. Hengstenberg[3] who mentions Seidel the Silesian as having promoted Jeremiah as the servant from a position of unbelief and Grotius,[4] who saw reference to Jeremiah "as a figure of Christ" in relation to his life and circumstances. The English deist Anthony Collins[5] thought that the words of Isaiah 53:12 could not possibly apply to Jeremiah. In slightly more recent times – the nineteenth century – Baron C. C. J. Bunsen[6] supposed that since features of the passages in Isaiah 52:13–53:12 fitted into the life of Jeremiah it might have been written by the prophet's amanuensis, Baruch.

Some early twentieth-century scholars also thought this way, including B. Duhm in his early work[7] who thought of the four servant songs (which he had already isolated as not written by the prophet himself) as a prophetic description of the life and work of Jeremiah, written by one of Jeremiah's younger contemporaries and taken over

---

[1] C. R. North, *The Suffering Servant in Deutero-Isaiah: An Historical and Critical Study* (Oxford; London 1948).
[2] Cited by S. R. Driver and A. Neubauer, *The Fifty-third Chapter of Isaiah according to the Jewish Interpreters* (Oxford, 1877) vol. 2, p. 551.
[3] E. W. Hengstenberg, *Christology of the Old Testament* (Edinburgh, 1858), vol. 2, p. 319.
[4] H. Grotius, *Annotata ad Vetus Testamentum*, Tomus II (Paris, 1644).
[5] A. Collins, *The Scheme of Literal Prophecy Considered* (London, 1727) pp. 208–20.
[6] Baron C. C. J. Bunsen, *Gott in der Geschichte* 1 (Leipzig, 1857); *Vollständiges Bibelwerk für die Gemeinde* (Leipzig, 1860), 2 Bd., p. 438.
[7] B. Duhm, *Die Theologie der Propheten* (Bonn, 1875).

by Deutero-Isaiah to relate to his ideal picture of God's servant.[8]
L. Itkonen[9] believed that there were a number of historical personages behind individual songs, Isaiah 50:4–9 referring to Jeremiah and
written by him. By the time North was writing in 1956, he was able
to state that "Jeremiah has no advocate today" (p. 192), although in a
footnote he qualified that statement when he said, "Beyond Sheldon
H. Blank's suggestion that the Servant is 'Israel in the guise of a martyr
prophet – of a prophet after the pattern of Jeremiah' ('Studies in DI',
HUCA 15 (1940), p. 29)" (p. 192). North also referred the reader to
F. A. Farley's article in the *Expository Times*[10] who believed the Servant
to be "idealized prophecy" based on the life of Jeremiah. North's own
comment on the Jeremiah suggestion was, "Although his claims are
in some respects attractive, it cannot be said that he suffered uncomplainingly. The most that can be said is that he contributed something
to the portrait (liii.7, cf. Jer. xi.19)" (p. 192).

In this article I wish to look afresh at the servant songs to seek to
understand why this suggestion was made. However, I do not wish
simply to reinvent the wheel of saying that the servant might have
been Jeremiah, as clearly there are problems over the lack of evidence
within the texts. If it had been obvious, then the problem of who the
servant was would have been solved a long time ago! There has been
a strong move away from finding one actual historical figure for this
role during the twentieth century. Most scholars have seen the servant as either a historically composite figure or as an idealized figure
or both. H. Gunkel, for example, wrote, "Many things have contributed to make up this figure: the experiences of Israel in exile, of great
prophets like Jeremiah, and the experiences of the Prophet himself;
not least the faith that at the end of things...a new Moses would arise
to free Israel and found a new covenant".[11] S. A. Cook[12] took the view
that the servant idea was an ideal figure, "neither necessarily limited
in its application (sc. to collective or individual), nor confined in its
reference solely to past events or to ideals in the future" (p. 493).
He stated that actual individuals were being thought of by those who

---

[8] The three Isaiahs were isolated by Döderlein in 1775 and Eichhorn in 1780–3.

[9] L. Itkonen, *Deuterojesaja (Jes 40–55) metrisch untersucht* (Helsinki, 1916).

[10] F. A. Farley, "Jeremiah and 'the suffering servant of Jehovah' in Deutero-Isaiah",
ExpT 38 (1926–7) pp. 521–524.

[11] H. Gunkel, "Der Knecht Jahwes", *RGG* (1912), cols. 1540ff. (quotation: col.
1543).

[12] J. B. Bury and S. A. Cook, *Cambridge Ancient History* 3 (London, 1970).

wrote the passages, and that, among such possibilities, Jeremiah was foremost. He believed, however, that the servant was not Jeremiah on the grounds that Jeremiah did not suffer martyrdom, "the Servant is certainly not Jeremiah himself, but 'Jeremian'". He continued, "he is greater than Jeremiah...His identity remains unknown...Not a Messianic figure whether conquering (Jer. xxii:4), or conspicuous for his humility (Zech. ix. 9). Indeed he is more than that; he is at once prophet and priest, missionary and intercessor; and his attributes make him almost more than human" (p. 494).

More recently there has been a move towards favouring the idea that Deutero-Isaiah himself was the servant.[13] C. Seitz, for example, argues that the historical servant is Deutero-Isaiah, the prophetic voice in these chapters, but the language used is veiled because the prophet has taken up the mantle of a long line of prophets.[14] The idea of intentionally veiled language was first made by C. Westermann.[15] He described the language used to describe the Servant as "cryptic and veiled" (p. 93). Seitz argues that the servant represents "the culmination of prophetic Israel, whose testimony he takes up and whose suffering he willingly embraces" (p. 190). The mantle of other prophets includes Jeremiah along with Moses, and Seitz notes the similarity of Isaiah 49:1–6 with the call narrative of Jeremiah.[16] However, Seitz argues that in this passage's nature as past reminiscence, "the servant's career picked up where Jeremiah left off, at the end of his career" (p. 188).

Another recent scholarly move is towards denying that the four songs are distinctive and separate. This often leads to the preference for a collective interpretation (the servant is Israel) that fits in with other passages where that identification is made. Or it leads to a mixture of collective and individual – e.g. P. Wilcox and D. Paton-Williams[17] who

---

[13] R. N. Whybray, *The Second Isaiah* (Old Testament Guide, Sheffield, 1983) amongst many others.

[14] C. Seitz, "How is the Prophet Isaiah Present in the Latter Half of the Book? The Logic of Chapters 40–66 within the Book of Isaiah" in *Word Without End: The Old Testament as Abiding Theological Witness* (Grand Rapids, MI, 1998), pp. 168–193.

[15] C. Westermann, *Isaiah 40–66* (London, 1969).

[16] Seitz, 1998, even suggests that 49:1–6 could be classified as a "call narrative" but notes that "the lack of a serious, present encounter with the divine" (p. 185) makes it fall short. He argues that it has the character of a past reminiscence, of a person called once and then recommissioned: "Our passage sounds more like an interim report, with a fresh charge being delivered, than the initial call of a prophet" (p. 187).

[17] P. Wilcox and D. Paton-Williams, "The Servant Songs in Deutero-Isaiah", *JSOT* 42 (1988), p. 95.

favour a collective interpretation for the first song, but see the others as styled in an individual fashion and referring to the prophet himself. However, the distinctive feature of these four passages is the way they present the servant as a male individual who suffered uncomplainingly even when faced with death. Somehow the view that seeks to deny the distinctiveness of these four passages does not ring true.

An attempt has been made to move away from historical identification towards a literary reading of the passages. So to come right up to date in the twenty-first century, M. Gignilliat in a recent article speaks in Ricoeurian terms of narrative identity, putting an emphasis on the character of the Servant within the plot of Isaiah 40–55.[18] His conclusion is that the literary technique of the Servant figure is a means used by the author to express God's reconciliation of both Zion and the nations. He writes, "the divine action and description of YHWH and the Servant begin to blend in such a way that the Servant can be described as a unique member of the divine identity" (p. 125). He concurs with Seitz regarding this figure as the culmination of prophetic tradition but argues against seeing any historical figure behind the book – he writes, "the witness is silent" (p. 134). This kind of approach takes attention away from historical reconstruction and allows for the possibility of literary archetypes or veiled composite personages, as have all been suggested.

I wish in this paper to revisit the case for Jeremiah. I do not wish entirely to exclude a historical personage whose memory may have contributed to the picture of the Servant. However I am essentially dealing here with parallels between two texts that are now in their final form, so that in that sense it is a literary analysis. I believe that there are echoes of Jeremiah in the text and I shall divide my analysis of the relevant passages into two categories: the first, passages with verbal thematic connections; second, passages with links to Jeremiah's life and thought. The songs are found in Isa. 42:1–4; 49:1–6; 50:4–9; 52:13–53:12. The Jeremiah tradition itself is eclectic, sometimes echoing other texts, such as psalmic ones (especially in the confessions). One needs therefore to be aware of wider inter-textual connections. I shall also look at other connections between the two texts outside the

---

[18] M. Gignilliat, "Who is Isaiah's Servant? Narrative identity and theological potentiality", *SJT* 61/2 (2008), pp. 125–136.

servant songs, notably at the technique of the reversal of motifs that has been found between the two.

1. *Passages with strong verbal and thematic connections*

A) *Isa. 49:1b:* יְהוָה מִבֶּטֶן קְרָאָנִי מִמְּעֵי אִמִּי הִזְכִּיר שְׁמִי

> The Lord called me before I was born, while I was in my mother's womb he named me (NRSV)

cf. Jer. 1:5a: בְּטֶרֶם אֶצָּורְךָ בַבֶּטֶן יְדַעְתִּיךָ וּבְטֶרֶם תֵּצֵא מֵרֶחֶם הִקְדַּשְׁתִּיךָ

> Before I formed you in the womb I knew you, and before you were born I consecrated you (NRSV)

In Isaiah 49:1b the surprise element is that it is not God that is speaking (as has been the case up until this point in the book), but rather God is being spoken about as the one who called the speaker. In the Jeremiah passage, on the other hand, God is speaking to the prophet in the context of his call. Interestingly both of these verses come in the wider context of, first, a call to the "coastlands" and "peoples" (Isa. 49:1a; cf. the previous servant song in 42:1–4) and, second, to the prophet's appointment "to the nations" (Jer. 1:5b), a passage that has proved problematic in Jeremiah studies since Jeremiah's message is so clearly for Israel itself and he is essentially seen as a nationalistic prophet. Clearly Isa. 49:1b suggests the context of a prophetic call, but it is interesting that the verbal overtones are of Jeremiah's call and not that of Second Isaiah (40:1–8 (if indeed this passage is a call narrative)). The speaker in Isa. 49:1 is summoned into service by Yahweh before birth. The second colon in the line reiterates the first in less familiar language, מעה being a rarer word for 'womb' than בטן (cf. Isa. 44:2 in reference to Jacob/Israel being called from the womb). Naming (זכר) often refers to the name of Yahweh (12:4; 48:1). J. Goldingay[19] suggests that the use of naming here initially suggests designating someone by name, but that it has wider overtones. He writes, "Having pronounced the name, Yhwh will see it is kept in mind and not forgotten... The reference to uttering the name will also have

---

[19] J. Goldingay, *The Message of Isaiah 40–55: A Literary-Theological Commentary* (London and New York, 2005).

the implication of summoning to service, like talk of calling by name (see 40:26)" (p. 366). Duhm[20] suggested that here it refers to Yahweh naming the speaker as his servant. There is a reiteration of the sentiment about being formed in the womb to be God's servant in Isa. 49:5 which makes explicit that the task of this servant is "to bring Jacob back to him and that Israel might be gathered to him", clarifying that it is not the collective Israel that is the servant here (despite elsewhere Jacob/Israel being described as having a relationship with Yahweh that goes back to the womb, clearly itself a favoured expression to define the long-standing nature of the relationship, e.g. 44:2, 24; 46:3; 48:8), but rather it is an individual, modeled upon a prophetic figure. As B.S. Childs[21] writes, "The imagery of the call is prophetic and reminiscent of Jeremiah's call (chapter 1): called from the womb, named by name, mouth like a sharp sword" (p. 383). The Jeremiah passage is the opening sentence of his call, making it clear that he was always intended for this task. The connection between these two passages is an interesting one, but one should bear in mind that the language of God calling from the womb is used in a number of contexts in Deutero-Isaiah – often to describe Jacob/Israel or Zion (49:15), or Abraham (51:2). This is a fresh context for such language in that the collective designation has given way to an individual one here (the two of which need not be incompatible with each other). Israel's servanthood is now described in a more individual way. However, most scholars of recent times have sought to find the identity of this individual in Deutero-Isaiah himself, or in a very generalized portrayal of a prophetic figure. My contention is that the echo is chiefly of Jeremiah here, although, of course, other resonances are clearly present.

B) *Isa. 53:7b* כְּשֶׂה לַטֶּבַח יוּבָל וּכְרָחֵל לִפְנֵי גֹזְזֶיהָ נֶאֱלָמָה וְלֹא יִפְתַּח פִּיו

> Like a lamb that is led to the slaughter and like a sheep that before its shearers is silent, so he did not open his mouth (NRSV)

cf. Jer. 11:19a וַאֲנִי כְּכֶבֶשׂ אַלּוּף יוּבַל לִטְבוֹחַ

> But I was like a gentle lamb led to the slaughter (NRSV)

---

[20] B. Duhm, *Die Theologie der Propheten* (Bonn, 1875).
[21] B. Childs, *Isaiah* (OTL; Louisville KY, London and Leiden, 2001).

Isaiah 53:7 is in the third person, reporting events that are past. The image is of a sacrificial lamb on the one hand and a sheep at the mercy of the shearers on the other. The striking aspect of the verse is the silence of the person involved. In fact the passage is framed by the repeated "he did not open his mouth" (53:7a; 53:7b). There was no complaint or crying out as he was led to his fate. As Goldingay[22] writes, "The third person form does slightly distance the prophet from the servant role" (p. 281). This, and the fact that it is a past event that is being described, makes it unlikely that the prophet Deutero-Isaiah is in mind. However, there is also a problem with the Jeremiah suggestion too, as he certainly did not behave uncomplainingly in his suffering. Goldingay continues, "Verses 7–8 follow Jer. 11:19, though the servant's silence distinguishes him from Jeremiah" (p. 506). Psalm 39 is a closer parallel as a picture of silence in the face of suffering (esp. v. 9). This sufferer is a willing one – he is passive and has no choice in his fate. His suffering is at the hands of other human beings. Westermann points out, citing North, that the use of נָגַשׂ in v.7a may denote physical violence (cf. Exod. 3:7; Isa. 58:3) and that not opening one's mouth only makes sense in the context of violent action by others which leads to fear and submission (cf. Ps. 38:14). This is in contrast to the picture of illness depicted earlier in the passage (esp. v. 4). In similar fashion Jeremiah 11:19 is placed in the context of hostile action from individuals (Jer. 11:18). Another point is the sacral context of "lamb led to the slaughter" which is what is picked up in Jeremiah 11:19 – as P. D. Hanson[23] writes, "the Servant was a victim of a sacral decision over which he had no control" (p. 160). This may suggest the hand of God is involved as well as human beings. There are overtones here of the kind of sentiment of Psalm 44:11, 12. In the Jeremiah passage the word אַלּוּף "gentle" (i.e. pet) is found to describe the lamb, which somehow heightens his innocence and vulnerability. He may have been a pet lamb such as is described in 2 Sam. 12:3 and hence more trusting of human beings than an ordinary lamb would be. The context in Jeremiah – where the prophet is speaking – is part of a confession in which the prophet describes how, even when God showed him the evil deeds going on around him, he did not realize, in his naivety, that it was geared towards him. He was "like a gentle

---

[22] J. Goldingay, *Isaiah 40–55* (ICC; London and New York, 2006).
[23] P. D. Hanson, *Isaiah 40–66* (Interpretation; Louisville KY, 1995).

lamb led to the slaughter" by hostile enemies who plotted to kill him.
He was innocent and defenceless in the face of his enemies. As W.
McKane[24] writes, "His instincts of self-preservation are undeveloped
and he is unable to envisage the moves which are being made against
him, far less to take steps to ensure his safety in a dangerous world"
(p. 256). Therefore there are strong parallels between these passages in
the sheep and sacrificial imagery used, and the context of hostile enemies. The theme of the silence of the Servant is a problem in relation
to Jeremiah who comes across as fairly argumentative (although he is
at times a passive victim of events, when, for example he is imprisoned
(Jer. 38)), and yet it might well describe an initial response to one's
enemies in a frightening situation, as in Psalm 38:14, and so could be
a short-term rather than a long-term reaction, thus not ruling echoes
of Jeremiah's situation out completely.

C) *Isa. 53:8b:* כִּי נִגְזַר מֵאֶרֶץ חַיִּים מִפֶּשַׁע עַמִּי נֶגַע לָמוֹ

> For he was cut off from the land of the living, stricken for the transgres-
> sion of my people. (NRSV)

cf. Jer. 11:19c: וְנִכְרְתֶנּוּ מֵאֶרֶץ חַיִּים וּשְׁמוֹ לֹא־יִזָּכֵר עוֹד

> Let us cut him off from the land of the living, so that his name will no
> longer be remembered! (NRSV)

Isaiah 53:8 continues the third person of reported speech of a past
event. There is some debate about whether "cut off from the land of
the living" indicates death or whether it means social exclusion. In the
light of verse 9 about his grave and tomb, there seems little doubt that
it is to be taken at face value to refer to death. There is also perceived
to be a problem with "my people", as this suggests that it is Yahweh
(or the prophet) who is speaking, yet the rest of the passage is in the
third person. This has led to amendment to "his people". In Jeremiah
11:19 being cut off from the land of the living is clearly a reference
to being killed – the verb used is כרת "cut" rather than the rarer גזר
in the Isaiah passage (used in Ps 88:5 to describe being cut off from
God's hand by death, but can mean "as good as dead"). Goldingay
acknowledges, when discussing the Jeremiah parallel, that it refers to
a fate which all but overtook Jeremiah and hence the Isaiah passage

---

[24] W. McKane, *Jeremiah* (ICC; Edinburgh, 1996).

"refers, moreover, to a prophet whose experience contributed to the portrayal of the servant" (p. 507). The reason given for the death is different in each passage – the Isaiah passage gives the "transgression of my people" as the reason, consistent with the earlier oppression of the Servant at the hands of others. The Jeremiah passage quotes the words of those who wish to harm Jeremiah and the reason given is so that his name will be remembered no more. This is the worst fate imaginable in Hebrew thought. However in the half verse before v.8b in Isa. 53 the same sentiment is found as in the Jeremiah passage – NRSV "Who could have imagined his future?"; NIV "And who can speak of his descendants?" The term דור indicates "lot, state" (Driver, cited by Westermann) or the time of a generation/circle of one's contemporaries (Childs). However one translates this, the point is that his future has just been wiped away, which is the same effect as not being remembered by anyone or through any descendants. So there is arguably a second link here between the two passages. Clearly the Isaiah passage describes someone who has been killed at the hands of enemies, whereas the Jeremiah passage is simply expressing a threat that nearly came to pass (and indeed Jeremiah's final fate after he was kidnapped and taken away to Egypt is unknown). However the verbal links are interesting and add to the cumulative evidence of echoes of the prophet Jeremiah in this picture of the Servant.

2. Passages with possible links to Jeremiah's life and thought

I now move on to the more circumstantial evidence of passages in Deutero-Isaiah's servant songs that seem to link with Jeremiah's life and thought, rather than with the text of Jeremiah. Such connections have been noted by scholars, such as Farley[25] and Lindblom.[26] Whilst Farley finds "direct references" to Jeremiah and is at times rather overconfident about the connections, I plan to be more cautious, noting his points of linkage during my discussion. Lindblom argues that the servant songs are allegories and draws out a few interesting links between the servant songs and Jeremiah's confessions, but does not do a passage by passage analysis as I plan to do here.

---

[25] F. A. Farley, "Jeremiah and 'the suffering servant of Jehovah' in Deutero-Isaiah", *ExpT* 38 (1926–7), pp. 521–524.
[26] J. Lindblom, *The Servant Songs in Deutero-Isaiah* (Lund, 1951).

A. *Isaiah 42:1–4 The First Song*

The first servant song is in 42:1–4 and in it the repeated injunction to the servant is to "bring forth justice" (vv. 1b and 4b),[27] in the first instance to the nations and in the second place "in the earth". In verse 1b God "puts his spirit" upon the servant, echoing a prophetic call such as Jeremiah's which uses the language of consecration and of God putting his words into the prophet's mouth (Jer. 1:5, 9). Farley sees an echo of Jeremiah's reluctance to accept his call in Isaiah 42:1–4, but I fail to find any such hint. Rather the promise of "justice to the nations" is arguably echoed in the phrase "prophet to the nations" in Jer. 1:5, 10. As noted above, Jeremiah's mission to the nations is an interesting further link, something slightly out of place in Jeremiah's usual profile, but very much at the heart of the mission of the servant. There are some images in this song that do not suggest a prophet, notably in verse 2 where the figure "will not cry in the street", indicating that this is not a public role. One imagines on the other hand that the prophet spoke out publicly on every occasion possible, knowing in reference to Jeremiah that he did so (Jer. 7:1–4; 26:1–6). In verse 3 the servant's call is not to violence. Nor is that of the prophet, although he sometimes incited violence without intending it (e.g. when Jeremiah was captured and thrown into a cistern in Jer. 37:11–21). However, the servant image is a much more passive one than would be usual with prophets (cf. Jer. 51:11 – his exhortation to "Sharpen the arrows! Fill the quivers!" in reference to destroying Babylon). Many scholars have suggested a kingly link in this passage, but these two objections seem to me also to apply to a kingly figure. Clearly verse 4 fits well with a king with mention of the establishment of justice, however the situation described suggests a wider "kingdom" than just one country.

There is some debate whether verses 5 and 6 of Isaiah 42 also form a part of the servant song. They may be a secondary redaction, as is also 49:7–12, which is inspired by the main song. Farley argues that 42:6b (cf. 49:8b) "I have given you as a covenant to the people" recalls Jeremiah 1:8 which is God's promise to deliver the prophet. I find that point less than convincing. However he makes a second point that in the wider context there is an echo of Jeremiah's desire for a "covenant written on the heart" (Jer. 31:33–34). The language of covenant is used,

---

[27] Lindblom (*The Servant Songs*) points out a verbal link with Isa. 51:10.

although in the Isaiah passage the servant himself is the covenant, whilst Jeremiah is calling for a metaphorical "covenant written on the heart" in order to inspire a new obedience and allegiance to Yahweh. However, I fall short of agreeing with Farley when he says of Jeremiah, "Since he was so active in seeking to promote this covenant of the spirit he might well be thought of as 'a covenant of the people'..." (p. 522) which sounds a little too much like special pleading. Therefore this particular attempt to make a link from 42:6 is somewhat unconvincing.

B. *Isaiah 49:1–6 The Second Song*

The second song in Isaiah 49:1–6 may yield slightly more fruit on this issue. I have already discussed 49:1b at some length, which leads Farley to claim that Isaiah 49:1–6 "seems to be directly connected with the call and experience of Jeremiah" (p. 522). Many commentators have argued that the phrase "made my mouth like a sharp sword...a polished arrow" (v. 2) is a reminder of the commissioning of Jeremiah, where in 1:6 he does not know how to speak and then in 1:7 he is told that God will give him the power to speak "whatever I command you" (cf. Jer. 1:17), touching his mouth to put the words in it in 1:9. This is a contrast to Isaiah 42:2 where the servant is not to raise his voice. Here in Isaiah 49:2a God empowers the servant in a similar way – "He made my mouth like a sharp sword". The sword is hidden in God's hand until needed, in verse 2b. There is an overtone of protection in verse 2 in the "hidden" aspect of it, which also comes out in the Jeremiah passage in 1:8 where "I am with you to deliver you, says the LORD" (cf. 1:19b). Jeremiah too is waiting in readiness to be given the order by God to "Gird up your loins; stand up and tell them everything that I command you" (Jer. 1:17, cf. Jer. 23:29).

Farley argues that Isaiah 49:4 is "just the kind of language Jeremiah employed in...his 'Confessions'. He might well have said, 'I have laboured in vain, I have spent my strength for nought and vanity'". He might well, indeed, but he didn't! The point is taken however, that this kind of sentiment resembles that found in the confessions in passages where the prophet speaks in the first person, describing his spiritual turmoil in the face of his difficult task and his turbulent relationship with God (e.g. Jeremiah 15, 17, 20). Lindblom points out that, as in Isaiah 49:4, "Jeremiah felt tempted to give up. He said, "I will not make mention of Him, nor speak any more in His name (XX:9)"

(p. 25) and the servant of this song also describes a crisis in verse 4a from which he recovers when he realizes that his "cause" and his "reward" are both "with my God" (cf. Psalm 31:22 and Psalm 73:17 both of which describe a key turning point). Jeremiah too had moments of optimism (e.g. Jer. 20:12) and had an intense personal relationship with his God.

In Isaiah 49:6 the mission of the servant is clearly beyond Israel itself and it extends to the whole world. Farley points out that in Isaiah 49:6, "we see an enlarged mission and unexpected success foretold as the reward of the Servant's fidelity through discouraging times, but the wider field here promised to the Servant is not beyond the scope of Jeremiah's own ordination (see Jer. 1:5, 10)" (p. 522). I have already noted Jeremiah's witness to the nations, beyond Israel itself.[28]

In 49:1–6 then, the main link is in 49:1 with Jeremiah 1:5, however there is a spiritual/theological link between 49:4 and Jeremiah's confessions and a flavour of the wider mission of both prophets in 49:6 and in Jeremiah's call.

C. *Isaiah 50:4–9 The Third Song*

A striking aspect of the third song is the overtly male imagery in verse 6. In this song the language of God giving the servant "the tongue of a teacher" is found – again indicating the importance of words given by God (cf. Jeremiah's call). Verses 5–6 indicate the passive response of the servant, but also it is clear that he was tormented by others who struck him, pulled out his beard and insulted him with spitting. The language of setting one's face hard recalls both Jeremiah and Ezekiel (Jer. 1:18–19; Ezek. 3:8–11). Farley writes optimistically of this poem that it "might, without any modification of language, have been written of Jeremiah himself" (p. 522). He compares Isaiah 50:4 and Jeremiah 1:9 – the endowment of words in the call. He also compares Isa. 50:6–9 in more general terms with Jeremiah's confessions – Jer. 17:17–18; 20:7–12 and 26:14 (not itself a confession, but expressing the sentiment of his life being in the hands of others). Again speaking in the first person of "oneself" very much recalls the confessions of Jeremiah,

---

[28] Seitz, "How is the prophet Isaiah present…", argues that Jeremiah's witness to the nations was not fully accomplished and hence this lack of resolution led to the passing on of the role to Deutero-Isaiah: "This mantle of painful witness is simply handed over to another (ch. 45)" (p. 188).

but the links are more spiritual and theological. In the confessions Jeremiah is asking God all the time for strength, longing to be justified, as he describes the difficult present situation for him. By contrast in the servant song there is a quieter confidence in the midst of persecution at the hands of others that "The Lord God helps me; therefore I have not been disgraced" (v. 7a). The link of clear persecution and reliance on God in the face of it in both texts is nevertheless clear.

D. Isaiah 52:13–53:12 The Fourth Song

Farley states optimistically, "The great poem in Isaiah 52:13–53:12 is very rich in passages which seem to owe their language as well as thought to reflection upon the experiences of Jeremiah" (p. 522). I have already noted the parallels in Isaiah 53:7–8 with Jeremiah 11:19. Farley suggests that in Isaiah 52:15, "kings shall shut their mouths because of him", there is a reference to the respect paid to Jeremiah by the court and especially by King Zedekiah" (p. 522). This is a circumstantial possibility, but not a strong example in my view. Farley then draws a verse by verse comparison between Isaiah 53:1–9 and parts of Jeremiah, some of which are more interesting than others. He suggests that verse 1 of chapter 53 would have been "a suitable comment on the reception accorded to Jeremiah and his message, few among his contemporaries having perceived the Divine power behind the prophet" (p. 522). This is perhaps a possibility, but a rather far-fetched one in my view. Farley suggests in 53:2 that "a young plant" may refer to Jeremiah's shrinking from his task in Jer. 1:6. I would agree about the echo of 1:6, but rather put the emphasis on the reference being to Jeremiah's youth and naiveté itself. Farley suggests that "dry ground" may indicate Jeremiah's "apparently effete" family who were descendants of the deposed priest, Abiathar. He writes, "Jeremiah's origin and possibly his personal presence were heavy handicaps against his success as a prophet" (p. 522). Again, this ventures into a rather fanciful realm in my view. The verse may well have the meaning that this was a rare strike of a "root" in apparently barren ground. Likewise the servant was a rare person amongst a fairly unpromising lot. However, the hints of a particular person are not strong here. The rest of verse 2 goes on to describe his very ordinary looks – of course there is no record of what Jeremiah may have looked like or whether he was despised on that account.

Isaiah 53:3, according to Farley, describes the prophet's experience in similar terms to Jeremiah's confessions, e.g. Jer. 20:14–18. This passage is itself often compared to Job 3, with which the verbal parallel is closer than with Isa. 53:3. The general parallel is there, that Jeremiah was indeed despised in the way the servant is described and clearly suffered greatly as a result of that rejection. By contrast, however, the servant is accepting of that rejection rather than railing against it.

If there is a link between verses 4–5 and Jeremiah's suffering, it is a general, circumstantial one. Jeremiah had to suffer himself, but he also knew that his people would certainly suffer too. Farley points out that Jeremiah 15:11 and Jeremiah 17:16 have him praying for the people. In this sense he bore the infirmities of others (Isa. 53:4a). In his confessions, Jeremiah's "unceasing pain" and "incurable wound" are described in the context of his accusation to God of deceitful dealing with his prophet. As the servant in verse 5 was "wounded" and "crushed", so was Jeremiah, and yet there is never any suggestion in this servant song of blaming God, rather the Servant suffers on behalf of others – "he was wounded for our transgressions" (v. 5). Farley points to moments in Jeremiah's life that led to his suffering – such as his advice during the siege of Jerusalem to surrender to the Babylonians and his advice of non-resistance to them which were both seen as unpatriotic and deserving of punishment. Farley argues that his contemporaries would thus have said Jeremiah was "struck down by God" (v. 4b). The talk of healing in Isaiah 53:5b might echo Jer. 30:17 where God promises to restore Jeremiah's health and heal his wounds because of his rejection by others; or Jer. 33:6 where the Lord promises healing in general to Israel; or Jeremiah 3:22 where God will heal the faithlessness of his children. However it is again little more than a possible circumstance with many other alternatives. The first parallel with Jeremiah 30:17 is perhaps the most interesting with the idea that healing might be given by God directly to the prophet as a result of his treatment by others. The servant in verse 5 is himself the vehicle of healing suggesting that this intermediary figure[29] is able to effect God's healing for others, which is a rather different nuance.

Verse 6 appears to be a confession of guilt spoken by the people themselves. The message here is that the Lord has caused the servant

---

[29] The intermediary nature of this figure reminds me of woman wisdom in Proverbs 8:22–31.

to take the blame for these sins of the people. This again reminds us perhaps of how Jeremiah also bore the burden of the sins of others, mainly through suffering at their hands directly. Farley sees this sentiment as representing "the verdict of posterity reversing the judgement of Jeremiah's own generation" (p. 523). He thus sees the servant passage in the context of post-death vindication of God's prophet.

I have discussed Isaiah 53:7–8 above, although as an addendum one might note that it could be Jeremiah's imprisonment rather than his death that is referred to here (Jer. 33:1; 39:15). Of Isaiah 53:9 Farley has nothing to say in relation to this verse of links with Jeremiah despite his earlier opinion that "phrase by phrase" Jeremiah may be seen in Isaiah 53:1–9. This is clearly an overstatement, although, some interesting possibilities are raised by him. The circumstantial evidence of links with Jeremiah's life is on the whole rather thin, but the theological connections with the sentiments of the confessions seem to rest on slightly firmer ground.

Clearly the possible parallels with Jeremiah's life and thought break down after verse 9 (arguably after verse 8). Whilst Jeremiah too may have felt "crushed with pain" (v. 10), to view his life as an offering for sin is probably a step too far. And he did not have any wife or offspring, since in Jer. 16:1–2 he is forbidden to take a wife. The eschatological tone of verse 11 in the making of "many righteous" has been compared to Jeremiah 31:33–34, the covenant written on the heart. A number of scholars have suggested (since early times, including Saadya Gaon) that Isaiah 53:12, "I will allot him a portion with the great", may be a reference to the provisions with which Jeremiah was supplied on a daily basis in Jeremiah 40:5. This is another possible circumstantial overtone, but one which is by no means decisive.

Farley concludes that it is the prophetic element in Israel that is to fulfil the destiny of the people of Israel. He writes, "It is reasonable to suppose that the thoughts of the exiles would be much occupied with Jeremiah, the prophet who foretold, strove to avert, but lived to see the captivity under which they suffered. Jeremiah would naturally be thought of as 'The Servant of the Lord'; he would even furnish features for the picture of the ideal 'Servant' or 'prophet'" (p. 523). He therefore sees the poems as "songs of idealized prophecy", with Jeremiah as the historical figure most nearly approaching this ideal. Whilst I have shown that some of his parallels do not really work, I find myself in essential agreement with Farley here, that indeed Jeremiah may have been the historical figure most likely to have been in mind, mainly because of his close historical proximity to the exile and as the one who tried very hard to warn the people of their fate, suffering as he did so. His book was being redacted even after his own time and there is a possible context in the circles of redactors for the continuation of his memory and words. However, I am sure that the picture outweighs any one designation and goes beyond anything that can be claimed of any one prophet. If it is a composite picture of what it means to be a servant of Yahweh, then Jeremiah, the suffering prophet, is a recent model of the prophetic role that would have readily and naturally come to the mind of his prophetic successor or those who shaped his book.[30]

---

[30] It is a great privilege and pleasure to write this article for my colleague and friend, John Emerton, who has supported me over the years, both when I returned to the University at Cambridge (having been born there) and before that at Oxford and through the Society for Old Testament Study. He also knew my father, Robert Dell, who was at one time Vice-Principal of Ridley Hall. A particularly special experience for me was being in Jerusalem, at St George's College, where John was also residing as Canon, when he was most generous of his time in guiding a newcomer around Jerusalem and reliving some of the excitement of his own introduction to the holy city.

GOD AND THE GODS: PAGAN DEITIES AND RELIGIOUS CONCEPTS IN THE OLD GREEK OF ISAIAH*

Joachim Schaper

I should like to draw attention to some remarkable features of the Old Greek (OG) of Isaiah. Since it presents a fairly faithful, yet creative, translation of its Hebrew *Vorlage*,[1] one of its great attractions lies in the fact that it serves as a mirror of the Hellenistic Jewish world that produced it. I. L. Seeligmann observes the translator's inclination to bring "geographical facts and names" up to date and points out "another general tendency which has caused the Isaiah translation, more than any other part of the Septuagint[,] to show the historical background of the smaller and larger Hellenistic states":[2] its rendering of אֶרֶץ as οἰκουμένη, which occurs eight times in Isaiah and only once (!) in all the other books of the Greek Bible. The translator uses this term, which is so typical of the political world of the Hellenistic Mediterranean, "either in a context in which God's punishment is prophesied to all

---

* I am happy to be able to express my gratitude to John Emerton, from whose teaching I have benefited so much, by collaborating in this *Festschrift*. John's contribution to the study of the Old Testament and of Semitic philology is a shining example and a source of inspiration for all his colleagues and friends.

[1] On categorizing the character of the "translation technique" informing the OG of Isaiah, and on the translation's use of mythological terminology, cf. S. J. Schweitzer, "Mythology in the Old Greek of Isaiah: The Technique of Translation", *CBQ* 66 (2004), pp. 214–30. Schweitzer claims (p. 217, n. 16) that "[n]o previous analysis of mythological elements in any OG book has been published, to my knowledge, so this analysis will be the first such investigation on a topic important for study of both the LXX and the Hebrew Bible"; he obviously overlooked J. Schaper, "Die Renaissance der Mythologie im hellenistischen Judentum und der Septuaginta-Psalter", in E. Zenger (ed.), *Der Septuaginta-Psalter: Sprachliche und theologische Aspekte* (HBS 32; Freiburg im Breisgau a.o., 2001), pp. 171–83. Schweitzer also fails to mention the discussion of mythological concepts in the LXX found in J. Schaper, "The Unicorn in the Messianic Imagery of the Greek Bible", in *JTS* N.S. 45 (1994), pp. 117–36. Most remarkably, there is another work omitted by Schweitzer, one in which we find numerous detailed discussions of mythological terminology in the Septuagint: I am referring, of course, to W. Bousset and H. Gressmann, *Die Religion des Judentums im späthellenistischen Zeitalter* (HNT 21, 3rd edn.; Tübingen, 1926).

[2] I. L. Seeligmann, *The Septuagint Version of Isaiah: A Discussion of Its Problems* (MVEOL 9; Leiden, 1948), p. 81.

peoples, or where the central figure of an (Assyrian) world ruler loudly puts forward his claim to world sovereignty".[3]

Apart from "[r]eminiscences of the diaspora of the period of the translator, of the frontier towns of Hellenistic Egypt, of the terminology of the Hellenistic administration, of the hostility of the Greek coastal towns towards Palestine, and of the ambitions of a king to acquire the sovereignty over the οἰκουμένη", the Septuagint of Isaiah "also contains allusions to historical personalities and events, enabling us to assign a more exact date to this translation", as Seeligmann points out.[4] He assumes that the mighty ruler threatening Israel in the Hebrew original of the Isaianic prophecies "was transmuted in the translation into a Hellenistic ruler of the translator's own period".[5] He is able to demonstrate that the translation of Isaiah 10:24 may be understood as an "echo of the idea of a Jewish emigration from Palestine to Egypt to escape the religious persecution of Antiochus Epiphanes",[6] given that the way the Greek translation renders the passages about the fearsome Assyrian ruler makes it likely that it refers to Antiochus. Seeligmann dates the Greek Isaiah to the mid-second century B.C.[7] and assumes Egypt, and more precisely Alexandria, as its place of origin.[8]

In the present paper I shall, taking Seeligmann's observations as my starting-point, investigate the way in which the Old Greek text of Isaiah introduces pagan deities and religious concepts that are not mentioned in its Hebrew *Vorlage* and shall try to understand them against the background of the religious history of Hellenistic Egypt in the second century B.C. It is my aim thus to throw some light on the relationship between Alexandrian Jews and the dominant non-Jewish culture which surrounded them. In so doing, I hope to contribute to the exploration of a significant aspect of Jewish religious history in Hellenistic Egypt and thus to follow the lead of such great scholars as Z. Frankel and I. L. Seeligmann, who have taught us to use the Septuagint not just as a tool for the textual criticism of the Hebrew Bible but as a – if not *the* – major cultural and religious monument of Hellenistic Judaism.

---

[3] Seeligmann, p. 81.
[4] Seeligmann, pp. 81–2.
[5] Seeligmann, p. 82.
[6] Seeligmann, p. 85.
[7] Cf. Seeligmann, p. 91.
[8] Cf. Seeligmann, p. 86.

Although it is impossible to do justice to our topic within the limits of this paper, I shall be able to draw attention to some characteristic features of pagan deities and religious concepts as represented by the Old Greek of Isaiah. Let us start with a few passages that deal with what seem to be not just concepts but actual divine beings. It makes sense to start with Isa 14:12. The Hebrew reads:

אֵיךְ נָפַלְתָּ מִשָּׁמַיִם הֵילֵל בֶּן־שָׁחַר נִגְדַּעְתָּ לָאָרֶץ חוֹלֵשׁ עַל־גּוֹיִם:

> How you are fallen from heaven, O Day Star, son of Dawn! How you are cut down to the ground, you who laid the nations low! (RSV)

The term הֵילֵל is derived from the root הלל I hiph., "to shine", and is used as an "epithet of the Morning Star, Venus".[9] As Watson points out, it is likely "that Isa 14:12–15 reflects the episode in Ugaritic myth where Athtar failed to replace Baal on the throne".[10] According to Watson "[i]n Isa 14, the King of Babylon is designated mockingly as Hêlēl in the guise of Athtar; but there is no evidence for the acknowledgement of Hêlēl's real existence or of his cult".[11] Similarly, Shahar may have been revered as a god.[12] Although the context of the passage in Isa 14 is doubtless mythological and the address "Morning Star, Son of Dawn" may thus be mythological too, we cannot be sure whether Shahar actually refers to a deity.

The Jewish Greek translator rendered the passage in question as follows: πῶς ἐξέπεσεν ἐκ τοῦ οὐρανοῦ ὁ ἑωσφόρος ὁ πρωὶ ἀνατέλλων;. As we shall see, this will give us some insight into the Hellenistic pagan world and the way Alexandrian Judaism engaged with it. In our passage, ὁ πρωὶ ἀνατέλλων translates בֶּן־שָׁחַר. There is only one likely way to account for this rendering: the intention seems to have been to get rid of the ancient mythological concept of a *deity* Shahar. בֶּן־שָׁחַר may have suggested to the translator that שַׁחַר referred to a divine being. In any case, the translator obviously wanted to circumvent a meaning that went contrary to his own understanding. Why else would he have wanted to avoid providing a straightforward translation of a perfectly straightforward text?

---

[9] W. G. Watson, "Helel", in *DDD*, pp. 392–94, here p. 392.

[10] Watson, p. 393.

[11] Watson, p. 394. For a yet more detailed exploration cf. J. W. McKay, "Helel and the Dawn-Goddess: A re-examination of the myth in Isaiah XIV 12–15", *VT* 20 (1970), pp. 451–64.

[12] Cf. S. B. Parker, "Shahar", in *DDD*, pp. 754–55, here p. 754.

What he did translate, however, was the term הֵילֵל. Here again, he did not opt for the most obvious rendering, i.e. a Greek term signifying "Bright One", "Shining One", but for ὁ ἑωσφόρος. Now this was a heavily-laden term. In Alexandria, ἑωσφόρος seems to have been considered a divine being. In the *Ptolemaia*, i.e. the πομπή, the festal procession in honour of Ptolemy I Soter and his successors, ἑωσφόρος led the procession,[13] as described by Kallixenos and as pointed out by E. Visser in her study on gods and cults in Ptolemaic Alexandria.[14] Seeligmann sees in our Isaianic passage "possible traces of polemics against contemporaneous Hellenistic heathendom".[15]

There are some more examples of unexpected renderings of perfectly "normal" Hebrew passages. Let us therefore turn to other pagan mythological beings mentioned in the Greek Isaiah, namely, the σειρῆνες καὶ δαιμόνια mentioned in Isa. 13:21, 34:13 and 43:20 LXX. In the MT Isa 13:21 reads:

וְרָבְצוּ־שָׁם צִיִּים וּמָלְאוּ בָתֵּיהֶם אֹחִים וְשָׁכְנוּ שָׁם בְּנוֹת יַעֲנָה וּשְׂעִירִים יְרַקְּדוּ־שָׁם

But wild beasts will lie down there, and its houses will be full of howling creatures; there ostriches will dwell, and there satyrs will dance. (RSV)

The Greek version renders the passage:

καὶ ἀναπαύσονται ἐκεῖ θηρία, καὶ ἐμπλησθήσονται αἱ οἰκίαι ἤχου, καὶ ἀναπαύσονται ἐκεῖ σειρῆνες, καὶ δαιμόνια ἐκεῖ ὀρχήσονται.[16]

But wild animals will rest there,/ and the houses will be filled with noise;/ there sirens will rest,/ and there demons will dance. (NETS)

Isa. 34:13 LXX presents a similar rendering:

וְעָלְתָה אַרְמְנֹתֶיהָ סִירִים קִמּוֹשׂ וָחוֹחַ בְּמִבְצָרֶיהָ וְהָיְתָה נְוֵה תַנִּים חָצִיר לִבְנוֹת יַעֲנָה

---

[13] This point, which is essential to understanding the use of ἑωσφόρος in Isa 14:12, is missed completely by Schweitzer in his discussion of the term (Schweitzer, pp. 226–27).

[14] Cf. E. Visser, *Götter und Kulte im ptolemäischen Alexandrien* (Archaeologisch-historische Bijdragen 5; Amsterdam, 1938), pp. 32, 86.

[15] Seeligmann, p. 100.

[16] In the present paper the quotations from the Greek Isaiah follow the text established in *Septuaginta: Vetus Testamentum Graecum Auctoritate Academiae Litterarum Gottingensis editum*, 14: *Isaias* (ed. J. Ziegler; Göttingen, 1967), and those from the Septuagint of Deuteronomy that *Septuaginta: Vetus Testamentum Graecum Auctoritate Academiae Litterarum Gottingensis editum*, 3, 2: *Deuteronomium* (ed. J. W. Wevers, adiuvante U. Quast; Göttingen, 1977).

Thorns shall grow over its strongholds, nettles and thistles in its fortresses. It shall be the haunt of jackals, an abode for ostriches. (RSV)

The Greek reads:

καὶ ἀναφύσει εἰς τὰς πόλεις αὐτῶν ἀκάνθινα ξύλα καὶ εἰς τὰ ὀχυρώματα αὐτῆς, καὶ ἔσται ἔπαυλις σειρήνων καὶ αὐλὴ στρουθῶν.

Thorn trees shall grow up in their cities/ and in her fortresses./ It shall be a habitation of sirens/ and a courtyard of ostriches. (NETS)

We thus get δαιμόνια and σειρῆνες where we would have expected more straightforward renderings. Readers get the impression that the beings referred to here have been "enculturated" into the Hellenistic world by the translator(s). Also, perfectly normal animals like the יַעֲנָה are "promoted" to the status of σειρῆνες, and a haunt of jackals turns into a habitation of sirens. These renderings give us a flavour of the translator's concept of bringing his parent text "up to date". They provide us with some items taken from the abundant treasures of Hellenistic mythology. However, they are among the lesser examples of the characteristic religious-historical peculiarities of the Greek Isaiah.

Isaiah 65:11–12 is yet more interesting. It mentions further pagan deities, and, as we shall see, the Greek translation deals with them in a peculiar way. In verse 11b of the Hebrew, reference is made to the deities Gad and Meni:

וְאַתֶּם עֹזְבֵי יְהוָה הַשְּׁכֵחִים אֶת־הַר קָדְשִׁי הַעֹרְכִים לַגַּד שֻׁלְחָן וְהַמְמַלְאִים לַמְנִי מִמְסָךְ:
וּמָנִיתִי אֶתְכֶם לַחֶרֶב וְכֻלְּכֶם לַטֶּבַח תִּכְרָעוּ יַעַן קָרָאתִי וְלֹא עֲנִיתֶם דִּבַּרְתִּי וְלֹא שְׁמַעְתֶּם

But you who forsake the Lord, who forget my holy mountain, who set a table for Fortune and fill cups of mixed wine for Destiny;
   I will destine you to the sword, and all of you shall bow down to the slaughter; because, when I called, you did not answer; when I spoke, you did not listen, but you did what was evil in my eyes, and chose what I did not delight in. (RSV)

It seems that Gad, who was a "deity of good luck",[17] was venerated together with Meni, who also was "credited with the ability to determine destiny".[18] S. D. Sperling is able to demonstrate that Gad and Meni are here seen as rivals to YHWH since "the verb עזב...is regularly

---

[17] Cf. S. Ribichini, "Gad", in *DDD*, pp. 339–41, here: p. 339.
[18] S. D. Sperling, "Meni", in *DDD*, pp. 566–68, here: pp. 566–67.

employed in contexts where Israel leaves Yahweh for other gods (Judg
2.12, 13; 10:6; 1 Sam 8:8), as is the verb שלח...(Deut 8:14; Jer 13:25;
Hos 2:15)".[19] The scene portrayed in Isa. 65 is that of a banquet for the
deities; those who entertain Gad and Meni instead of supporting the
cult of YHWH are denounced.[20]

Let us now compare the Greek version of these verses:

> ὑμεῖς δὲ οἱ ἐγκαταλείποντες με καὶ ἐπιλανθανόμενοι τὸ ὄρος τὸ ἅγιον
> μου καὶ ἑτοιμάζοντες τῷ δαίμονι[21] τράπεζαν καὶ πληροῦντες τῇ τύχῃ
> κέρασμα,
> ἐγὼ παραδώσω ὑμᾶς εἰς μάχαιραν, πάντες ἐν σφαγῇ πεσεῖσθε, ὅτι
> ἐκάλεσα ὑμᾶς καὶ οὐχ ὑπηκούσατε, ἐλάλησα καὶ παρηκούσατε καὶ
> ἐποιήσατε τὸ πονηρὸν ἐναντίον ἐμοῦ καὶ ἃ οὐκ ἐβουλόμην ἐξελέξασθε.

> But as for you who forsake me and forget my holy mountain, and prepare
> a table for the demon and fill a mixed drink for Fortune,
> I will deliver you over to the dagger; all of you shall fall by slaughter;
> because I called you and you did not answer, I spoke and you misheard,
> and you did what was evil before me and chose the things I did not
> desire. (NETS)

The Greek translation is, on the whole, not surprising, but the rendering
of the names of the deities Gad and Meni deserves attention. Δαίμων
renders Gad; τύχη is employed as the equivalent of Meni. This translation is not arbitrary, but rather a "daring contemporization"[22] of the
original reference to the Semitic deities Gad and Meni found in the MT,
and its reference points are not abstract concepts of a demon or of fate/
Fortune (as NETS renders it) but distinct deities worshipped in Alexandria (so correctly in Septuaginta Deutsch), as we shall soon see.

In Seeligmann's view Δαίμων refers to the Ἀγαθὸς Δαίμων of Alexandrian religious practice, and Τύχη to the goddess Τύχη universally
worshipped in the Hellenistic world. G. J. Riley does not share Seeligmann's opinion. Rather, he thinks that, "[a]s the gods of the nations
were demonized, so 'demon' in the dualistic sense is found in the Septuagint...as a designation of pagan deities and spirits"[23] and he adduces
Deut 32:17, Psa 95:5, Psa 105:37 LXX, Bar 4:7 and Isa 65:11 in support

---

[19] Sperling, p. 567.

[20] Cf. Sperling, p. 567.

[21] My reading, which follows Rahlfs, is based on Codex Sinaiticus. Rahlfs's decision
to follow Sinaiticus is to be preferred to that of Ziegler here.

[22] Cf. Seeligmann, p. 99, followed by D. Baer, When we all go home: translation and
theology in LXX Isaiah 56–66 (JSOTSup 318; Sheffield, 2001), p. 177.

[23] G. J. Riley, "Demon", in DDD, pp. 235–40, here p. 238.

of his thesis. Interestingly, he traces the concept of table fellowship with YHWH, as contrasted with table fellowship with demons, into the New Testament, where it plays an important role in 1 Cor 10:20–21.[24] We shall come back to that later.

Seeligmann claims that the use of Δαίμων and Τύχη is considerably more specific than Riley's view suggests. As indicated above, Seeligmann thinks that Δαίμων actually refers to the Ἀγαθὸς Δαίμων of the Alexandrian tradition, a deity that was of utmost importance to the city. The importance of this deity and its sanctuary to the Alexandrian population even in the fourth century A.D. (!) is indicated by the remarks of Ammianus Marcellinus (22.11.7). Writing about Bishop Georgius, Ammianus Marcellinus remarks:

> Ad haec mala id quoque addiderat, unde paulo post actus est in exitium praeceps. Reversus ex comitatu principis cum transiret per speciosum Genii templum multitudine stipatus ex more, flexis ad aedem ipsam luminibus "quamdiu", inquit, "sepulcrum hoc stabit?" Quo audito velut fulmine multi perculsi metuentesque ne illud quoque temptaret evertere, quicquid poterant in eius perniciem clandestinis insidiis concitabant.

J. C. Rolfe translates:

> To these evil deeds he had added still another, which soon after drove him headlong to destruction. As he was returning from the emperor's court and passed by the beautiful temple of the Genius, attended as usual by a large crowd, he turned his eyes straight at the temple, and said: 'How long shall this sepulchre stand?' On hearing this, many were struck as if by a thunderbolt, and fearing that he might try to overthrow even that building, they devised secret plots to destroy him in whatever way they could.[25]

This shows the extraordinary commitment of ordinary Alexandrians to the founding traditions of their city, to the founder himself and to the Ἀγαθὸς Δαίμων. Some scholars have claimed the Ἀγαθὸς Δαίμων to have been the personal δαίμων of Alexander.[26] As E. Visser rightly points out, the link between Alexander and the concept of the Agathos Daimon certainly was, in the eyes of the common population, indissoluble. In

---

[24] Cf. Riley, p. 238.

[25] J. C. Rolfe (ed.), *Ammianus Marcellinus*, 2 (LCL; London and Cambridge, MA, 1972), p. 261.

[26] Cf. P. Schnabel, "Zur Frage der Selbstvergötterung Alexanders", *Klio* 20 (1926), pp. 398–414; successfully refuted by H. Berve, *Das Alexanderreich auf prosopographischer Grundlage*, 1: *Darstellung* (Munich, 1926), p. 340.

her analysis, she makes an interesting distinction between the actual
history of the *concept* of Ἀγαθὸς Δαίμων and the way that concept was
perceived in the general populace. There was a cult devoted to Alexander
as the city's god or ἥρως κτίστης. Visser writes:

> Noch in römischer Zeit gibt es einen Priester Ἀλεξάνδρου κτίστου τῆς
> πόλεως, und dass der Kult des Agathos Daimon damit in irgendeiner
> Verbindung steht, ist völlig unbewiesen. Die einzig mögliche Erklärung
> scheint mir die, dass, während die Kulte Alexanders und des Agathos
> Daimon ursprünglich verschieden waren..., die beiden in den Gedanken
> der weniger rationellen (*sic*) Schichten der Bevölkerung, und vielleicht
> auch im Kult, nicht streng getrennt sind. Der Heros Ktistes und der
> Genius loci sind beide Beschützer der Stadt; so ist es leicht zu erklären,
> dass sie zu einander in Beziehung gebracht werden.[27]

The point is that it was easy for the average person to link their reverence for Alexander with that for the Agathos Daimon. However, it is
clear that the Agathos Daimon had always led a life of his own and
must not be understood as the personal δαίμων of Alexander. As Berve
has pointed out, there is no evidence for the veneration of the Agathos
Daimon of a person – in the sense of the Roman concept of a person's
genius – in Greek culture; the Agathos Daimon of Alexandria, he states,
"ist eben der ἀ.δ. der Stadt, bestenfalls Alexander selbst, niemals aber
der ἀ.δ. Alexanders".[28]

As Visser demonstrates, Ἀγαθὸς Δαίμων had a cult of his own up
to the late period. Although there was the connection with Τύχη, and
Τύχη had been equated with Isis, Ἀγαθὸς Δαίμων did not disappear
from the scene. The opposite seems to be true: whereas in the early
period he does not appear on official monuments and is not depicted on
coins, his image is used on coins of the Roman period from the time of
Nero.[29] Indeed there seems to have been a connection between the cult
of Ἀγαθὸς Δαίμων and the foundation of the city of Alexandria, as is
claimed in the Alexander Romance (Pseudo-Callisthenes) 1.32.6–10:

---

[27] Visser, p. 8.
[28] Berve, p. 340. Cf. Visser, pp. 6–7, especially p. 6: "Wie aus vielen Stellen hervorgeht,
ist Agathos Daimon nicht bloss der alte Stadtgott Alexandriens, sondern durch alle
Jahrhunderte Schutzgeist der Stadt. Nur so ist die Erzählung bei Ammianus Marcellinus
zu verstehen: offenbar verband das Volk von Alexandrien das Schicksal des Tempels
mit dem eigenen."
[29] Cf. Visser, p. 6, n. 5.

Then Alexander gave orders for the perimeter of the city to be marked out so that he could get an impression of it. The workmen marked out the limits with wheat flour, but the birds flew down, ate up the meal and flew away. Alexander was very disturbed at the possible meaning of this omen; he sent for interpreters and told them what had happened. Their reply was:
"The city you have ordered to be built, O king, will feed the whole inhabited world, and those who are born in it will reach all parts of the world; just as the birds fly over the whole earth."
So he gave orders for building work to begin.
When the foundations for most of the city had been laid and measured, Alexander inscribed five letters: A B G D E. A for "Alexander"; B for *Basileus*, "king"; G for *Genos*, "descendant"; D for *Dios*, "Zeus"; and E for *ektisen*, "founded an incomparable city". Beasts of burden and mules helped with the work. As the gate of the sanctuary was being put in place, a large and ancient tablet of stone, inscribed with many letters, fell out of it; and after it came a large number of snakes, which crept away into the doorways of the houses that had already been built. Nowadays the doorkeepers reverence these snakes as friendly spirits when they come into their houses – for they are not venomous – and they place garlands on their working animals and give them a rest day. Alexander was still in the city when it and the sanctuary were being built, in the month of Tybi, which is January. For this reason the Alexandrians still even now keep the custom of celebrating a festival on the twenty-fifth day of Tybi.[30]

P. M. Fraser points out that, most likely, the cult of Ἀγαθὸς Δαίμων, the aetiology of which is presented in this passage, "was early established both as a purely domestic cult, and also in a wider context", and bases his judgement on the evidence of Phylarchus and the Potter's Oracle.[31] The probable early origin of the Ἀγαθὸς Δαίμων also militates

---

[30] Translation taken from R. Stoneman, *The Greek Alexander Romance* (Harmondsworth, 1991), pp. 64–65. For the critical edition of the Greek text cf. W. Kroll (ed.), *Historia Alexandri Magni* (*Pseudo-Callisthenes*), 1: *Recensio vetusta* (Berlin, 1926), pp. 32–33.
[31] P. M. Fraser, *Ptolemaic Alexandria*, 1: *Text* (Oxford, 1972), pp. 209–10: "Although this aetiology of the cult of Agathos Daimon is certainly largely fictitious, there are good grounds for supposing that the cult was early established both as a purely domestic cult, and also in a wider context. On the first point we have the express testimony of Phylarchus, who wrote in the third century B.C., that 'the Egyptians', by whom he primarily, no doubt, means the Alexandrians, treated their snakes much as the Romance suggests: leaving special mixtures of barley and wine on their tables at the end of meals, which the snakes consumed at their leisure after the diners had departed. Secondly, the 'oracle of the Potter', which contains a prophecy of the approaching desolation of Alexandria written early in the history of the city, and which is probably the one surviving tangible product of the native hostility to Macedonian rule, prophesies the departure of the Agathos Daimon from the city 'now being built', that is, Alexandria,

in favour of an early date for the introduction of the cult to Alexandria. Rohde understands the Ἀγαθὸς Δαίμων as an originally chthonic deity. Like other chthonic deities, he appears as a snake,[32] and there is a plethora of passages in classical and Hellenistic texts that witness to the protective function of the Ἀγαθὸς Δαίμων. Also, it is important to note, with Rohde and in the light of Pausanias 9.39.4, that in the sanctuary of Trophonios near Lebadea Ἀγαθὸς Δαίμων was venerated in conjunction with a number of chthonic deities, and that there he appeared alongside Tyche, in conjunction with whom Ἀγαθὸς Δαίμων is sometimes named in funeral inscriptions. Tyche herself also appears alongside chthonic deities.[33]

Thus it seems that Ἀγαθὸς Δαίμων had rather humble origins but then set off on a rather meteoric political "career". Certainly Alexandrians hearing or reading of Ἀγαθὸς Δαίμων thought of him as the patron deity of their city. P. M. Fraser rightly points out that "[i]n Athens and elsewhere from the fifth century onwards, Agathos Daimon was a minor or household god, to whom, as to Zeus Soter and others, libations were made at the end of meals, as they were made to Hestia, goddess of the Hearth, at the beginning".[34] Furthermore, it is remarkable that, as in the private inscriptions just mentioned, Ἀγαθὸς Δαίμων and Τύχη occur together. Fraser draws attention to the fact that "altars, dedicatory stelae, and other monuments frequently bear the inscription Ἀγαθοῦ Δαίμονος Ἀγαθῆς Τύχης in which it is not possible to distinguish between the two deities" even in the fourth century B.C.[35] We shall see in a moment, with regard to the classical and even the pre-classical history of Tyche, that

---

for Memphis, 'the Mother of God'. This passage appears to show that the Agathos Daimon was already regarded as symbolic of the city, its 'patron deity', as Sarapis, perhaps through identification with his predecessor, became in the Roman period."

[32] E. Rohde, *Psyche: Seelencult und Unsterblichkeitsglaube der Griechen*, 2nd edn. (Freiburg im Breisgau, 1898), pp. 254–55, n. 2.

[33] Cf. Rohde, p. 255, n. 2. Rohde points to *CIG* 2465–66 and *CIG* 1464.

[34] Fraser, p. 210.

[35] Cf. Fraser, p. 210: "The early associations of the Agathos Daimon with the fate of the city, attested by the 'Oracle of the Potter', may be due to another aspect of the Daimon, familiar from the mainland and the Islands. Already in the fourth century Agathos Daimon and Agathe Tyche had become so closely associated as to be almost identified: altars, dedicatory stelae, and other monuments frequently bear the inscription Ἀγαθοῦ Δαίμονος Ἀγαθῆς Τύχης in which it is not possible to distinguish between the two deities. This fusion, partial or complete, probably extended to other contexts than the purely domestic, and it appears probable that the Agathos Daimon, like the Agathe Tyche, came to personify the Fortune of cities. The hostile Egyptians in prophesying the departure of the tutelary deity from Alexandria prophesied the fall of the city."

Fraser is probably right. The main point for the moment is to realise that there was a private as well as a public aspect to the cult of Ἀγαθὸς Δαίμων and Ἀγαθὴ Τύχη, that both deities were venerated together, both privately and publicly, from an early time onwards, and that the cult had its origin in the private sphere.

Τύχη is to be understood as a less specifically Alexandrian deity since, "[i]n contrast to the traditional association of Greek deities with particular cities, *tyche* could be associated with any city because of her comprehensiveness and by the third century she possessed temples in nearly all large Greek cities".[36] No specific myth is connected with Τύχη: although Hesiod in his *Theogony* (360) calls her a daughter of Okeanos and Tethys, and Pindar (*Olympian* 12.1–2) regards her as a daughter of Zeus, this is of no consequence to her religious function.[37] She often occurs alongside other deities or powers, like Moira (Archilochos, *IEG* fr. 16; Pindar, fr. 41), Kairos (Plato, *De legibus*, 709b), or, indeed, Daimon (Euripides, *Iph. A.* 1136; Lysias 13.63). Pausanias (9.39.5) bears witness to Τύχη being revered in conjunction with Ἀγαθὸς Δαίμων. Even in pre-classical times Τύχη was thought of as a protector of cities, as is obvious from Pindar who describes her as φερήπολις, "carrying/ protecting the city" (fr. 39). However, she is by no means exclusively a "political" deity, but is also thought of as accompanying every human being individually. Cults of Τύχη sprang up in numerous important Greek cities from the fourth century B.C. onwards; among those cities were Athens, Thebes, Megara, Corinth and numerous others.[38]

In Alexandria, too, Τύχη was of great importance. The main source concerning her Alexandrian cult is, as Visser points out, Libanius.[39] He describes the Alexandrian temple of Τύχη, and although his description was written in the fourth century A.D., the contents of the temple pictured in that description take us back, as Visser rightly concludes, to the Ptolemaic period: "Denn im Mittelpunkt steht Alexander und neben ihm Ptolemaios Soter; ausserdem sind die wichtigsten der Könige mit Bronzestatuen geehrt; das alles führt uns auf die Ptolemäerzeit, wo wir ähnliche Aufstellungen aus der Pompe des Philadelphos und dem theokritischen Hymnus auf Ptolemaios kennen. Wir dürfen also

---

[36] L. H. Martin, "Tyche", in *DDD*, pp. 877–78.
[37] Thus N. Johannsen, "Tyche", in *DNP* 12/1, cols. 936–37, here col. 936.
[38] The preceding sketch of the significance of Tyche is indebted to Johannsen.
[39] Libanius, *Descr.* 25 (ed. Foerster, 8, pp. 530–31); cf. Visser, p. 99.

das Tychaion zu den frühptolemäischen Heiligtümern rechnen."[40] The cult of Τύχη can be considered one of the foundational cults of Alexandria.

It is important to keep this in mind when returning to the Septuagint text denouncing table fellowship with the (Ἀγαθὸς) Δαίμων and with Τύχη. Thus, Isa 65:11 does not denounce "table fellowship with pagan gods who are in reality demons"[41] – which is Riley's interpretation of Isa 65:11 LXX, and which we have been able to reject by pointing out what the Ἀγαθὸς Δαίμων really was considered to be – but table fellowship with the actual *tutelary deities* Ἀγαθὸς Δαίμων and Τύχη, thus trying to prevent Alexandrian Jews from communing with the patron deity of their city and another one of its centrally important deities.

This was not simply an issue of ritual purity and the subject matter of what seems to have been an internal dispute amongst Alexandrian Jewry. It went far beyond the boundaries of Alexandria's Jewish community. Participation or non-participation in the cult of Ἀγαθὸς Δαίμων and Ἀγαθὴ Τύχη was potentially highly divisive on the *political* front. If Seeligmann was right in pointing out that the Greek of Isa. 65:11 alludes to Ἀγαθὸς Δαίμων and Ἀγαθὴ Τύχη, this would also imply that the translator consciously and openly dissociated himself from the protective deity of his city, Alexandria, and encouraged others to do likewise. This would amount to a refusal to accept his religious and civic duties, a serious matter in a Hellenistic city state. Isa. 65:11 would thus give expression to a clash between what the translator thought of as the religious duty of observant Jews and the civic duties of the inhabitants of a Hellenistic πόλις.

There is another way of interpreting the renderings Δαίμων for גַד and Τύχη for מְנִי. As we have seen, the term Ἀγαθὸς Δαίμων also denotes the "Good Deity" predominantly found in private cults where, as in the Alexandrian public cult, the god often occurs together with Ἀγαθὴ Τύχη.[42] The same conjunction in our LXX passage strongly supports this understanding. This is further confirmed by the fact that an Ἀγαθὸς Δαίμων in a Greek household was offered a measure of unmixed wine after every meal (cf. Aristophanes, *Equites*, 105–07), which reminds us

---

[40] Visser, p. 42.
[41] Riley, p. 238.
[42] Generally, cf. G. Sfameni Gasparro, "Daimon and Tyche in the Hellenistic Religious Experience", in P. Bilde *et al.* (eds.), *Conventional Values of the Hellenistic Greeks* (Studies in Hellenistic Civilization 8; Aarhus, 1997), pp. 67–109.

of our Isaianic verse: καὶ πληροῦντες τῇ τύχῃ κέρασμα. Although in our passage it is the Τύχη, not the Δαίμων, who is offered the wine, the parallel with pagan Hellenistic practice is too striking to be dismissed.

We know that, in Hellenistic times, in many houses altars were dedicated to the Ἀγαθὸς Δαίμων.[43] The cult of Ἀγαθὸς Δαίμων and Ἀγαθὴ Τύχη was a popular one. There are numerous instances of their veneration in the Greek world. We have epigraphical evidence that on the island of Rhodes there was a cult conducted by a group of so-called Ἀγαθοδαιμωνιασταί.[44] The cult of such Ἀγαθοδαιμωνιασταί, which existed in a number of places in the Greek world,[45] seems to have been centred on the dedication of offerings to the deified dead. Cults were installed in honour of a given deified person, a ἥρως. Later on even some living persons were considered worthy of such honours.[46] The inscription of the Halikarnassian association of Poseidonios provides us with an example of the veneration of both the Ἀγαθὸς Δαίμων of living persons and the Τύχη Ἀγαθή of deceased human beings. In some interesting details it reminds us of Isaiah 65:11 and the κέρασμα offered to Tyche: the same practice prevailed in the community of Agathodaimoniastai on Rhodes.

We have seen that cults of Ἀγαθὸς Δαίμων and Ἀγαθὴ Τύχη could serve different religious needs and give expression to different concepts of Ἀγαθὸς Δαίμων and Ἀγαθὴ Τύχη. In some cases the names were used to refer to gods, in others, to refer to the deified dead or even to the *genii* of living human beings. The cults which were devoted to

---

[43] Cf. M. P. Nilsson, "Griechische Hausaltäre", in *id., Opuscula Selecta* 3 (Lund, 1960), pp. 265–70.

[44] Cf. F. Poland, *Geschichte des griechischen Vereinswesens* (Preisschriften gekrönt und herausgegeben von der Fürstlich Jablonowskischen Gesellschaft zu Leipzig 38; Leipzig, 1909), p. 57.

[45] Cf. Poland, p. 227.

[46] Cf. Poland, p. 227: "Die erste Stufe dieser interessanten Erscheinung im Vereinsleben wird uns durch die Verhältnisse des Poseidoniosvereins von Halikarnaß...vermittelt. Hier werden Opfer gefordert für den Ἀγαθὸς Δαίμων des noch lebenden Gründers und seiner Frau....Es liegt hier offenbar dem Ἀγαθὸς Δαίμων dieselbe Vorstellung zu Grunde, wie sie der Römer von seinem Genius hatte und wie sie eine Stelle des Menander (Clem. Alex. Strom. V, 260) ausspricht....Im interessanten Gegensatze aber zu dem Ἀγαθὸς Δαίμων des noch Lebenden steht in unserer Inschrift die Τύχη Ἀγαθή der verstorbenen Eltern des Stifters, für die ebenfalls Opfer bestellt werden...Ähnlich könnte auch der Name der Agathodaimoniasten...erklärt werden, die es mehrfach in der griechischen Welt gab und deren Brauch es war, in mäßiger Weise unvermischten Wein zu trinken..., wofern hier nicht an die allgemeinere Bedeutung der Gottheit als eines Segensspenders gedacht werden muß."

offering sacrifices to these gods, heroes or *genii* were often conducted by associations founded especially for that purpose.

So, while the terms Ἀγαθὸς Δαίμων and Τύχη do not refer to demons, they also do not always indicate gods, but can be used with reference to heroes and *genii*. In any case, these gods, heroes and *genii* were at the centre of cults in which, according to the Jewish Greek translators of Isaiah, Jews must not participate – which indicates that some Jews *did* participate in such cults. The cults were conducted by associations whose table fellowship Jews must not share – but which they obviously did share.

Since there are astounding parallels between our passage and actual Hellenistic private religious practice, one is tempted to ask whether Isa. 65:11 was intended, not just to encourage Alexandrian Jews not to participate in public rituals devoted to Daimon and Tyche, but also to fight a current private cultic practice that had possibly found its way even into Jewish houses in Hellenistic Alexandria.

It must be said that there is no need to opt for an either-or interpretation of the reference to Δαίμων and Τύχη in Isaiah 65:11. We do not have to choose between a "political" and a "non-political" interpretation, since they are not mutually exclusive. With reference to the roles of Agathos Daimon in both public and private cults, Fraser rightly points out that "[t]hese two roles…may not have been wholly distinct in practice, in so far as the civic attributes are not incompatible with the domestic, but it seems clear that the civic role was unknown to the earlier Greek world".[47] Tyche, by contrast, had been associated with the welfare of cities from a very early time onwards, but she also had, as we have seen, private and personal aspects. Daimon and Tyche had been linked even before their Alexandrian cult was inaugurated, and because of their earlier cultic histories they could both be venerated in public and in private. Public and private devotion to the Ἀγαθὸς Δαίμων and Ἀγαθὴ Τύχη were practised side by side in Alexandria, where they were considered the city's tutelary deities. The cult of Ἀγαθὸς Δαίμων, which was considered to have been inaugurated by Alexander himself,[48] was practised not just in the public domain, but also in private households, and remained inextricably linked with that of Ἀγαθὴ Τύχη.

---

[47] Fraser, p. 210.
[48] See above, p. 143.

In any case Isaiah 65:11 provides us with an instance of the translator taking a tough line against a Hellenistic religious practice that is,
from his decidedly non-syncretistic Jewish point of view, unacceptable.
As in the case of the rather selective translation of הֵילֵל בֶּן־שָׁחַר in Isa.
14:12, Hellenistic pagan deities are made the object of religious polemic,
a polemic validated, from the point of view of the translator and his
readers and/or hearers, by the authority of scripture. The translation
thus seems to have been considered a legitimate weapon in the hands
of the defenders of Yahwistic orthodoxy, devised not just as a means
of bridging a linguistic and cultural gap but as a vehicle of internal
Jewish *propagatio fidei*.

How did the translator go about his business? So far we have discussed some concepts of divine beings in Alexandria, and how they
may have been linked to our Isaianic passage. But what is there to say,
if anything, about the translator's hermeneutics, or maybe even his
exegetical pursuits? In order to answer that question let us place Isa
65:11 LXX alongside a text upon which, in my view, it is dependent.

Deut 32:17–19 LXX:

> ἔθυσαν δαιμονίοις καὶ οὐ θεῷ, θεοῖς οἷς οὐκ ᾔδεισαν· καινοὶ πρόσφατοι
> ἥκασιν, οὓς οὐκ ᾔδεισαν οἱ πατέρες αὐτῶν.
>   θεὸν τὸν γεννήσαντά σε ἐγκατέλιπες καὶ ἐπελάθου θεοῦ τοῦ τρέφοντός
> σε,
>   καὶ εἶδεν κύριος καὶ ἐζήλωσεν, καὶ παρωξύνθη δι'ὀργὴν υἱῶν αὐτοῦ
> καὶ θυγατέρων…

> They sacrificed to demons and not to God, to gods they did not know.
> New, recent ones have come, whom their fathers did not know.
>   You abandoned God who bore you, and you forgot God who nurtures
> you.
>   And the Lord saw it and was jealous, and he was provoked on account
> of the wrath of his sons and daughters. (NETS)

Let us now compare the evidence to that provided by Isa. 65:11–12. The
use of ἐγκαταλείπω and ἐπιλανθάνομαι in both passages is interesting. In Deut 32:18 the Hebrew reads צוּר יְלָדְךָ תֶּשִׁי וַתִּשְׁכַּח אֵל מְחֹלְלֶךָ
("You were unmindful of the Rock that begot you, and you forgot the
God who gave you birth": RSV); ἐγκαταλείπω and ἐπιλανθάνομαι
thus render נשה (if we follow Driver's emendation and read תִּשֶּׁה)[49]

---

[49] S. R. Driver, *A Critical and Exegetical Commentary on Deuteronomy*, 3rd edn.
(ICC; Edinburgh, 1902), p. 364.

and שׁכח. In Isa 65:11–12, the same Greek verbs are used to render
עזב and שׁכח. The intriguing question is whether the translators of
Isa 65:11 were influenced by the Septuagint rendering of Deut 32:18.
I think it is highly likely that they were. In both cases, we have the
same sequence of ἐγκαταλείπω and ἐπιλανθάνομαι, which is likely
to be more than a mere coincidence. The subject matter of both passages is very similar, which would explain why the translator of Isaiah
looked up Deuteronomy 32. That there is a network of texts dealing
with "demonology" has been noted before, for example, by H. Lietzmann who refers to texts that denounce pagan cults as cults devoted
to demons and mentions earlier examples of that view in Deut 32:17,
Psa 95:5 and also in 1 Enoch 19:1; 99:7 and Jubilees 1:11.[50] Similarly,
M. Hengel thinks that there was a concept in Hellenistic Judaism that
attempted to give a "demonological" explanation for the existence of
pagan cults. He traces the supposed demonological explanation back
to apocalyptic circles and mentions, as typical examples, texts like 1
Enoch 19:1; 99:7, Jubilees 11.3–4; 19:28; 22:16–17; Deut 32:17 LXX;
Sib. Or. 3:547,554; and 1 Cor 10:20.[51]

However, neither Lietzmann nor Hengel refers to Isa 65:11 LXX. It
seems to me that the Isaianic passage is, on the one hand, part of the
above-mentioned tradition which is trying to come to terms with the
significance of pagan deities. On the other hand, it is a straightforward
attempt to deal with a concrete problem in second century B.C. Jewish
Alexandria, the problem of acclaiming the pagan tutelary deities of the
city and of having table fellowship with pagan gods, with the additional
problem of possibly being tainted by a cult of the dead. There is a clear
parallel with the situation which provoked Paul's statement in 1 Cor
10:20–21. In fact, 1 Cor 10:20–21 echoes not just Deut 32:17 – which
has been pointed out in earlier research – but also, and even more so,
Isa 65:11 LXX.

---

[50] Cf. H. Lietzmann, *An die Korinther I–II* (HNT 9; Tübingen, 1949), p. 49, with
reference to W. Bousset, *Die Religion des Judentums im neutestamentlichen Zeitalter*,
2nd edn. (Berlin, 1906), p. 351.

[51] M. Hengel, *Judentum und Hellenismus: Studien zu ihrer Begegnung unter beson-
derer Berücksichtigung Palästinas bis zur Mitte des 2. Jh.s v. Chr.*, 3rd edn. (Tübingen,
1988), pp. 485–86, especially p. 485, n. 54.

In 1 Cor 10:20–21 we read:

τί οὖν φημι; ὅτι εἰδωλόθυτον τί ἐστιν ἢ ὅτι εἴδωλόν τί ἐστιν;
ἀλλ᾿ὅτι ἃ θύουσιν, δαιμονίοις καὶ οὐ θεῷ [θύουσιν]· οὐ θέλω δὲ ὑμᾶς
κοινωνοὺς τῶν δαιμονίων γίνεσθαι.
οὐ δύνασθε ποτήριον κυρίου πίνειν καὶ ποτήριον δαιμονίων, οὐ δύνασθε
τραπέζης κυρίου μετέχειν καὶ τραπέζης δαιμονίων.

What do I imply then? That food offered to idols is anything, or that an
idol is anything?
    No, I imply that what pagans sacrifice they offer to demons and not
to God. I do not want you to be partners with demons.
    You cannot drink the cup of the Lord and the cup of demons. You
cannot partake of the table of the Lord and the table of demons. (RSV)

Several reasons which motivate the rejection of table fellowship with
Daimon and Tyche in Isa 65:11 LXX are also at the basis of the Pauline
passage. It is fellowship with demons that is to be rejected, and, more
specifically, it is the eating of the sacrificial meat which is at issue.
1 Cor 10:21, just like Isa 65:11 LXX, refers to the Hellenistic practice of
cultic associations having table fellowship with divine beings, associations like the Agathodaimoniastai mentioned earlier. It is that practice
which Paul rejects, just like the Alexandrian translator of Isaiah. Paul
does not present us with an abstract criticism of pagan cults and does
not just provide a "demonological" explanation of the significance of
pagan cults, but attacks a concrete practice which many of the Corin-
thian Christians seem to have followed. He thus goes to the root of
the problem. He attempts to dissuade his Corinthians from a practice
they cherished – witness the enormous number of cultic associations
all over the Hellenistic world – because he thinks it to be contrary to
the faith. The same had happened roughly two hundred years earlier
when the Jewish Greek translator of Isaiah had tried to dissuade his
fellow Jews from taking part in such celebrations.
    Let me now sum up my observations. I have so far concentrated on
two aspects of the Greek Isaiah in particular, that is, translations of
הֵילֵל בֶּן־שָׁחַר and of גַּד and מְנִי. In the case of its use of Δαίμων and
Τύχη to render גַּד and מְנִי we have an example of a highly interpretative
and significant translation which brings a reference to ancient pagan
deities up to date by alluding to a pair of deities known to just about
everyone in the Hellenistic world. By the insertion of this reference
into an unchanged context Δαίμων and Τύχη are explicitly depicted as
unworthy of Jewish adoration. This in turn implies that some Jews –
presumably in Alexandria – *did* in fact pay homage to them. This is

not surprising since the deities in question were, in Alexandria, of immense importance in public life as well as in private devotion. The translator or translators thus must have been of a fairly purist Yahwistic persuasion, since they were not willing to compromise their faith even if that implied dissociating themselves from the rest of the Alexandrian population by refusing to adhere to one of the central symbols of its political theology and to one of its most important private cults.

All our observations, by the way, tie in very well with the date suggested for the Greek Isaiah by Seeligmann on the basis of other observations. We have, in the Greek Isaiah, a religious message imparted by pious, purist followers of the Yahwistic faith who, in view of the sharpness of that message, may well have produced their translation under the more or less direct impact of religious persecution going on in the motherland.

Be that as it may, the Greek Isaiah's references to pagan deities open a window on to some particularly interesting aspects of Jewish Hellenistic religious history,[52] thus adding further pieces to the mosaic of the history of Hellenistic Judaism which is being assembled by contemporary scholarship.

---

[52] Schweitzer, p. 230, sees things differently: "There is no evidence that *any* of these mythological elements were utilized to engage in 'actualizing exegesis'. Although these terms often occur in prophetic oracles, there is *no evidence* that they were construed by the translator as references to new historical realities." He can say this only because he has completely failed to realize the significance of the use of Δαίμων and Τύχη in Isa 65:11 LXX; also, there is no reference in his study to Seeligmann's discussion of Δαίμων and Τύχη in Isa 65:11; cf. Schweizer, pp. 222–23.

FRANTS BUHL AS AN OLD TESTAMENT SCHOLAR: THE ISAIAH COMMENTARY IN DANISH

Knud Jeppesen

Frants Peder William Buhl (1850–1932) is best known to the learned world as an Orientalist. He studied theology and graduated in 1874 at the University of Copenhagen, but already as an undergraduate he read Semitic Languages, especially Arabic, along with the theological disciplines. In the same year that he graduated he wrote an essay, in which he compared the negatives in Arabic and Hebrew.[1] A few years later, in 1878, he earned his doctorate from the Faculty of Arts with a thesis in Danish entitled, "Linguistic and historical contributions to Arabic Grammar".

In 1880 Frants Buhl was appointed docent and in 1882 Professor of Old Testament at the Faculty of Theology in Copenhagen, and when Franz Delitzsch retired he was called to the Old Testament chair in Leipzig in 1890. But in 1898 Buhl returned to Copenhagen, where he became Professor of Semitic-Oriental Philology.

His most important contribution to Semitic philology is his publishing of the 12th to the 17th editions of W. Gesenius, *Hebräisches und Aramäisches Hand-Wörterbuch über das Alte Testament* (Leipzig, 1895–1921). He made it the most important Hebrew dictionary at that time, and the etymological material from other Semitic languages here gathered is still a useful source for students of Hebrew. The list of literature given at the end of almost every entry shows that he mastered both the philology and the contemporary Old Testament field.

Another important contribution of his which remains useful to scholars and students of Old Testament language and literature is his editing of the Hebrew texts of the Psalms and the Book of Esther in R. Kittel, *Biblia Hebraica* (Stuttgart, 1906 and later). After he returned to Copenhagen to become the Professor of Semitic philology, he took up his Arabic studies and published in Danish, among other works,

---

[1] A prize paper submitted to the University of Copenhagen, for which Buhl was given the mark "accessit".

two important volumes about Muhammed's life and his religious preaching according to the Koran.[2]

Most of Buhl's work mentioned so far is known outside Scandinavia, but how much he did for Old Testament exegesis in Denmark and Scandinavia is probably not so well known. As already mentioned above, Buhl was very well informed about contemporary Old Testament research, and it is not too much to claim that he was the scholar who first introduced modern critical research to Denmark. What he did in this field is probably not very different from what other scholars in other countries did during the same period. But rereading the works of a scholar like Buhl you get a picture of the period. As a point of departure, he was convinced that the history as told in the Old Testament was the true history. However, many new ideas were presented and the scholars were very eager to discuss them, even when questions were raised about what was written in the Bible. At that time the volume of secondary literature was still manageable, and therefore it was not as necessary as it is nowadays for scholars to give exact references or to make indexes in the books they published. That is true for the Isaiah commentary dealt with here.

It became important for Buhl's development that he was studying Old Testament and Arabic in Leipzig when Julius Wellhausen's *Geschichte Israels I* (Berlin, 1878) was first published, and soon after he wrote an extensive article in Danish,[3] in which he was very reserved towards new ideas about the genesis of the five books of Moses. But a few years later, in a series of articles in *Theologisk Tidsskrift* (1884–86)[4] he developed his own view on these themes. Although he still had reservations, he nevertheless accepted the basic ideas of the theory that the Pentateuch was put together from texts of different origin and from different sources, and he accepted too the suggested dates of these sources. Ten years later, when he wrote his own history of Israel, he used the documentary hypothesis to assist the dating of events and ideas in both the Israelite people's and their country's history.[5]

---

[2] F. Buhl, *Muhammeds Liv* (København, 1903; German edn. 1930) and *Muhammes religiøse Forkyndelse efter Qurānen* (København, 1924).

[3] F. Buhl, "When was Deuteronomy written?", in Danish, "Naar er femte Mosebog affattet?", *ThT* 1878, pp. 129–168, 193–277.

[4] F. Buhl, *ThT* 1884, pp. 63–111 (on the Immanuel sign); *ThT* 1885, pp. 256–82, and 1886, pp. 250–77 (on Pentateuchal criticism).

[5] F. Buhl, *Det israelitiske Folks Historie* (Kjøbenhavn, 1893). The book was published in six editions over the following years, and in the different editions one can follow

Buhl considered the history of Israel a unique history, and one of the reasons for that lies in his opinion concerning the phenomenon of biblical prophecy. Through prophecy it becomes clear that Israel was, what Buhl in Danish named *Aabenbaringsfolket*, "the revelation-people". The Prophets' foretelling of the future implied for him that the religion of Israel pointed to a more complete form of belief beyond the Old Testament. These ideas were developed in his monograph about messianic promises in the Old Testament.[6] In this book he distinguished the historic element from the eschatological element in the prophetic preaching (see pp. 24–26). The prophecies which dealt with contemporary history were only fulfilled in a relative way and this often caused disappointment. The history seemed time and again to ignore prophetic warnings about coming catastrophes and the subsequent messianic age; these things did not happen immediately and believers had to be patient. But to be found in eschatological preaching was an absolute and complete idea about events that were to take place at the end of the world, and this idea kept the prophets from falling into doubt, when historic prophecies were not fulfilled. It is obvious that Buhl wrote this from a Christian point of view, as he himself stated.

The book about the prophets' messianic preaching was published in the same year that Buhl finished the first edition of his commentary on Isaiah in Danish.[7] He started to release ideas contained in the commentary a few years earlier, as he had worked on books on the messianic promises and Isaiah during the same period of time. Thus, the two works share the above-mentioned ideas about prophecy. Buhl was well aware that most prophecies are to be interpreted and understood against the background of their contemporary history. But he is also clear that one cannot solve all problems using history as a tool. Any attempt to read and understand the prophecies of the book of Isaiah as if they were transmitted in a chronological order ultimately breaks down. This is clear from the beginning of his book. He rejected Isa.

---

the development of research into the history of Israel. He refers briefly to the documentary hypothesis in the chapter about the sources of the history of Israel (cf. e.g. 5th edn., p. 3), and the section about Moses and his work (pp. 62–104) is built upon this hypothesis.

[6] F. Buhl, *De messianske Forjættelser i det gamle Testamente* (Kjøbenhavn 1894).

[7] F. Buhl, *Jesaja oversat og fortolket* (Kjøbenhavn, 1894).

13:1–14:23; 21:1–10; 34–35; 40–66 as genuine Isaiah prophecies. They reflect a time other than the time of Isaiah the prophet (pp. 16–17).

In what follows I will present Buhl's understanding of some of the parts of Isaiah which have played an important role in the history of the Isaiah research. In the introduction to Isaiah 40–66 (pp. 530–540) he rejects all attempts to prove Isaianic authorship for these chapters. He finds, after a thorough investigation, that the relevant historical background for these chapters is the exile, and he cannot believe that Isaiah could have foreseen this period in the way it is referred to in these chapters, not even prophetically "in the spirit". Apart from a few exceptions he is sure that the whole text of chs. 40–66 is exilic. He is open to the possibility that some of it could have been edited at home in Judah, but rejected other suggestions for the place of editing, such as Egypt. He also rejects the idea that there was more than one author, only acknowledging a few later editorial additions.

Isaiah 24–27 – "this strange eschatological text" – resists all attempts to fit these chapters into a historical framework. Many scholars have tried, but all have failed (see pp. 26; 358–59). After his analysis of these chapters, Buhl refrains from giving them a date; it seems that for him this text is among the prophetical texts which deal with absolute and not historical truths.

It is obvious that Buhl, when he wrote most of his commentary, did not know the theory about the four Ebed-Yahweh hymns. When he worked on Isa. 42:1–7, he realised that the text in 41:21–29 continued in 42:8ff. This means that the text is an insertion, and Buhl cannot find the reason why it is placed here. Ebed-Yahweh cannot here, as in some other cases in Isa. 40ff, mean the people, but is an image dealing with a minority within the people. In Isa. 53 the servant, Israel's personified ideal, is transformed into a person, in whom this ideal becomes a full reality. The text has its own mystical character, "and from its historic ground it rises to pure prophetic, extra-historical heights".[8]

Almost twenty years after the first edition was finished, Buhl published the second edition of the Isaiah commentary.[9] In the preface he

---

[8] This and other quotations are translated from the Danish by the present author. Frants Buhl wrote these books more than a hundred years ago, and it is often difficult to translate his ideas into modern language, and, in a few cases, the words he used have developed a new meaning in modern Danish.

[9] F. Buhl, *Jesaja oversat og fortolket* (2nd rev. edn.; København and Kristiania, 1912).

writes that this revision was not his personal wish; he would have liked to carry out other plans. But in the years between the two editions he had worked intensively with the Old Testament and not least with the prophets. In 1910 he had edited a modern translation of the Old Testament into Danish in cooperation with a Norwegian and three other Danish scholars.[10] This translation made use of the newest insights in textual and literary criticism and was later on very much used by others, such as the committee responsible for the new authorised version of the Old Testament in Danish released in 1931. A remarkable difference between the two translations is, however, that the ordering of Old Testament books in Buhl's edition follows that of the Hebrew Bible, whilst the authorised version follows the order known from Lutheran tradition.

I observed earlier in this article, when I dealt with Buhl's view on the documentary hypothesis, that he was not a scholar who stubbornly stuck to the opinion he had first held, being unwilling to learn from other scholars. On the contrary, he read new commentaries and learned from them. He had already modified several of his earlier ideas and reached new insights, and that was why he felt that a new edition was necessary. He probably believed it possible that scholars, through careful research, would one day learn the final truth about the text and history of the Old Testament. However it seems that he did not regard his own results as arriving at this final truth. At least he never stopped refining his research and results, and what he wrote contributed to the ongoing debate among scholars. He believed that it was his duty to introduce Danish students of the Bible at that time to modern understandings of the text by referring to other scholars, discussing with them and learning from their results.

In the preface to the first edition Buhl mentions that he regretted that he did not know "Duhm's bold, but to a high degree stimulating interpretation" until he was working on the last part of the commentary, which, according to him, starts on p. 675, i.e. just before he commented on Isa. 53. It is clear that in the years from 1894 to 1912 he had

---

[10] F. Buhl (ed.), *Det gamle Testamente* (with the cooperation of Prof. Theol. J. C. Jacobsen in København, Pastor lic.theol. Martensen-Lassen in København, and Professor Dr. Michelet in Kristiania and Cand.theol. Johannes Pedersen; København and Kristiania, 1910).

profited not only by working with Duhm's commentary, but also from both Marti's commentary and Cheyne's introduction to Isaiah.[11]

The material had gradually become, if not overwhelming, then at the very least much greater in quantity during these years, and in the preface to the new edition Buhl writes that he wanted the second edition of his commentary to remain about the same size as the first edition in spite of this increase. Therefore some of the themes dealt with in the first edition were cut out of the second. Paragraphs which had to do with the relationship between prophecy and fulfilment were removed and the reader was asked to look for answers to these questions in Buhl's other book concerning the messianic promises. Some of the philological remarks in the first edition were now replaced by references to the latest edition of Gesenius's *Lexicon*. In the rest of this article some of the problems considered in the second edition in relation to the first edition will be discussed again in order to see how Buhl saw them after twenty years of exegetical work.

The first part of the second edition, a little less than fifty pages (pp. I–XLIV), is the introduction and follows almost the same pattern as the introduction to the first edition, although much of it is rewritten. First Buhl collects the surviving biographical material about Isaiah, and then follows the historical background for his prophecy; this part is very much like the corresponding paragraphs in the earlier edition. But in coming to the chapter which deals with Isaiah's prophetic writings there are many new ideas presented and discussed. For example, when it comes to the prophecies about salvation, Buhl comments, "One would like to attribute to him (Isaiah) the magnificent prophecies Isa. 2:2–4; 9:1ff, and 11:1ff, but only dullness and lack of consciousness can close the eyes to the weight of doubt which is claimed against their authenticity" (p. XVII). However, Buhl continues, it is a sign of "unwisdom" to regard these results as a devaluing of the religious content of these promises. Furthermore, in spite of the fact that authenticity to the prophet is denied in these cases, it is still true that Isaiah both preached about Israel's destruction by the Assyrian armies and prophesied the doom of this world power and the ultimate salvation of purified Israel.

---

[11] B. Duhm, *Das Buch Jesaia übersetzt und erklärt* (HKAT; Göttingen, 1892); T. K. Cheyne, *Introduction to the Book of Isaiah* (London, 1895), and Karl Marti, *Das Buch Jesaja* (KHAT; Tübingen, 1900).

In the first edition Buhl gave a short list of prophecies in the book of Isaiah which he, in the 1890s, considered inauthentic. In the second edition there is a longer list (p. XIX), but in this case the pericopes mentioned are, following principles developed on previous pages, certainly or at least probably genuine. Less than fifty shorter or longer texts are in this list, and even some of these were reworked before they reached their present form. Eight more texts are not certainly genuine, and among them Buhl includes the messianic texts in chapters 2, 9, and 11, mentioned above. Here there seems to be some kind of contradiction. Whereas Buhl, in 1894, found that by far the majority of texts in Isa. 1–39 were genuine, by 1912 he did not find any genuine Isaiah prophecies in Isa. 11, 12, 13, 15, 16, 19, 21, 23, 24, 25, 26 and 27; after chapter 32 no texts from the prophet Isaiah in the 8th century are found. By 1912 he is convinced that the present Book of Isaiah has a very complicated history of origin.

In a new chapter in the second edition, "The religious content of the Book of Isaiah" (pp. XXV–XXX), Buhl reached the conclusion that one can no longer speak about the theology of the Book of Isaiah but only the different religious ideas contained in the parts of which the book is composed. There are characteristic differences between the ideas in, for example, the beginning of the book and chapters 40–55, and that is additional proof that the results of critical research into the book are correct. It is not the same author in the two parts.

However, from the texts that in Buhl's opinion are proven to be genuine it is still viable to reconstruct the prophet's ideas and thoughts. It is possible to isolate the preaching of the prophet Isaiah himself, and that preaching is, in the oldest parts of the book, close to the prophecies of Amos and Hosea. He prophesied about imminent doom and punishment and described the sins which would lead to the catastrophe. However, what is special for Isaiah is that he not only preached doom and the need for repentance, he also, at a few critical points, gave advice to the king and people about what to do in specific situations. In the group of people he gathered around him the prophet identified the remnant, which in his understanding was the basis for the purified Israel, which would emerge from the coming doom.

The prophet's thoughts were closely linked to his understanding of God. Yahweh is *God* in the definitive meaning of that word; he was, as stated in Isa. 6:3, the three-fold holy one, whose glory fills the whole world. The world power and its magnificent army were magnificent only because both were tools in the hand of God. Consequently the only way to salvation was through unconditional trust in God. "Maybe Isaiah was not the first one to preach belief in God, but he was certainly the first who consciously made belief the centre of man's relation to God" (p. XXVI).

The prophet known from the first part of the book by the name Isaiah was a prophet with a live audience, while the person behind Isa. 40–55 was, according to Buhl, a writer who addressed an imaginary group of readers (pp. XXVII–XXIX). The main motivation behind this work was to bring comfort to the people who lived in Babylonian captivity, by preaching an immediate salvation. Deutero-Isaiah's concept of God is not identical with the concept of the first Isaiah. It was as grandiose as the first Isaiah's concept, but there is more theological reflection contained therein, for example when the writer talks about Yahweh as the only one, the first and the last, and the almighty creator of the world.

One part of the Book of Isaiah, which was used above as an example of Buhl's method of argumentation in the first edition of the Isaiah Commentary, is Isaiah 24–27. In the second edition this section is dealt with under the heading "The great doom and the salvation of the people of God".[12] In dealing with this text, Buhl did not arrive at many new results as compared with his answers to problems discussed some twenty years earlier. He considers these chapters post-prophetic, but cannot accept any other scholarly attempts to date the text exactly. No real historical events are reflected in the text, a central idea being the Lord's feast for all peoples of the world at Mount Zion when all suffering and pain will disappear. But he is not as sure as he was earlier that this section is one unit. Duhm's idea that these chapters are made up of four psalms, each with a different metre,[13] made Buhl hesitant. In the end he rejected Duhm's thesis as uncertain, but admitted that the text was not as coherent as he had earlier thought.

About Isaiah 40ff Buhl writes in the preface:[14] "I would have liked to drop most of the introduction to chs 40ff, because the recognition that these chapters are of late origin has been widely accepted to such a degree that detailed proof is no longer necessary. But after all I have kept this part unchanged because these chapters have played a

---

[12] See F. Buhl, *Jesaja oversat og fortolket*, 2nd. edn. 1912, pp. 314–315, and the subsequent translation and verse for verse commentary on pp. 316–369.

[13] Duhm, 1892, pp. XII and 148–176.

[14] The Preface is unpaginated.

fundamental role in the development of critical research." To this he adds that a presentation of this development is useful for introducing beginners to the problems related to this kind of investigation and for providing them with an accurate method.

However, what he wrote in this paragraph does not mean that he had not changed his mind about Isaiah 40–66. The two parts of the Book of Isaiah have expressions and phrases in common, but there are differences too. Whilst, in Buhl's day, there were still scholars who found enough material to argue for the unity of the whole book, in Buhl's own opinion there were so many differences that the book of Isaiah could not be the work of one author. The main argument against unity is that Isa. 40ff relates to a different historical situation from Isa. 1ff. It is obvious that the beginning of the book of Isaiah points to events in the eighth century B.C., but from chapter 40 onwards the situation is different. That Jerusalem and the temple were in ruins, the people in captivity in Babylon, and that the coming liberator was Cyrus, who had the task of bringing the people back, all point in the same direction. The background is the exile. Buhl was not any longer in doubt himself about this theory, because in his understanding the prophets always addressed a contemporary audience. But even if it was clear to him, he felt obliged to argue at length against those scholars who were not yet convinced.

Buhl also did not believe any longer that Isaiah 40–66 is one unit. In this case he was again influenced by Duhm's commentary. The collection of prophecies in Isa. 56–66 are admittedly close to Deutero-Isaiah, but cannot have been composed by the same prophet. Buhl had now realised that the magnificent salvation, about which the prophet wrote in Isa. 40–55, had according to Isa. 56–66 not yet occurred, even though the prophet behind these chapters had clearly returned to the land. The return to the country was only a foreshadowing of what was to come in this preaching. The reasons for the delay of salvation were the sin of the people and the outward form the cult had taken. Some of the expectations which Deutero-Isaiah had of the Servant of the Lord were now applied to the peoples of other nations. The theology is, as in Isa. 40–55, universalistic, but here too there are differences. A radical change of the whole world is expected in the form of a re-creation of Heaven and Earth.

The last example I will give of a difference between the first and second editions of Buhl's Isaiah commentary, under the influence of Duhm's commentary, is the origin and form of the so-called

Ebed-Yahweh-hymns and their relationship to other parts of the section in which they are found in Isaiah 40–55. Buhl's treatment of these problems is not a reproduction of Duhm's writing and understanding, for he had to work through the text himself before he was able to decide how far he was able to follow his German colleague.

After the translation of Isa. 42:1–7 (p. 528) Buhl presents the scholarly discussion about the Ebed-Yahweh-hymns as it took place in the period between the two editions of his Isaiah commentary. Earlier in the history of research scholars had disagreed about whether "servant" in these four texts is a designation of the Messiah or a personification of Israel or at least a part of Israel. With Duhm's commentary, a new way of understanding the servant was opened up. The servant was understood as a historical personage in all four texts, not only in Isa. 53 as several scholars thought before Duhm. He also concluded that the servant songs were not genuine Deutero-Isaiah texts (p. 529).

After his exegesis of the Servant Songs, 42:1–7; 49:1–9, 50:4ff, and 52:13–53:12, in the context in which they are found, Buhl tries to give, in connection with his interpretation of Isa. 53:12 (pp. 648–656), an answer to the problems related to these texts. His conclusion is that in the first three servant songs there may have been historical models behind the portrayal of the servant. But when it comes to Isa. 53 and the glorification of the servant we are not dealing with a text about a single person. Therefore Isa. 53 could be a text from a different author from the one who wrote the other three songs. In any case probably none of them were written by Deutero-Isaiah.

Buhl cannot give an answer to the question, how the servant songs came into the second part of the Book of Isaiah. But in the end that is not the most important thing to say about these texts. For Buhl the servant songs mark a culminating point in the Old Testament. They are a bridge which connects the Old Testament with the New Testament. Christ saw in these poems a direct image of himself, unlike other images of messiahship from the Old Testament which he changed. This insight is Buhl's personal reason to continue his research into these and other prophetic texts in the Old Testament, as he went on to do.

PART C

PSALMS

EDITORIAL ARRANGEMENT IN BOOK IV
OF THE PSALTER

Anthony Gelston

Much time and energy has been expended on explaining hypothetical processes of editorial arrangement by which originally separate blocks of material came to be assembled into the final text of the Hebrew Bible. It is important to recognize at the outset that such reconstructions are inevitably hypothetical, since, with rare exceptions, the editors have left no record of how they set about their work, and only occasional parallel texts afford a glimpse of how the earlier components of the final text may have appeared. An example of the former may be seen in the note appended to Ps. 72, to the effect that this marks the end of the prayers of David, although this is not true of the actual Psalter, in the second half of which several further psalms are attributed to David. An example of the latter may be seen in the case of Ps. 108, which consists entirely of a combination of passages from Pss. 57 and 60.

Despite the case of Ps. 108, and of other cases of partial overlap, such as that between the whole of Ps. 70 and the closing verses of Ps. 40, it seems overwhelmingly probable that the unit of composition in the Psalter is the individual psalm. This immediately suggests the questions how, when, by whom, and on what principles individual psalms came to be grouped together, and such particular groups of psalms subsequently combined into what ultimately became the Psalter. The existence of occasional overlap between some individual psalms, and the virtual duplication of Pss. 14 and 53, indicate one negative conclusion that can be drawn. It is evident that there was no final process of editing the Psalter, by which such duplications might have been removed, and textual inconsistencies between parallel passages ironed out. In all probability this should not be ascribed to editorial negligence, but rather to respect for texts hallowed by long usage in worship, which had already acquired a degree of sacrosanctity.

While the Psalter is unique in consisting of a large number of clearly defined individual compositions, some inferences may be drawn from other parts of the Hebrew Bible about processes which took place as smaller blocks of material were gradually combined into groups on the way to becoming complete books. The obvious method of chronological sequence, adopted in the main in narrative books, was hardly applicable in assembling material of a prophetic, poetic, or wisdom nature. It is possible, however, to trace with some plausibility sub-collections of material which were ultimately combined to form a book.

Within the book of Isaiah, for instance, it is easy to discern certain blocks of material such as the oracles against foreign nations in chs. 13–23, a section with an apocalyptic flavour in chs 24–27, the historical narratives in chs. 36–39, and the section regularly ascribed to Deutero-Isaiah in chs. 40–55, within which certain themes are confined to chs. 40–48 and others to chs. 49–55. Occasional titles, such as those in 2:1 and 13:1, indicate the beginnings of new collections, while the placing of Isaiah's call vision in ch. 6 suggests that this also may have once introduced a sub-collection. The way in which material on similar topics is distributed within a wider section, such as the respective passages on the incomparability of God, the futility of idolatry, the "former" and "new" things, the references to Cyrus, and the suggestions of a new exodus within chs. 40–48, suggests that the basic unit of material is often quite short, and that there has been no editorial attempt to bring the individual units into some kind of orderly progression.

In the case of the book of Jeremiah there is much to suggest that it was produced in successive stages by the simple expedient of adding further blocks of material. Ch. 36 records the occasion of the writing of the first scroll of Jeremiah's oracles in the year 605 B.C. This scroll was notoriously destroyed by king Jehoiakim, and replaced with another expanded version. To quote one particular analysis by way of example, J. R. Lundbom identifies the following stages in the growth of the final book of Jeremiah: (a) chs. 1–20, possibly with ch. 45 as a final colophon, (b) chs. 21–23, an appendix on kings and prophets, (c) chs. 24–36, within which (d) chs. 30–33 are a separate insertion, (e) chs. 37–44, (f) chs. 46–51 consisting of oracles against foreign nations, and (g) ch. 52, a historical appendix.[1] It is noteworthy that the oracles against foreign nations are located at a different point in the LXX, after 25:13a. It is difficult to resist the conclusion that the earliest collection has been supplemented by a series of later collections of

---

[1] J. R. Lundbom, *Jeremiah 1–20* (AB; New York, 1999), pp. 92–101.

material, which have either been appended respectively to the previous "edition", or, as in the cases of chs. 30–33, or the oracles against the foreign nations in the LXX, inserted at what was felt to be an appropriate point within it.

These last examples afford an illustration of one particular editorial method, whereby a whole block of material seems to have been inserted into an already existing block, whose continuity is thus disrupted. The clearest example of this method is probably to be seen in the last four chapters of 2 Samuel, which break the natural narrative sequence from 2 Samuel 20 to 1 Kings 1. These chapters seem to consist of a series of supplementary passages, which would be more likely in a modern book to be set apart as excursuses or appendices.

In the light of these wider considerations we may approach the question of editorial arrangement within the Psalter with four provisional hypotheses. The first is that the basic unit is normally the individual psalm. The second is that we may expect to find small groups of psalms with common features of form and/or content, which may well have been a reason for their collocation. The third is that occasionally one such group may have been inserted within another, in such a way as to obscure the homogeneity of the latter group. The last is that, although Pss. 1 and 146–150 may have been deliberately placed to open and close the final Psalter, there are plenty of indications that there was no attempt at a final editing of the complete Psalter; it seems simply to have grown by accretion.

At this point something needs to be said about attempts to discern an overall arrangement of the individual psalms within the Psalter as a whole. Space prevents more than a very limited survey of some of the work that has been done in this area, among which attention is drawn especially to a series of publications by G. H. Wilson.[2] He makes some useful observations about the division of the Psalter into five books, and draws attention in particular to a clear difference of arrangement between the first three and the last two books.[3] This is based on a thorough study of the titles of the psalms. Titles indicating author and

---

[2] G. H. Wilson, "Evidence of Editorial Divisions in the Hebrew Psalter", *VT* 34 (1984), pp. 337–52; *The Editing of the Hebrew Psalter* (SBLDS 76; Chico, CA, 1985); "The Use of Royal Psalms at the 'Seams' of the Hebrew Psalter", *JSOT* 35 (1986), pp. 85–94; "Understanding the Purposeful Arrangement of Psalms in the Psalter: Pitfalls and Promise", in J. C. McCann Jr. (ed.), *The Shape and Shaping of the Psalter* (JSOT-Sup 159; Sheffield, 1993), pp. 42–51.

[3] Wilson, 1984.

genre are plentiful in the first three books, but far less frequent in the last two books. He envisages the first three books as "the result of a gradual process of collection", while the last two books are later additions to this earlier unit.[4]

It is when Wilson moves beyond the examination of titles, and tries to detect an overall development of theme within the Psalter as a whole,[5] that his argument becomes less convincing. He begins with an effective critique of the theory that the five books of the Psalter are thematically related to the five books of the Torah. He then turns to the marked difference in the editorial arrangement of the first three and the last two books of the Psalter. This suggests to him that Ps. 89, the last psalm in Book III, occupies a pivotal position in the Psalter as a whole. He notes the presence of royal psalms (2, 72 and 89) at the "seams" of the first three books, and traces a development in the treatment of the Davidic covenant in these psalms, noting that the concluding section of Ps. 89 reflects the anguished cry of the Davidic descendants at the failure of this covenant. The theme of divine kingship in Book IV is seen as part of the answer to this plea. Book IV itself ends with a plea of the exiles to be gathered from the diaspora (Ps. 106:47), while Book V in turn is seen in some sense as an answer to this plea, by emphasizing that deliverance is dependent on an attitude of trust in God alone, as illustrated in the Davidic psalms 108–110 and 138–145.

Wilson's most valuable contribution to this question is his detection of a marked difference in the editorial arrangement of the first three and the last two books of the Psalter. His characterization of Ps. 89 as occupying a pivotal position in the Psalter, however, rests primarily on his selection of the Davidic covenant as a major theme, particularly within the first three books. His theory that the "seams" of these books are marked by royal psalms is weakened by the absence of such a psalm at the seam between the first two books, which he has to explain by the hypothesis that these two books were already combined before this principle of editorial arrangement was adopted. His argument for the thematic structuring of the Psalter as a whole seems to depend too much on a highly selective choice of themes. It also ignores the way in which thematic elements, like indications of authorship and

---

[4] Wilson, 1986, p. 92.
[5] Wilson, 1985, pp. 199–228.

genre, are in fact distributed widely through the Psalter, transcending the divisions between the five books.

The present study is concerned with Book IV of the Psalter. One reason for this choice is the remarkable paucity of editorial titles within this book. Only three psalms are attributed to particular authors (Ps. 90 to Moses, and Pss. 101 and 103 to David). Ps. 92 is described as a song for the sabbath, and Ps. 100 as a psalm of thanksgiving, or possibly as a psalm for the thank-offering. The remaining title, that of Ps. 102, is evidently inferred from the content of the psalm. Otherwise Pss. 90 and 102 are described as prayers, and Pss. 92, 98, 100 and 101 as psalms. Little can be learnt from these titles about the editorial arrangement of the psalms within this book.

One particular study of Book IV of the Psalter is that of M. D. Goulder.[6] He proposes that the arrangement of these psalms follows their actual use in the autumn festival, albeit with an admitted "strong element of speculation". Wilson, however, draws attention to the fact that Mowinckel developed his theory of the autumn festival and its thematic content on the basis of these psalms.[7] Goulder's hypothesis, although in many ways attractive, is thus shown to be based on a circular argument.

One detail of Goulder's theory, however, merits further consideration. It is based on the assumption that the even numbered psalms in Book IV were used in the evenings, and the odd numbered psalms in the mornings, of the consecutive days of the festival.[8] Goulder himself admits that only five of the seventeen psalms (Pss. 90, 95, 97, 101 and 102), contain such a reference, and that of these only Pss. 90 and 101 "yield any confidence". On closer examination, however, even this conclusion seems to run ahead of the evidence. Ps. 90 refers to a watch in the night (v. 4), to the transition from morning to evening (vv. 5–6), and to the hope of satisfaction with God's steadfast love in the morning (v. 14). While the psalm is undoubtedly suitable for use in the evening, it can hardly be claimed that such use is required by its content. Ps. 91, which is not considered by Goulder in this context, contains references to night and day, darkness and noonday (vv. 5–6), clearly a comprehensive time reference comparable with that to be found in

---

[6] M. D. Goulder, "The Fourth Book of the Psalter", *JTS* N.S. 26 (1975), pp. 269–89.

[7] Wilson, 1993, pp. 45–46.

[8] Goulder, pp. 271–72.

Ps. 55:18. Another psalm which contains references to both morning
and night is Ps 92 (v. 3). It is doubtful whether the reference to "today"
in Ps. 95:7 is sufficient to establish its use as a morning psalm. Ps. 97: 11
may contain a reference to the dawn, if, with the NRSV, the reading
of the LXX and Jerome is preferred to that of the MT, but, even so,
it is essentially metaphorical. Goulder's most convincing instance is
Ps. 101:8, but even this would not be inconsistent with the use of the
psalm in the evening. Ps 102:12 likens the psalmist's days to an evening shadow, but the main point is not the actual time of day, but the
brevity of human life. Ps. 104:19–23 is a sustained passage about day
and night, sunrise and evening, seen as one aspect of the Creator's
work. In the light of this review of the references to different times of
day and night it would be hard to maintain that this was a major factor in the editorial arrangement of the psalms in Book IV.[9] Ironically
the most convincing instance of an alternating morning and evening
sequence is to be found not in Book IV but in Book I (Pss. 3:6, 4:9 and
5:4), although even in this case Ps. 3:6 contains a double reference to
both morning and evening.

   The hypothesis proposed in the present essay is that the strongest clue
to the principles underlying the editorial arrangement of the psalms
in Book IV is to be found in the presence of thematic and sometimes
verbal links between adjacent psalms. These correspondences will
repay detailed consideration. We shall consider first some correspondences between two groups of psalms within Book IV: Pss. 90–92+94
and Pss. 102–104. The most significant ones concern the themes of the
transience and frailty of human life, contrasted with the transcendence
of God the Creator. Three recurrent images expressing this theme are
to be found in these psalms.

   Ps. 90:3 speaks of God turning human beings back to dust, a passage reminiscent of Genesis 3:19. Ps. 103:14 says that God remembers
that we are but dust. Ps. 104:29 speaks of all living creatures returning
to their dust when God takes away their breath, but states in the next
verse that, when God sends forth his breath/spirit, the effect is a new
act of creation. The Hebrew word translated "dust" in Ps. 90 is the
rare word דכא, used as a noun uniquely here in the Hebrew Bible. In
Genesis and Pss. 103–104 the much more common word עפר is used.
Ps. 104:29–30 uses the word רוח in two contrasted senses, denoting

---

[9] See further Wilson, 1993, p. 46.

first the breath of life in all living creatures, which distinguishes the living from the dead, and secondly the breath or spirit of God, which has the power to create and to bestow new life.

The imagery of "breath" recurs in a slightly different form in Ps. 94:11, where human thoughts are described as "but an empty breath". The Hebrew word used here, הבל, does not recur within Book IV, but is found in similar contexts in other parts of the Psalter (Pss. 39:6, 12; 62:10; and 144:4).

A third image is that of "grass", for which two Hebrew words – חציר and עשׂב – are used, or that of a "flower (ציץ) of the field" (Ps. 103:15). Ps. 90:5–6 draws out the relevance of this image. The grass flourishes in the morning, but fades and withers in the evening. This image is applied to human life in general, as it is again in Ps. 102:5, 12 and Ps. 103:15–16. It reappears in a more restricted application to the wicked in Ps. 92:8, a concept found also in Ps. 37:2. The use of the word חציר (Pss. 37:2, 90:5 and 103:15) recalls the similar descriptions of humanity in Isaiah 40:6–8 and 51:12. Two words are used to denote "flourish": ציץ, cognate with the "flower" in Ps. 103:15, is used in Pss. 90:6, 92:8 and 103:15, while פרח is used in Ps. 92:8 of the wicked and in Ps. 92:13, 14, as also in Ps. 72:7, of the righteous.

There are a few other fairly distinctive expressions to be found in some of these psalms, although none are so characteristic of the group as those considered above. The "dullard" (בער) and "stupid" (כסיל) are paired in Pss. 92:7 and 94:8, as also in Ps. 49:11. On the other hand God is described under a range of images. He is a "rock" (צור) in Pss. 92:16, 94:22 and 95:1, a "dwelling-place" (מעון) in Pss. 90:1 and 91:9, and a "refuge" (מחסה) in Pss. 91:2, 9 and 94:22. What is interesting in these cases is that all the instances occur within Pss. 90–94, except for one occurrence of "rock" in Ps. 95:1. None of them occur in Pss. 102–104. This may suggest a distinction between the earlier and later groups of psalms under immediate consideration.

At this point we need to note that each of the psalms within this group has its own theme, and that the recurrent material does not reflect a dominant theme that runs throughout the group. The main theme of Ps. 90 is certainly the contrast between the transcendence and eternity of God and the transience and frailty of humankind. The psalm also stresses the theme of divine judgement in connection with human finitude in its echo of Genesis 3. In v. 12 it introduces the theme of the wise human use of finite time, and in its closing verses it appeals to the divine compassion and prays for prosperity in human activity. Ps. 91 is much more concerned with the various dangers to which human life is exposed, and looks to God as a source of protection and security. Ps. 92 celebrates the steadfast love and faithfulness of God, and draws a sharp distinction between the experience of the wicked and that of the righteous. Ps. 94 is also deeply concerned with the distinction between the wicked and the righteous. It strongly emphasizes the theme of God as judge, and particularly as rescuer of the righteous from the machinations of the wicked.

Ps. 102 depicts three aspects of human affliction – the taunts of enemies, the anger of God himself, and the finitude of human life. Against this it sets both the eternity and the compassion of God, and the divine intervention anticipated is focused more on the future of the community than on that of the psalmist himself. Ps. 103 is essentially a hymn of praise and thanksgiving, celebrating God's compassion, and particularly his intervention to vindicate the oppressed. This is set over against human adversity and sin as well as human finitude. The psalm ends with a summons to all creation to bless the Lord. Ps. 104 is another hymn, this time celebrating the magnificence of God's work in creation, within which special emphasis is laid on his providential care for his creatures, and on their dependence on him for life and renewal. It includes a brief reference (v. 35) to the fate of the wicked.

Each of these psalms is thus seen to have its own particular theme, within which the common material is sometimes used in different ways and in different connections. It may also be noted that common themes are not always expressed in identical vocabulary, and that material that is similar, both in thematic content and in verbal expression, is often to be found elsewhere in the Psalter. All these factors suggest that thematic overlap seems to have played a part in the formation of small groups of psalms rather than in the overall arrangement of the Psalter.

We turn now to a different group of psalms within Book IV, Pss. 93 and 95–100. This time there is no doubt that a common theme, that of divine kingship, pervades the whole group and renders it more homogeneous than the previous group. No less than three of these psalms (Pss. 93, 97 and 99) begin with the affirmation, "The Lord is king" (מלך יהוה), which is also found at a climactic point in Ps. 96:10, and in an expanded form in Ps. 95:3, while the title "king" is applied to the Lord in Ps. 98:6. Only Ps. 100 within this group makes no explicit mention of the divine kingship. Much has been written about these psalms, particularly in connection with the hypothesis that the autumn festival was an enthronement festival, which we do not need to examine here. Ps. 47, with its repeated affirmation of the universal kingship of God, has often been included with this group, but its main significance for our present purposes is that it provides another instance of a close thematic parallel outside Book IV with this group of psalms.

There are also particularly close parallels between certain psalms within this group. Ps. 95 stresses the creative role of God, and uses the terminology of sheep and pasture, as well as that of "people", to denote Israel's relationship to God. These features recur in Ps. 100:3, but also in Ps. 79:13 in another book. Although the term "covenant" does not occur in Pss. 95 and 100, the theme seems to be implicit in both psalms, and probably accounts for the admonitory conclusion to Ps. 95, which is without parallel within the group. Pss. 96 and 98 both begin with the summons to sing a new song to the Lord, found also outside Book IV at Pss. 33:3 and 149:1, and at Isaiah 42:10. Other resonances between these psalms and Deutero-Isaiah include notably the verbal identity between Ps. 98:3b and Isaiah 52:10b, and the theme of publishing God's deeds among the nations. The question of the direction of dependence between Deutero-Isaiah and these psalms has been much but inconclusively debated; if this could be resolved, it would have useful implications for the date of these psalms, and possibly for the date of the formation of Book IV and its addition to Books I–III. Both of these psalms end on the note of God's coming to judge the earth, inspiring joy in the natural order.

The most distinctive psalms within the group are Pss. 97 and 99. Ps. 97 begins with a theophany, reminiscent of prophetic passages such as Micah 1:3–4. Ps. 99 refers to historic figures: Moses, Aaron and Samuel. One feature these two psalms have in common is that of Zion (Pss. 97:8 and 99:2). Ps. 99 in particular seems to evoke the Temple: God sits enthroned on the cherubim (v. 1), and the refrain summons the people to worship at his footstool (v. 5) or his holy mountain (v. 9). God's sanctuary is mentioned also, however, in Ps. 96:6 and implicitly in Ps. 100:4.

Ps. 93 is separated from the rest of this group by Ps. 94, but in addition to its opening affirmation it has close links with other psalms in the group. It celebrates the stability of the world created by God, mentions God's decrees (עדת), and refers to the Temple and its holiness, for which compare respectively Pss. 96:9, 99:7 and 99:9.

D. M. Howard, however, has drawn attention, among others, to two particularly significant verbal links between Pss. 93 and 94.[10] Both "majesty" in Ps. 93:1 and "proud" in Ps. 94:2 are derived from the root גאה, and there is an assonance between "roaring" (דכי) in Ps. 93:3 and "crush" (דכא) in Ps. 94:5. Although Ps. 94 has closer links with Pss. 90–92 than with Pss. 93, 95–100, its links with the latter group may be thought to suggest that it is well placed as a "bridge" between the two groups of psalms. Wilson goes so far as to speak of "the transposition of the final psalm of the first group and the beginning psalm of the second group" as "an accepted editorial technique to bind two segments together into a new whole".[11]

Further links between the two groups of psalms so far considered may be found in the references to the universal divine kingship in Ps. 103:19, and in the theme of God clothing himself in majesty in the opening verses of Pss. 93 and 104.

Ps. 101 is the most distinctive psalm in Book IV. It has no obvious links with either of the two main groups so far considered, but, since the theme of judgement is found in both of them as well as in Ps. 101:8, the editors may have decided that a position at the junction between the second group and the resumption of the first group would be the most suitable for it.

The last two psalms in Book IV have an obvious similarity in that they both contain substantial reminiscences of the early history of Israel. Ps. 105 covers the period of the patriarchs and the Exodus, with a brief reference to the wilderness wanderings and the occupation of the promised land. The overall theme is thanksgiving for God's providential and saving care for his people. Ps. 106, on the other hand, has a penitential tone, focusing attention on the repeated faithlessness and apostasy of Israel, mostly during the wilderness wanderings, but moving on in the last third of the psalm to the period after the settlement, including the experience of subjection to foreign power and eventual exile. The two psalms thus form a contrasting pair.

The opening verse of Ps. 106 combines two formulae: "Halleluyah" and "O give thanks to the Lord, for he is good; for his steadfast love endures for ever". The second is found also at the beginning of Pss. 107

---

[10] D. M. Howard, "A Contextual Reading of Psalms 90–94", in McCann (ed.), 1993, pp. 108–23 (114–16).
[11] Wilson, 1993, p. 50.

and 136, and at both the beginning and the end of Ps. 118. The first is found at the end of Pss. 104, 105 and 106, as well as at the beginning or end or both of Pss. 111–113, 115–117, 135 and 146–150. Wilson examines the use of these formulae, and draws the conclusion that the second formula is used to introduce segments, and the first to conclude them, within the last two books of the Psalter.[12] It may be questioned whether the use of these formulae, which may well have had a wider traditional use (as implied for the second by Jeremiah 33:11), is so distinctive as to establish their significance as a consistent indication of editorial arrangement within the Psalter. The occurrence of "Halleluyah" in Pss. 104, 105 and 106 may, however, have been a reason for placing these three psalms at the end of Book IV, providing a link between the group ending with Ps. 104 and the two historical psalms that follow. One may note also, for instance, the formula "Bless the Lord, O my soul", found at the beginning and end of both Pss. 103 and 104, which may well have served as a reason for the editorial collocation of these two psalms.

This necessarily brief survey of possible indications of reasons for the order of the psalms in Book IV has confirmed the expectation that the most convincing evidence is to be found for the collocation of small groups of psalms on grounds of thematic and verbal similarity. In particular, sufficient common material has been found to suggest a preliminary collection of three groups (Pss. 90–92, 94, and 102–104; Pss. 93 and 95–100; and Pss. 105–106), of which the first two were combined by the insertion of the second within the first. The last two psalms stand rather apart from the rest of the book, as does also Ps. 101, but tenuous links have been found to explain the inclusion of these psalms too within the book as a whole. Our attention has been confined to the more striking correspondences between psalms. Many more could be, and indeed have been, adduced, but some are of so general a nature as to carry little weight as evidence for editorial arrangement, while allowance must surely also be made for sheer coincidence in some cases. The larger the group of psalms under consideration, the harder it is to trace a convincing overall thematic arrangement. The evidence we have surveyed, therefore, points to a degree of careful editorial arrangement at the level of the small group, but the larger growth of the Psalter out of these small groups of psalms

---

[12] Wilson, 1984, pp. 349–52.

seems more likely to have been the result of a series of additions to a growing collection than of any overall editorial thematic design.

John Emerton's encyclopaedic knowledge and meticulous scholarship have long been an inspiration to all students of the Hebrew Bible. His readiness to offer advice, encouragement and constructive criticism of their work to colleagues and specially to younger scholars has also been widely appreciated. It is a pleasure to offer this small study in his honour.

G. H. WILSON'S THEORIES ON THE ORGANIZATION OF THE MASORETIC PSALTER

Yee Von Koh

I

The late Gerald H. Wilson is often credited by many for opening the floodgates of canonical criticism to Psalms study. He is generally acknowledged as the first to apply canonical criticism to the study of the Psalter in the clearest and most comprehensive way. Mainly through his monograph[1] but also in his many essays thereafter,[2] Wilson contended that there was a purposeful unity to the Hebrew Psalter and made the argument that the "book" had been redacted to represent a developing sequence of ideas. From his survey of a select group of Mesopotamian hymns (Sumerian Temple Hymns) Wilson saw, as some had also observed earlier, a purposeful intent behind the arrangement of adjacent units of hymns. He also observed in his study of several catalogues of Hymnic Incipits (catalogues containing only the first lines of hymnic compositions) the flexibility reflected in the classification of hymns which allowed for modification in their super-scriptions in order to accommodate the various purposes for which the individual catalogues were produced.[3] Wilson took his cue from the Mesopotamian hymnic literature to examine the Hebrew Psalter to see if there was any notable way in which the titles and postscripts of the individual psalms were arranged. Further comparative work on

---

[1] G. H. Wilson, *The Editing of the Hebrew Psalter* (SBLDS 78; Chico, CA, 1985) and previous to this, "The Qumran Psalms Manuscripts and the Consecutive Arrangement of Psalms in the Hebrew Psalter", *CBQ* 45 (1983), pp. 377–88; "The Qumran Psalms Scroll Reconsidered: Analysis of the Debate", *CBQ* 47 (1985), pp. 624–42.

[2] See especially G. H. Wilson, "The Use of Royal Psalms at the 'Seams' of the Hebrew Psalter", *JSOT* 35 (1986), pp. 85–94, reprinted in D. J. A. Clines (ed.), *The Poetical Books: A Sheffield Reader* (Sheffield, 1997), pp. 73–83; "The Shape of the Book of Psalms", *Int* 46 (1992), pp. 129–142; "11QPsᵃ and the Canonical Psalter: Comparison of Editorial Technique and Shaping", *CBQ* 59 (1997), pp. 448–464; "A First Century C.E. Date For the Closing of the Hebrew Psalter?", *JBQ* 28 (2000), pp. 102–110; "The Structure of the Psalter", in D. Firth and P. S. Johnston (eds.), *Interpreting the Psalms. Issues and Approaches* (Downers Grove, IL, 2005), pp. 229–46.

[3] Chapters 2 and 3 of Wilson, 1985.

the Qumran Psalms Scrolls led him to observe several parallel patterns in the arrangement of the psalms in the MT-150 Psalter which cumulatively suggested, to him, that there was a single and purposeful arrangement to the whole collection. There were others who had previously made similar suggestions regarding the purposeful arrangement of smaller groupings of psalms in the Masoretic Psalter though none went as far as to speak of the entire "book" as reflecting editorial unity nor provided as comprehensive a study for their argument as Wilson.[4] This new method of interpretation which shows a concern for identifying literary linkages and demonstrating the editorial unity of the Psalter in its final form had gained particular prominence through Brevard Childs, who was also Wilson's teacher. Childs had earlier applied the new approach called "canonical criticism" to the study of Psalms and acknowledged the influence of Claus Westermann[5] who himself offered a few interesting thoughts on the formation of the Psalter following his observation of the placement of certain psalms.[6] However, it was Wilson who made significant inroads with this "new" approach as he offered meticulous analyses, particularly in his comparative study of the psalms of the LXX, MT-150 Psalter, and the Qumran Psalms

---

[4] Most notably J. P. Brennan, P. Auffret, G. Sheppard, although there were also others who had observed the similarity of themes and links between adjacent psalms (e.g. Delitzsch, Alexander) without drawing any further conclusions.

[5] B. S. Childs, "Reflections on the Modern Study of the Psalms", in F. M. Cross, W. E. Lemke and P. D. Miller (eds.), *Magnalia Dei: The Mighty Acts of God. Essays in Memory of G. Ernest Wright* (Garden City, NY, 1976), pp. 377–88; *Introduction to the Old Testament as Scripture* (London, 1979), pp. 508–23. Childs does mention the influence of Westermann who had pondered about the presence and possible function of some of the royal psalms (e.g. Psalms 2 and 89 as marking the limits to the collections of Psalms 3–41 and 42–88), and certain psalms of praise (as conclusions of the individual collections and smaller groups), and their presence as evidence of editorial activity on the present and final form of the Hebrew Psalter. See C. Westermann, *Lob und Klage in den Psalmen* (5th ed., Göttingen, 1977), ET K. R. Crim and R. N. Soulen (tr.), *Praise and Lament in the Psalms* (Atlanta, 1981) which includes *Das Loben Gottes in den Psalmen* (Göttingen, 1961), ET K. R. Crim (tr.), *The Praise of God in the Psalms* (Richmond, VA, 1965), and three previously published German articles – see especially "Zur Sammlung des Psalters" which appears as "The Formation of the Psalter"; also idem, R. H. Boyd (tr. and ed.), *Handbook to the Old Testament* (Minneapolis, 1967), pp. 210–225 (the introduction and OT sections of the author's *Abriss der Bibelkunde*). A. Arens, *Die Psalmen im Gottesdienst des Alten Bundes* (Trier, 1961), also suggested looking at those psalms that are at the so-called seams of the Psalter to discover the possible editorial purpose behind the arrangement of the Psalter.

[6] Westermann was in fact following in Gunkel's footsteps in working meticulously on the genre analysis of the psalms, particularly on the praise and lament kind (see his *Loben* and *Lob*) and was not deliberately departing from the form-critical method of analysis when he made these observations.

manuscripts, and pulled together earlier views which supported his main thesis. Even critics of this new method of interpretation have lauded Wilson for presenting a thorough and systematic study of texts which has brought forth several valuable insights, particularly on the Qumran material. Wilson is also recognised for his important contribution to the argument for a two-stage process of canonization of the Masoretic Psalter. His arguments for a two-segment Masoretic Psalter are based on his observation of the difference in the organization of the psalms in Books I, II, and III and that of Books IV and V, and the important comparative data from Qumran. Wilson's work encompasses both studies on a textual level (e.g. noting the occurrence of superscriptions and postscripts, and repetitive phrases within groups of psalms) and the overall thematic and theological interpretation of the Psalter, the latter being what has attracted most criticism and generated many alternative theses. Wilson's suggestion that in the final form of the Psalter we find a clear move to obscure the precise cultic origins of the individual psalms whilst building a new context which emphasises the private life of devotion and individual access to YHWH has not, however, achieved majority agreement.[7]

II

In recent years there has been an increasing number of scholars who have followed after Wilson in attempting to establish further the case for seeing the Masoretic Psalter as a work of unity and reflecting a purposeful arrangement. Yet there are many others who remain unconvinced of the validity of this new "holistic" approach to Psalms study as it is said that there appears to be a lot of reworking of the arguments even among contemporary scholars which makes it unclear whether significant progress has been made in some of the topics discussed. Furthermore, it is charged that most of the contextual readings rely heavily on a priori theological assumptions rather than on detailed study of the texts at hand. Added to this is the criticism that many of the arguments that are offered in support of the canonical method of interpretation are presented in a garbled manner with many showing

---

[7] Wilson, 1985, pp. 170–3.

serious contradictions with one another.[8] There have been calls for greater controls to be applied in the works of this kind in order to avoid creating greater confusion and for them to go beyond the narrow focus of merely identifying "lexical" links between neighbouring psalms.[9] Interestingly, Wilson himself has voiced a similar concern.[10] Wilson's work continues to be considered as one of the main models of the canonical approach to Psalms study today. In this paper I shall review several of Wilson's theories which include his arguments on the arrangement of the small groupings of psalms and the alleged editorial activity behind the final "shape" of the Masoretic Psalter.

III

In his study of the Qumran Psalms manuscripts, Wilson made several observations about the structure and pattern of organization of smaller groups of psalms which he argued were also present in the MT. He suggested that the superscripts and postscripts held a special function of binding groups of psalms together. Wilson was convinced from his study that there was clear evidence to show that the work of the final redactor of the MT-150 Psalter was not only limited to the arranging of certain psalms using external texts (such as the superscripts and postscripts) but also included editorial additions and interpolations for the purpose of shaping the message of the Psalter in a particular theological way. According to Wilson, several levels of redaction may be discerned in the Psalter, although the influence of the final redactors on the earlier and already fixed collections of psalms is limited to only the reorganization and placement of a few psalms, the adding of superscripts and postscripts, and a few other minor textual interpolations. We will now take a closer look at two of his theories that relate to the pattern of organization of the smaller groups of psalms in the Masoretic Psalter.

---

[8] Howard, who is a proponent of this new approach to Psalms study, has also noted the many disagreements and divergence in the views of the canonical critics. See D. M. Howard, Jr, "The Psalms and Current Study", in Firth and Johnston, pp. 23–40.

[9] E.g. R. E. Murphy, "Reflections on Contextual Interpretation of the Psalms", in J. C. McCann Jr. (ed.), *The Shape and Shaping of the Psalter* (JSOTSup 159; Sheffield, 1993), pp. 21–28.

[10] G. H. Wilson, "Understanding the Purposeful Arrangement of Psalms in the Psalter: Pitfalls and Promise", in McCann, pp. 42–51.

1. The use of titles and postscripts to assist in the organization of the psalms corpus

(a) *Genre categories in titles*[11]

Wilson argues that, especially in Books I, II, and III, we find evidence of "editorial use of genre categories in the superscriptions" which help to "soften" the transition between groups of psalms which otherwise show a different genre or theme. Wilson lists, as examples of this phenomenon, psalms from the second and third book of the Psalter: Psalms 47–51, 62–68, 82–85. In the case of Psalms 62–68, the use of the genre categories of *mzmwr* and *šyr* in various combinations in the titles of Psalms 62–68 helps to bind the non-David Psalms 66 and 67 to an otherwise interrupted Davidic collection which begins at Psalm 51 and ends at 70/71. Wilson's hypothesis looks persuasive at first sight. However, a closer look reveals a significant problem. In the example just described, Wilson does not address why Psalm 61, which does not share the use of any of the said genre categories, finds itself isolated from the other "bound" groups within the Davidic collection.

Wilson's other example, which shows a step-paralleling of genre titles (i.e. A→B, B→C, C→D) between the Asaph collection (Psalms 73–83) and the second Korah collection (Psalms 84–88), is even less persuasive because there is a far less obvious pattern of organization here than in the previous example. We find here the use of a mixture of genre titles (in no systematic or observable order) in Psalms 73–80 and in the case of Psalm 81 there is none. In the four consecutive psalms following (Psalms 82–85) the term *mzmwr* is found in all of their superscriptions. As for the final three psalms (Psalms 86–88) we find another round of mixed genre titles on display, with Psalm 88 having three genre categories described which Wilson is unable to explain along the lines of his own hypothesis.

The observation of the omission and non-systematic distribution of genre titles in the Asaphite and Korahite collections can only be taken to suggest the priority of authorial ascriptions over genre titles in the grouping of the psalms belonging to, as in this particular example, Book III. To make more out of this general observation would be dangerous. There is also doubt over the suggested importance of the use of genre titles in this particular example of psalms in the Third Book:

---

[11] Wilson, 1985, pp. 163–66.

whilst the use of genre titles in the pulling together of the Asaphite
(Psalms 82–83) and Korahite (Psalms 84–85) collection of psalms is
observable, the question arises why the same redactor did not make
any attempts to pull together the only two *mśkyl* psalms (Psalms 74
and 78) which belong to the same genre within the Asaphite collection? This latter observation questions the actual importance of the use
of the genre titles as Wilson claims, since the redactor himself did not
see it necessary to group together those psalms with the same genre
titles, despite using the very same genre title elsewhere to bind other
disparate groups of psalms.

(b) *The pattern of use of* hôdû *and* hallelujah *in superscripts and
postscripts as reflecting an organizing principle behind some groupings
of psalms in Books IV and V*[12]
This next theory arose out of Wilson's study of the Qumran Psalms
scrolls and in particular out of his observation of a similar occurrence
in 11QPs[a]. On two occasions in the Qumran text Wilson observed the
grouping of psalms according to a "decidedly chiastic structure" which
contained elements of hallelujah and the phrase *hwdw lyhwh ky ṭwb ky
l'wlm ḥsdw* (i.e. Psalms 135–136–Catena, and Psalms 118–104–147–
105–146–148).[13]

Psalm	Superscript	Postscript
135	-----	hllwyh
136	hwdw lyhwh ky ṭwb	-----
Catena	hwdw lyhwh ky ṭwb	hllwyh
118	hwdw lyhwh ky ṭwb[14]	-----
104	ldwyd	hllwyh
147	[-----]	[hllwyh]
105	hwdw lyhwh ky ṭwb	[?]
146	[?]	hllwyh
148	-----	[hllwyh]

Wilson then suggested that a similar pattern of arrangement could
be seen in a few groupings of psalms in Books IV and V where the

---

[12] Wilson, 1985, pp. 125–29.
[13] Wilson, 1985, pp. 125–26.
[14] This is reconstructed by Wilson based on its occurrence in the MT and the
Catena in col. XVI. See P. W. Flint, *The Dead Sea Psalms Scrolls and the Book of
Psalms*, (VTSup 17; Leiden, 1997), p. 178, n. 35.

element of hallelujah is used to help form an inclusio for the group. Wilson explains with charts that are reproduced below.[15]

Pss 111–117
   111   hllwyh....
   112   hllwyh....
   113   hllwyh....
   114   -----....-----
   115   -----....hllwyh
   116   -----....hllwyh
   117   -----....hllwyh

Ps 135 (stands alone)
   135   hllwyh...hllwyh

Pss 146–150
   146   hllwyh...hllwyh
   147   hllwyh...hllwyh
   148   hllwyh...hllwyh
   149   hllwyh...hllwyh
   150   hllwyh...hllwyh

This hypothesis holds more persuasion in the Qumran examples, especially as we see in the second example given of 11QPs[a] that a second *hôdû* phrase is likely to have been added to Psalm 105 (which is missing in the MT version of this psalm) to complete the chiastic pattern. Wilson's observation of the groups of psalms in the fifth book of the Masoretic Psalter which have "hallelujah" at the beginning and at the end of the psalm is nothing special and the examples of Psalm 135 and Psalms 146–150 which Wilson refers to here cannot be used as evidence to corroborate the hypothesis, which strictly has to do with the hallelujah or *hôdû* phrase helping to form chiastic patterns for the group to which they belong. The only example in the MT that Wilson provides in support of this theory is the group of Psalms 111–117 where he argues that the location of the hallelujah at the beginning and at the end of the individual psalms within the group, with the exception of Psalm 114, produces an inclusio for the group. Wilson's argument, on a closer look, is based on an incorrect observation. The hallelujah praise in Psalm 113 in the MT occurs both at the beginning and at the end of it and not just at the start as Wilson

---

[15] Wilson, 1985, pp. 126–27.

observes.[16] Thus, this hypothesis of the use of the praise phrase(s) to form chiastic patterns within groups of psalms, whilst helpful for the understanding of the arrangement of them in the Qumran text, is inapplicable to the MT.[17]

IV

We now come to those signposts which Wilson argues the redactors have put throughout the Psalter and go beyond book divisions, which are supposed to function as interpretive clues to guide readers towards a particular theological understanding of the entire Psalter. As mentioned before, underlying his argument for the presence of a developing theological theme to the Psalter is the assumption or recognition of a two-segment Psalter. Some of the recognisable clues to the different levels of redaction are said to be found separately within the respective two sections whilst others go beyond the boundaries. Thus Wilson argues that certain royal psalms were placed at the seams of Books I, II, and III by the earlier redactor of the first segment of the Psalter in his attempt to reflect a particular theological emphasis for this earlier collection. Subsequently, the final shape of the entire Psalter was achieved by the addition of the last two books (Psalms 90–150) and the placing of wisdom psalms at strategic positions in the Psalter in order to provide the final influence on the interpretation of the Psalter. The final redactor of the Psalter is also responsible for placing Psalm 1 as the introduction to the whole Psalter, Psalms 90 and 107 to introduce Books IV and V respectively, and Psalm 145 to conclude the body of the Psalter proper, which also leads on to the extended hallelujah praise conclusion of Psalms 146–150. Wilson further argues that the work of placing the *YHWH mlk* psalms (Psalms 93, 95–99) to form the "core of the first answering book" (i.e. Book IV) and "indeed of the whole Psalter" also belongs to the same final redactor.

Many of the above observations have in fact been noted by others before, in addition to some others not detailed above, such as the presence of doxologies at the end of the first four Books. For example,

---

[16] The LXX has a different arrangement but Wilson's hypothesis here relates to the MT-150.

[17] Psalm 117 also begins with a hallel which, though not exactly the same (*hallĕlû 'et-YHWH*), is very similar to the hallelujah praise on which Wilson focuses.

Claus Westermann had earlier made the observation that certain psalms were found at particular points in the Psalter to mark the limits of book divisions and lesser groups of psalms.[18] Of the many arguments posited by Wilson the theory of the placement of royal psalms at the seams of the Psalter and that of wisdom and/or Torah material throughout the Psalter are the more significant.[19] Some brief and general comments on these will be offered below.

2. The placing of royal psalms at the "seams" of the Psalter

Wilson argues that Psalms 2, 72, and 89 are three royal psalms that have been placed to shape the understanding of this first segment of the Psalter to reflect the exilic response to the loss of the Davidic monarchy. The first segment of the Psalter begins with Psalm 2 which introduces the idea of the Davidic covenant (even though neither David nor the specific covenant is mentioned), which Wilson insists has its focus on the sovereignty of YHWH and the security that he extends to the king through the promise in 2:7–9.[20] The next stop is Psalm 41 which, though not a royal psalm, is argued by Wilson to bear "royal" elements and which has strong thematic parallels with Psalm 72. Wilson sees Psalm 41 as an appropriate end-piece to a collection which began with Psalm 2 since it speaks of David's assurance of God's continued protective action on his behalf. Psalm 72, a Solomonic psalm, shifts the focus of the Psalter from David to his descendants with a list of petitions for God's blessings on their behalf.[21] The concluding Psalm 89 adds the final and new perspective to the message of the Psalter. Here the Psalm shows the concern for the extension of the covenant to the descendants of David (vv. 4, 29, 36, 38–39, 44) and hope is further expressed in YHWH's ḥesed to remember his covenant and preserve the descendants of David (vv. 1, 46, 49–50). Wilson argues that at the conclusion of the first segment (i.e. Book III), the failure of the covenant is depicted, a plight which is further accentuated by the

---

[18] See n. 5.

[19] Of course many scholars in the past had a similar perception, e.g. Mowinckel believed that the Psalter had been composed and put together by temple personnel who were also learned scribes.

[20] Wilson, 1985, p. 209.

[21] "So the covenant which YHWH made with David (Ps. 2) and in whose promises David rested secure (Ps 41) is now passed on to his descendants in this series of petitions in behalf of 'the king's son' (Ps 72)" (Wilson, 1985, p. 211).

pleas of David's descendants and the implicit reference to YHWH's delay to act (v. 46). Wilson argues that Psalm 89 ends the first part of the Psalter with a plea to the problem of the failure of God to honour the Davidic covenant.

In response to this, the final redactors of the second segment saw it necessary to put together Books IV and V in such a way as to help direct the reader "*away* from trust in human kings and *toward* the kingship of Yahweh".[22] Wilson writes that the strong association of Psalm 2 with Psalms 72 and 89 (which readers are presumed to discern) "mitigates the status of David significantly and opens the way…for a new understanding of the anointed servant of Yahweh that focuses the reader instead on the kingship and kingdom of Yahweh".[23] Thus the final "shape" of the canonical collection of Psalms directs the establishment and rejection of the house of David (Books I, II, III) to its replacement by YHWH's theocratic rule (Books IV, V). Much discussion and debate has challenged the notion of the depiction of the rejection of David and his dynasty and the exclusive and absolute theocractic rulership of YHWH in the Psalter, both by critics of Wilson's method of reading (e.g. Whybray, Vincent) and also, and interestingly, by other canonical interpreters of the Psalter (e.g. Howard, Grant, Mitchell).[24]

Firstly, it is important to understand that Wilson's theory of the royal psalms at the seams relies on the assumption of a two-segmented Psalter. Hence, the presence of a royal psalm at the seams after Book III is not to be expected. The final redactors have instead chosen to develop the thrust of the earlier first segment, or rather answer the

---

[22] G. H. Wilson, "King, Messiah, and the Reign of God: Revisiting the Royal Psalms and the Shape of the Psalter", in P. W. Flint and P. D. Miller (eds.), *The Book of Psalms. Composition and Reception* (VTSup 99; FIOTL 4; Leiden, 2005), p. 396 (emphasis his).

[23] Flint and Miller, p. 395.

[24] R. N. Whybray, *Reading the Psalms as a Book* (JSOTSup 222; Sheffield, 1996); D. M. Howard Jr., *The Structure of Psalms 93–100* (BJSUCSD 5; Winona Lake, IN, 1997); M. A. Vincent, "The Shape of the Psalter: An Eschatological Dimension?", in P. J. Harland and C. T. R. Hayward (eds.), *New Heaven and New Earth: Prophecy and the Millenium, Essays in Honour of Anthony Gelston* (VTSup 77; Leiden, 1999), pp. 61–82; J. A. Grant, *The King as Exemplar. The Function of Deuteronomy's Kingship Law in the Shaping of the Book of Psalms* (SBLAB 17; Atlanta, Leiden, 2004); D. C. Mitchell, "Lord, Remember David: G. H. Wilson and the Message of the Psalter", *VT* 56 (2006), pp. 526–48.

theological dilemma thereof, by the addition and arrangement of psalms in their effort to present a coherent message whilst maintaining continuity between the two segments of the Psalter. As to the question of the absence of a royal psalm at the end of Book I, Wilson suggests that this rule of redaction did not apply in this particular case, since Psalm 41 belongs to a prior and longer collection (Psalms 2–72) whose end is marked by the colophon in Psalm 72:20.

Wilson's interpretation of the message of both of the segments of the Psalter is not agreed upon by many. The problems may be divided into two parts. First there is the question of whether the message of Books I to III is as dependent upon Psalms 2, 72, and 89 as Wilson suggests. Furthermore, much disagreement has been voiced over Wilson's suggestions that (1) the absolute failure of Davidic covenant and the rejection of the house of David is portrayed in Psalm 89, (2) the royal psalms, especially in Books IV and V, do not have an eschatological message, and (3) Books IV and V were written to admonish readers (exiled Israel) to trust in God alone and not in a Davidic messiah to come in the future. Wilson's views on some of these issues have recently changed. The failure of the Davidic covenant, which Wilson originally said was depicted in Psalm 89, could now be reprieved. Instead of a total rejection of the covenant and David's descendants, Wilson posits that any possible rise of the house of David in future would be subsumed under God's absolute and theocratic rule (i.e. he now allows for an eschatological interpretation). Nevertheless, Wilson is adamant that the emphasis of the last segment of the Psalter is solely on YHWH alone, in whom Israel is called to place their trust.

The major problem with Wilson's hypothesis here is that the second segment of the Psalter does not clearly develop the first in the way that Wilson has suggested it does, especially since there is a clear and continual presence of Davidic psalms in the final two books of the Psalter. Psalms 110, 122, 132, and 144, all of which are found in Book V pose a problem, since there is a clear reference to kingship and also to David in these psalms. Much criticism has been made of Wilson's interpretation, including his clear choice to down-play any possible Davidic reference in the latter collection of Psalms 90–150, which where found is creatively interpreted to support his thesis. It is unnecessary to repeat all that has been said of these issues here. However, general mention of some of the problems in Wilson's theory will be briefly made below.

In the interpretation of Psalms 110 and 132, it is clear that Wilson chooses to avoid reading allusions to a Davidic king whenever the possibility of doing so arises in these psalms. He argues, for example, that in Psalm 110 the earthly ruler who rules from Zion is a reference to an unidentified person who is not a Davidic scion but someone who has a priestly lineage (like the Hasmonean or Maccabean kings). However, an eschatological reading of this psalm, for which the text itself provides strong hints, would have us see in the psalm a reference to a new perspective on the role of the Messiah who now carries the role of a high-priest concurrent with his kingship.[25] Wilson further argues that, despite the initial hints to a royal context in verse 4a, and allusions there to the original text of the Davidic Covenant in 2 Sam 7:11–16, the proclamation in verse 4b with its reference to Melchizedek provides the interpretation that an unexpected reversal is observed, which speaks of the replacement of the eternal human kingship with an enduring priesthood.[26] In Wilson's latest (and last) review of his hypothesis, he suggests that "in this Davidic psalm, it is ultimately Yahweh who assumes the role of conquering monarch while the Davidic scion is affirmed as "priest forever".[27] Without going into a detailed study of what is commonly acknowledged as a difficult text, it is clear that Wilson's apparent suppression of some of the probable links to David and kingship in this psalm is artificial and forced. Even a simple and superficial reading of the psalm would lead one to see in it the picture of a Davidic ruler who is being honoured by YHWH in his role as king. D. C. Mitchell has also argued that reference to David cannot be ignored, since the conqueror who sits enthroned on Zion at the right hand of YHWH can only be a reference to David or his seed, since David's palace was on the spur of Mount Zion on the right, or south, of the Temple Mount.[28]

The royal Psalm 132 presents another difficulty for Wilson's hypothesis. Bernhard Anderson has questioned why such a psalm should

---

[25] J. C. McCann Jr.'s argument, that the psalm was put there by the final redactor to show that hope that is placed on the Davidic dynasty is misplaced, is unpersuasive: *A Theological Introduction to the Book of Psalms: The Psalms as Torah* (Nashville, 1993).

[26] Flint and Miller, pp. 399–400.

[27] Flint and Miller, p. 400.

[28] See Mitchell, pp. 535–36, for his arguments against Wilson's interpretation of the name "Melchizedek" in the context of the above argument in Flint and Miller, p. 400.

be found after the *YHWH mlk* collection especially since in Psalm 132 we find "a restatement of Davidic theology: the election of the Davidic king to a role in God's cosmic administration, and the choice of the temple of Zion as God's 'dwelling place'".[29] Its location in the final book of the Psalter clearly weakens Wilson's thesis on the royal psalms. Wilson, whilst willing to concede that verse 17 speaks of the anticipated raising up of a Davidic king, nevertheless argues that the clear reference in the verse to God's promises to "make a horn grow for David and set up a lamp for my anointed one" "stop[s] just short of an unambiguous declaration of David's kingship".[30] Wilson further tries to read the reference to the "crown" in verse 18 as alluding to other non–royal images (such as the sign for the dedication of priests or the adherents of the Nazirite vow). Against Wilson, Mitchell has suggested the possibility that the psalm may have been deliberately placed as "a counterpoise to the nadir of Psalm lxxxix" in that both recall verbatim the Davidic Covenant, both mention David four times, "(b)ut while Ps. lxxxix recalls the covenant to plead of its failure (vv. 39–46 [38–45]), Ps. cxxxii recalls it to reassert its eternal validity".[31] A similar kind of correspondence with Psalm 89 is arguably found in Psalm 148 with its reference to God raising up for his people a "horn" (v. 14). It may be added that Psalm 148 holds special kingly significance since the same word (*qrn*) is used of the Davidic king in Psalm 89:18.

Wilson's interpretation has been undoubtedly influenced by the observation that the Psalter moves from a mood of lament to one of praise (or from hurt to joy as argued by Brueggemann).[32] This general shift in the genre of the psalms would support Wilson's suggested presence of a thematic movement from the so-called rejection of the Davidic house and covenant to the praise of YHWH in the Psalter. However, such an observation needs to be qualified by the nature of the broad survey, since there is clearly evidence of both the lament and the hymns of praise being in both segments of the Psalter. There

---

[29] B. W. Anderson, *Out of the Depths. The Psalms Speak for Us Today* (Philadelphia, 2000), p. 209.

[30] Flint and Miller, p. 397.

[31] Mitchell, pp. 536–37.

[32] There are various other descriptions which W. Brueggemann gives to the broad movement found in the Psalter such as "from obedience to praise", "from duty to delight", "from death to life"; see "Bounded by Obedience and Praise: The Psalms as Canon", *JSOT* 50 (1991), pp. 63–92.

is one final question to ask of Wilson's theory, which is, in view of their task of collecting and arranging the psalms in the final segment of the Psalter, why the final redactors did not see it necessary and to their advantage to exchange the positions of the *YHWH mlk* psalms (Psalms 93, 95–99) in Book IV with the second Davidic collection in Book V (Psalms 138–145), which would have helped to develop their intended literary plot on clearer lines.

V

Wilson's thesis argues that the Psalter has undergone several levels of redaction, of which the last was the adding of wisdom and Torah emphases at various strategic points of the Psalter. Wilson posits that wisdom and Torah psalms have deliberately been placed at the beginning of the Book division (namely Psalm 1) as well as at "strategic" places throughout the Psalter to form a "cohesive sapiential framework".[33] These psalms are Psalms 1–2, 73, 90, 107, and 119.

3. *The cohesive sapiential framework*

Mitchell has recently spoken against this particular argument of Wilson. He points out that Wilson's argument that certain wisdom psalms have been added to form a wisdom framework (and he points to Psalms 1 and 73 as examples) does not constitute a proof. Applying Wilson's own line of argument to his own claims, Mitchell highlights that, whereas Wilson has elsewhere argued that superscripts and postscripts provide the clues to editorial activity, in the case of Psalm 73, if it were to be a later editorial addition as Wilson claims it is, then we would expect some indication of this in its title. Instead we find that it continues to hold to its Asaph title which "binds it firmly to the ten following psalms of the Asaph group".[34] Mitchell's argument makes a fair point but does not necessarily discredit Wilson's altogether, since Wilson maintains that one of the main purposes of adding titles to the psalms is to hide as much of the disjunctions in the divisions or groupings as possible (the smoothing effect). In this case, the supposed

---

[33] Firth and Johnston (see n. 1), pp. 237–240.
[34] Mitchell, p. 542.

inconspicuous nature of Psalm 73 does not particularly pose a problem for Wilson's thesis.

Whybray has conducted a more in-depth assessment of the argument that the Psalter was edited by sages and scribes and that evidence of wisdom interpolation and Torah emphasis can be found at strategic places in the work. In his study Whybray first looked at psalms containing interpolations of wisdom and/or Torah material (i.e. Psalms 18, 19, 27, 32, 37, 40, 78, 86, 92, 94, 105, 107, 111, 144, 146), followed by those that are "purely" wisdom and Torah psalms (i.e. Psalms 8, 14, 25, 34, 39, 49, 53, 73, 90, 112, 127, 131, 139).[35] In his detailed study Whybray made several observations and presented a number of conclusions. First, the extent of wisdom or Torah psalms or interpolations in the Psalter is large. Secondly, there are cases where wisdom psalms have been placed in their present context to influence the interpretation of the psalms surrounding it. Whybray lists, as examples, Psalm 86 for Psalms 84–88, Psalms 92 and 94 for Psalms 92–99, Psalms 107 for 105–107, and Psalms 111–112 which complement each other. The examples and arguments that Whybray gives in support of these are, on a closer look, persuasive, except for Psalms 92 and 94 which he suggests have been added to the group Psalms 92–99 as a "correction" to them. Whybray suggests that both Psalms 92 and 94 are placed in their current contexts to remind worshippers, who are in "cultic euphoria", of their present plight and the need "to learn the practical implications for God's people", whilst never to forget to hold God in fear (92:6–8). There are no clear and exclusive connections between Psalms 92 and 94 and the rest of the said group, and the argument for a connection given by Whybray is unconvincing and unnecessary. Whybray further explores the possible function of Psalms 1 and 2 as an introduction to the rest of the Psalter, which he eventually rejects. In the end, whilst Whybray is able to see the use of wisdom psalms in influencing certain neighbouring groups of psalms in a particular way and whilst the link between adjacent psalms on several occasions could be seen to show a development of a particular theme (e.g. Psalms 90–91–92), he nevertheless found that there was no systematic placement of wisdom and Torah psalms in such a way as to reflect a "wisdom book" or a book designed as a single work for consecutive reading.[36]

---

[35] Whybray, Chapter 2.
[36] Whybray, Chapter 2, and pp. 119–21.

Whybray concludes that although the phenomenon of wisdom and
Torah influence on the Psalter cannot be denied, nevertheless there is
no clear proof of an overall systematic ordering of the whole Psalter
which reflects a wisdom theme, since those separate instances where
it is observed did not necessarily come from the same editor.[37] After
Whybray's detailed study, Wilson's hypothesis, which is a lesser argument than the one Whybray examined, since its only focus is on a few
wisdom or Torah psalms found at the seams of the book divisions, can
at best receive the same evaluation. A selective emphasis on the presence of wisdom and Torah interpolation at the seams clearly renders
the theory one–sided and inconclusive.

VI

The above examination of Wilson's theories on the organization of
the Masoretic Psalter has shown that they are not as persuasive as
they first appear to be. Wilson's argument on the alleged use of titles
and postscripts by the final editor of the Masoretic Psalter to help
arrange the psalms in a particular way was found to be unconvincing
as was his hermeneutic which clearly holds many serious problems.
This assessment, however, does not affect the reputation of his work
on the Qumran Psalms scrolls, which is still held in high regard and
will clearly continue to be studied and referred to by students of both
the Qumran Psalms manuscripts and the MT-150 Psalter.

---

[37] Whybray, pp. 83–87. The issue at hand has been simplified here because, as many
scholars have observed before, the question of what constitutes a "wisdom psalm" is a
difficult one to answer. See the discussion of this issue by Whybray in "The wisdom
psalms", in J. Day, R. P. Gordon, and H. G. M. Williamson (eds.), *Wisdom in Ancient
Israel. Essays in honour of J. A. Emerton* (Cambridge, 1995), pp. 152–60.

PSALM 93: AN HISTORICAL AND COMPARATIVE SURVEY OF ITS JEWISH INTERPRETATIONS

Stefan C. Reif

Introduction

One of the particular pleasures of functioning as an academic colleague of John Emerton over a period of some thirty-five years has been the opportunity that this has occasionally provided of assessing the importance of the medieval commentators for various cruces in the Hebrew Bible that were being closely studied by him and in the interpretation of which he was anxious not to neglect the pre-modern Jewish exegetical tradition. The resulting discussions with him on the views expressed in these commentaries and on the manner in which they related to the relevant treatments offered by contemporary biblical scholarship often clarified for me the sense of both, and consequently contributed to the advancement of my own research in the field.

When honoured by an invitation to add a study of my own to the distinguished offerings being made by leading scholars of the Old Testament, it occurred to me that it would be appropriate to engage on a topic that would be pertinent to the many scholarly discussions that I had had with John and especially suitable if I could find a subject that, again, made a link between the medieval Jewish and the modern critical analysis of some verses from the Hebrew Bible. No sooner had this thought occurred when I found myself reciting Psalm 93 in the synagogue and asking myself, in an unconscionable departure from liturgical concentration, what Jewish exegetes had made of this short but undoubtedly challenging collection of five verses. A quick glance at some of the medieval commentators revealed such a singular lack of consensus that further serious enquiry became a highly desirable option. This was followed soon afterwards by a note from one of the editors of this volume suggesting that Psalms might be one of the books that would best feature in the collection of essays being planned. And so was born the present brief study which I offer to John in gratitude for the generous support he always offered to my plans for the promotion of Genizah research and with a sincere wish that we may share many more such fruitful discussions relating to the exegetical history of difficult verses in the Hebrew Bible.

Recent critical studies

A useful starting point for this survey are the conclusions reached in a number of modern scholarly commentaries, by both Jews and Christians, on the book of Psalms. Obviously it would take us greatly beyond the present remit to survey any more than a small sample of the relevant literature. I have therefore chosen two works from around the beginning of the twentieth century and two from its end, in the hope that this will provide a reasonable guide to the manner in which contemporary scholars have understood the literal meaning and religious message of Psalm 93. Against the background of such a guide, it will be possible to exemplify, summarize and assess earlier Jewish interpretations of the same psalm, and to offer a comparative evaluation of the various approaches.

The production of the "The Cambridge Bible for Schools and Colleges", published by Cambridge University Press, stands singular testimony to the degree to which Biblical Hebrew was regarded in many circles as part of a classical education in the late Victorian and early Edwardian years. The series was edited by A. F. Kirkpatrick (1849–1940) who served as Regius Professor of Hebrew (1882–1903), Master of Selwyn College (1898–1907) and Lady Margaret's Professor of Divinity (1903–1907) in the University of Cambridge, and the contributors included the finest scholars of the Hebrew Bible in the United Kingdom of his day. It was the editor himself who wrote the commentary on Psalms, the three volumes of which appeared between 1891 and 1901.[1]

Kirkpatrick describes Psalm 93 as a "prelude to the remarkable group of theocratic psalms 95–100" and argues that the stress on kingship is not part of a prophetic vision of the messianic period but a response to the sixth-century B.C.E. restoration after the Babylonian exile which represents proof to the psalmist of the divine sovereignty. He accepts as

---

[1] A. F. Kirkpatrick, *The Book of Psalms. Book I: Psalms I–XLI* (CBSC; Cambridge, 1891); *The Book of Psalms. Books II and III: Psalms XLII–LXXXIX* (CBSC; Cambridge, 1895); *The Book of Psalms. Books IV and V: Psalms XC–CL* (CBSC; Cambridge, 1901).

liturgically authentic the LXX's superscription noting its recitation on the sixth day (with its talmudic parallels) and suggests that the LXX's phrase about the peopling of the land may just as well refer to the restoration as to the creation. God's firmly established throne is a contrast to the "tottering order of the world" and the waters are a figure for the heathen nations who menace the kingdom of God, but to no avail. He interprets the testimonies of v. 5a as the revealed Torah rather than the prophetic promises and v. 5b as a promise that the Temple will never again "be defiled by Israel" or "desecrated by foreign invaders".[2]

Another series that has left a major mark on the scholarship of the Hebrew Bible until the present day is "The International Critical Commentary on the Holy Scriptures of the Old and New Testaments", edited by S. R. Driver of Oxford, A. Plummer of Durham and C. A. Briggs of New York, and published by T. & T. Clark. Charles Augustus Briggs, perhaps most famous for his part in helping S. R. Driver and Francis Brown to produce *A Hebrew and English Lexicon of the Old Testament* (Oxford, 1907), taught at the Union Theological Seminary in New York for most of his career and, influenced by the findings of German historical and literary scholarship, was committed to a critical view as to the textual reliability, authorship and historical fulfilment of Scripture. There was some doubt within the Presbyterian Church at that time about the acceptability of such views on the part of an ordained minister and this led to a trial for heresy from which he emerged bruised but not beaten. Briggs, with the assistance of his daughter, Emilie Grace, wrote the commentary on Psalms for the "ICC", which was published in 1906–07.[3]

The Briggs family team place Psalm 93 in the group of royal psalms represented by Psalms 96–100 but "separated from them for liturgical reasons". Their view of the LXX's superscription matches that of Kirkpatrick regarding liturgical use and the matter of repopulation but they see this psalm, and the others in the group, as dependent on Deutero-Isaiah and in accord with parts of its Servant Songs, comparing v. 1 with Isaiah 51:9 and 52:7, and v. 2 with Isaiah 44:8, 45:21 and 48:3, 5, 7–8. God has now "shown Himself to be king by a royal advent" and from his eternal throne has set aright the "whole order of

---

[2] Kirkpatrick, 1901, pp. 563–65.
[3] C. A. Briggs and E. G. Briggs, *The Book of Psalms*, 2 vols. (ICC: Edinburgh, 1906, 1907).

the habitable world". The powerful waters of vv. 3–4 are not symbolic of mighty foes but are "a graphic description of the majesty of the sea in a great storm", the magnificence of which is surpassed by that of God who can reduce it to order. They regard v. 5 as a liturgical addition, constituting a prosaic gloss that introduces "corresponding thoughts of the Law and the temple".[4]

Nahum Sarna's primary contributions to biblical Hebrew studies in the second half of the twentieth century lay in the major impact he had on generations of students at Brandeis University, the contribution he made to Jewish understanding of modern scholarship, and the part he played in the creation of the Jewish Publication Society of America's new translation of the Hebrew Bible.[5] Educated in Jews' College, London, and the University of London, as well as at Dropsie College in Philadelphia, he attempted to synthesize the best in scientific learning with the most valuable in Jewish traditional study, as especially exemplified in his commentaries on Genesis and Exodus.[6] His study of the book of Psalms appeared in 1993 and was republished as a paperback in 1995.[7]

Sarna cites the liturgical usage noted by the LXX and Talmud and also makes reference to the talmudic view (*b. Rosh Ha-Shanah* 31a) that the completion of creation with the formation of man on the sixth day established God's overall sovereignty. He does not regard the concept of God as king as emanating from the surrounding cultures of the ancient Near East but as an internal Israelite development that occurred after the establishment of the Israelite monarchy. He is sceptical about aspects of Sigmund Mowinckel's theory of enthronement psalms as the liturgy of an annual festival, borrowed from Mesopotamia, that celebrated God's victory over chaos and the establishment of his sovereignty.[8] He does, however, accept that the Jewish New Year festival's stress on God's kingship may owe something to an ancient pre-exilic holy day. This

---

[4] Briggs and Briggs, 1907, 2, pp. 299, 301–03, 311.

[5] *Tanakh = The Holy Scriptures: The New JPS Translation according to the Traditional Hebrew Text* (Philadelphia, 1985).

[6] N. M. Sarna, *The JPS Torah Commentary: Genesis.* בראשית (Philadelphia, New York and Jerusalem, 1989); *The JPS Torah Commentary: Exodus.* שמות (Philadelphia and New York, 1991).

[7] N. M. Sarna, *Songs of the Heart: An Introduction to the Book of Psalms* (New York, 1993); pb. *On the Book of Psalms: Exploring the Prayers of Ancient Israel* (New York, 1995).

[8] S. Mowinckel, *Offersang og Sangoffer* (Oslo, 1951); ET with revisions, *The Psalms in Israel's Worship* 2 vols., (Oxford, 1962).

psalm celebrates the eternal, indisputable fact of God's kingship and uses the image of royal apparel to emphasize God's eternal omnipotence and invulnerability and the manner in which he ensures the stability of the world. Later verses mention the chaos of the primordial waters and how God brought it to order, before concluding with a recognition of the eternity of God's reliability, holiness and celestial shrine.[9]

The tendency of the more traditional wings of Judaism and Christianity is to approach each of the biblical books in a more holistic fashion. This can of course be done without sacrificing academically acceptable levels of scientific understanding, as has been amply demonstrated by David M. Howard Jr. in his various studies of the historical and poetic books of the Hebrew Bible. Howard, who teaches Old Testament at Bethel Theological Seminary and is active in the Evangelical Church, completed a doctoral dissertation under the supervision of David Noel Freedman at the University of Michigan in 1986. His extensive revision of that dissertation appeared as *The Structure of Psalms 93–100* in 1997 and offers a thorough, synchronic and structural analysis of these psalms which identifies their similarities of theme and language and dates them all as pre-exilic.[10]

Howard sees Psalm 93 as a burst of praise for the eternally present and enthroned God as the sovereign king and proud creator. The psalm expresses total confidence in him and highlights the contrast between him and those who rebel against him and whom he crushes. Like the whole section of Psalms 93–100, it is concerned with the divine kingship and functions as an introduction to the theme and an appropriate transition between the more detailed and specific texts of Psalms 90–92 and 94. The psalmist affirms that God is sovereign even over the rebellious waters (of myth and cosmology) and stresses the ongoing importance of God's covenant and decrees (= Torah) and of his shrine. Primarily on linguistic grounds, and in view of the links with Ugaritic literature, Howard dates the psalm to the earliest stages of Hebrew poetic writing, no later than the tenth century B.C.E. and perhaps even two centuries earlier.[11]

---

[9] Sarna, 1995, pp. 177–88.

[10] D. M. Howard Jr., *The Structure of Psalms 93–100* (BJSUCSD 5; Winona Lake, 1997).

[11] Howard, pp. 34–43, 105–19, 171, 184–89.

Issues

These sample studies clearly identify at least some of the major issues that have confronted the modern exegete approaching Psalm 93. Does it have any liturgical function and, if so, from which period or periods? What is the background to its stress on the kingship of God and what is the nature of this latter divine quality? Is the psalm centred on the past, the present or the future? How does it relate to the other chapters in this part of the book and to other parts of the Hebrew Bible? Is the creation of the world one of its themes and are the references to the waters metaphorical or cosmological? In which way are God and the world here related and what precisely is conveyed by the allusions to the divine testimonies and God's house? With these questions in mind it will be interesting to survey the earliest history of Jewish interpretation as it relates to these five tantalising verses and their internal and external relationships.

Ancient Versions

The tradition of associating Psalm 93 with Friday is clearly an ancient one. The texts of the Septuagint and the Vulgate include a heading that describes it as a psalm of David "for the day before the sabbath when the earth was inhabited".[12] This same association with Friday is made in the Mishnah (*m. Tamid* 7:4) which lists the specific psalms said to have been recited in the Temple on each day of the week. The explanation for the connection with Friday by reference to the particular act of creation completed on that day is also to be found in the Babylonian Talmud (*b. Rosh Ha-Shanah* 31a), which notes that Friday was the day on which God completed his work (by creating man) and was therefore able to assume his kingship. This piece of exegesis goes beyond the mishnaic text and links v. 1 with the divine act of creation. Interestingly, 4QPs[b] reads נוה and not נאוה in v. 5, seeing here a noun yielding the sense of "habitation" rather than an epithet with the sense of "comely" and thus effecting a parallel with "your house" (ביתך).

---

[12] LXX: Εἰς τὴν ἡμέραν τοῦ προσαββάτου, ὅτε κατῴκισται ἡ γῆ. αἶνος ᾠδῆς τῷ Δαυιδ. Vulgate: *laus cantici David in die ante sabbatum quando inhabitata est terra.*

Talmud

Five passages, in addition to the two noted in the previous paragraph, also deserve attention in the present context. The first of these concerns the word וישרנה that describes an action on the part of the cows when they were bringing back the ark of the covenant to Beth-Shemesh (1 Sam 6:12). The word is linked in *b. 'Avodah Zarah* 24b with the Hebrew for a "song", and what the cows sang as they walked is variously identified by a number of *tanna'im* as Exodus 15, Isaiah 12:4, an anonymous (unidentified?) psalm, Psalm 98:1, Psalm 99:1, Psalm 93:1, and a *piyyuṭ*, possibly relating to Numbers 10:35. The identification with Psalm 93 is made by R. Samuel b. Naḥmani, an accomplished preacher in late third-century Lod, and appears to indicate his awareness of the liturgical importance of Psalm 93. Equally important is a tannaitic tradition (*b. Nedarim* 39b) that lists seven items that existed before the creation of the world, namely, Torah, repentance, heaven and hell (= "garden of Eden and Gehinnom"), God's throne of glory, the Temple and the name of the Messiah. The source for the primordial existence of the throne of glory is given as Psalm 93:2, indicating that the phrase נכון כסאך מאז and perhaps other parts of the psalm were given a cosmological interpretation.[13]

Three other talmudic texts are of no more than homiletical significance but should be cited for the sake of completeness. The later talmudic commentators are led a somewhat sorry dance by a playful piece of exegesis from the third-century teacher R. Yohanan (*b. Beṣah* 15b) which associates the tree with God's celestial power because of the use of the same stem (אדר) in both cases.[14] Secondly, the epithet אדיר is reported (*b. Menaḥot* 53a) to have been the subject of a homiletical discourse by the (third century?) *'amora* R. Ezra, grandson of R. Avtolos, which linked Psalm 93:4 with Psalm 16:3 and Exodus 15:10. Finally, the link made by a young pupil between Psalm 90:1 (תפלה למשה) and Psalm 93:5 (יהוה לארך ימים) helped the fourth-century Babylonian *'amora* R. Ḥagga to understand that Moses had to pray intensely before he succeeded in seeing divine patience restored. This midrash relates to the broader rabbinic view (Midrash Tehillim 90.3)

---

[13] תניא שבעה דברים נבראו קודם שנברא העולם ואלו הן: תורה, ותשובה, גן עדן, וגיהנם, כסא הכבוד, ובית המקדש, ושמו של משיח...כסא כבוד דכתיב 'נכון כסאך מאז'.

[14] See the summary of their attempted explanations in the Steinsalz edition of this tractate (Jerusalem, 1982) at the foot of p. 67.

that Psalms 90–100 represent eleven prayers of Moses. But precisely how this story (*b. Sanhedrin* 111b) relates to the one told in Midrash Tehillim (cited below) and what we are to make of the textual variants is not immediately clear and requires closer attention in an independent context.[15] What, at least, is demonstrated by these three homilies is that Psalm 93 was not an unpopular choice of text for the preachers of the early talmudic period. There appear to be no parallel homilies cited in the Talmud Yerushalmi.

Minor tractates

Those smaller post-talmudic tractates that are generally dated to the Geonic period (covering the seventh to the eleventh centuries) also contain some passages that are of interest to this discussion. Although there are some instances in which the traditions recorded there may have earlier origins, these particular passages appear to reflect developments that are post-talmudic. In the first of them, in 'Avoth de-Rabbi Nathan, the tradition about the use of Psalm 93 in the Temple, already encountered above, appears to have been slightly expanded. Although the Hebrew text (מהו אומר) is ambiguous, it is possible to explain it as reporting that Adam recited the same psalms that were recited in the Temple on each of the days of the week.[16] The attribution to Adam may reflect an interest in promoting the recitation of these daily psalms by adding to the custom's historical prestige.

Three liturgical instructions recorded in *Soferim* testify to a growing use, within the statutory rabbinic liturgy, of biblical verses in general and of verses from the book of Psalms in particular. In the first of these mention is again made of the psalms said to have been recited by the Levites in the Temple but it is then categorically explained that use of biblical verses in the appropriate liturgical context is equivalent to rebuilding the altar and making an offering on it (שכל המזכיר פסוק

---

[15] ר' חגא הוה סליק ואזיל בדרגא דבי רבה בר שילה שמעיה לההוא ינוקא דאמר עדותיך נאמנו מאד לביתך נאוה קדש ה' לאורך ימים וסמיך ליה תפלה למשה וגו' אמר ש"מ ארך אפים ראה. Genizah fragment Cambridge University Library, T-S F2(1).122 reads: צער גדול היה למשה רבינו עד שהחזירו ארך אפים למקומו.

[16] Recension A, ed. S. Schechter (Vienna, London and Frankfurt-am-Main, 1887; reprinted with a prolegomenon by M. Kister [New York and Jerusalem, 1997]), p. 5. In his English translation Eli Cashdan (London, 1965: p. 10) takes it as a reference to what Adam said each day while in his version Judah Goldin (New Haven and London, 1955: p. 11) refers it to the Levites in the Temple, as in the talmudic passage.

(בעונתו מעלה עליו כאילו בנה מזבח חדש והקריב עליו קרבן). The second
lists various verses to be recited on removing the Torah scroll from
the ark, including an amalgam of Psalm 10:16, Psalm 93:1 and Exodus
15:18 stressing God's eternity. In the third, reference is made to the use
(in whole or in part) of Psalm 93 among the selection of chapters from
the book of Psalms used as introductory material to inspire the correct,
spiritual frame of mind before the recitation of the prayers proper.[17]

Two comments in *Kallah Rabbathi* are based, respectively, on the
opening and concluding verses of Psalm 93. The verse about God's royal
clothing inspires the explanation, in Aramaic, that the exercise of God's
great power and glory includes being eternally exalted in his heights
and robed in excellency as in a cloak. This may be seen as part of the
attempt being made in this post-talmudic anthology to offer various
forms of ethical and spiritual edification, in this case by expatiating on
the nature of God's power. The phrase יהוה לאורך ימים is expounded in
the context of a commendation of the Torah for its manifold qualities.
It is said to indicate that one of the Torah's many attributes is that its
protective power is everlasting, providing reward in both this and the
next world. What is here being demonstrated is an interest in using
appropriate biblical verses to develop theological notions concerning
the divine nature.[18]

Midrashim

This theological tendency is also to be found in Midrash Tehillim which,
again, may include some earlier material but reflects, on the whole,
post-talmudic thinking. It constitutes an anthology of comments on
each psalm which probably represents an edited version dating from
the late Geonic period in the land of Israel, at least as far as the first
section, including our psalm, is concerned. On the word מלך in v. 1, it
argues, by reference to Jeremiah 10:6–7 and 1:5, that God's sovereignty,
as Jeremiah's prophecy, is directed not only to Israel but to the whole
world, thereby stressing the universal aspect of the Psalmist's message.

---

[17] M. Higger (ed.), *Massekheth Soferim* (New York, 1937), 18.2 (p. 312), 14.4 (p. 256),
18.1 (p. 308); ET (London, 1965), 18.1 (p. 300), 14.8 (p. 278), 17.11 (p. 298).
[18] 52b and 54b; ET (London, 1965), 3.4 (p. 449) and 8 (p. 507). On Kallah Rabbathi see M. B. Lerner, "The External Tractates", in S. Safrai and P. J. Tomson (eds.),
*The Literature of the Sages, First Part: Oral Tora, Halakha, Mishna, Tosefta, Talmud,
External Tractates* (Assen/Maastricht and Philadelphia, 1987), pp. 393–97.

In his comment on לבש in v. 1 the homilist cites seven scriptural instances in which God is described as being clothed. In five of these (Exodus 15, Isaiah 59, Jeremiah 51, Esther 8, Isaiah 63) he is clothed as a warrior who defeats the Egyptians, Babylonians, Medes, Greeks and Edomites, while the remaining two relate to the messianic age (Daniel 7:9) and to the revelation at Sinai (Psalm 93:1).[19] The phrase עז התאזר describes how Israel received the benefit of the divine strength during that revelation.[20]

The word כסא in v. 2 elicits the comment that God's throne of glory was one of the six (not seven) things already in existence before the creation of the world. While this list follows the passage in *b. Nedarim* 39b in including – as well as the throne – the Torah, the Temple, the Messiah and repentance, it adds Israel but omits the garden of Eden and Gehinnom. The notion of God's throne is therefore seen as standing outside the normal worlds of nature and history. The references to water in vv. 2–4 indicate that primordial waters praised God. During the process of creation the mighty waters had threatened to overpower the whole universe but God set controls on them so that they were limited to seas and lakes, as well as to the depths of the oceans. The waters are also said to represent the arrogant Philistines who captured the ark and were punished by God, in addition to those who destroyed the Temple and the nations who carried Israel off into exile, who will ultimately be wiped out by waters sent by God against them. The aggadic interpretation therefore wavers between the waters associated with the act of creation and waters as a metaphor for the enemies of Israel.[21]

The homilist takes the word עדתיך in v. 5 to mean that Moses advises God that what He does to the Jewish people accurately testifies to his evaluation of Israel and her adversaries. The success of the Temple and the Torah silences the wicked nations while the humiliation of these two Jewish institutions strengthens the voice of Israel's enemies.[22] God is asked to restore the holiness of the Temple, but on this occasion on a permanent basis. The phrase יהוה לארך ימים is understood to allude

[19] S. Buber (ed.), *Midrasch Tehillim (Schocher Tob)* (Vilna, 1891), p. 413; ET by W. G. Braude, *The Midrash on Psalms* (New Haven, 1959), pp. 124–25, 498.

[20] The Buber text refers to Psalm 29:11 but, as Braude suggests, following Reifmann, a more appropriate reference would be to Psalm 93:1, then followed by the phrase: כנגד עוז שנתן לעמו בסיני.

[21] Buber, pp. 414–16; Braude, pp. 125–29, 499.

[22] אמר משה לפני הקב"ה רבש"ע השפלת קולה של תורה וקולו של בית המקדש והגבהת קולן של רשעים.

to God's patience, that is, his ארך אפים (Exodus 34:6). In the context of a discussion of some of God's attributes, the issue is raised of this great divine quality. The story is told that R. Ḥaggai was once walking through a double colonnade in Tiberias when he heard the youngsters in the synagogue class reciting Psalm 93:5 (יהוה לארך ימים), followed immediately by Psalm 94:1 (אל נקמות יהוה). From this he derived that God takes his time in taking revenge on the wicked but punishes the righteous immediately. The midrashic lesson is apparently that the Jews have paid the price of their wrongdoing while the wicked nations have their punishment awaiting them in the future, evidently intended as some sort of consolation to the long-suffering Jewish listener.[23]

This reference would appear to be to the third-century *'amora* R. Ḥaggai and the question arises as to how this can be harmonized with the similar story told in *b. Sanhedrin* 111b and cited above. It is unclear whether there were two such teachers with this name, one in third-century Palestine and the other in fourth-century Babylonia, or only one, who spent time in both centres. The talmudic text, as already indicated above, is in any event problematic, so it would not be surprising to find that errors have crept into one or both of the transmissions.

Summary of rabbinic interpretations

What emerges, unsurprisingly, from these talmudic, post-talmudic and midrashic sources is that Psalm 93 was from the earliest times regarded as of liturgical importance – at least potential if not actual – and that this importance grew during the Geonic period. It was also seen as belonging to the group Psalms 90–100, comprising the prayers of Moses. Parts of Psalm 93 were associated by the exegetes with the creation of the world and with their notions of cosmology while others were regarded as conveying central teachings about the power, sovereignty and patience of God and the special qualities of the Torah, as well as the universalism of God's message. The references to water were understood as a metaphor for the enemies of Israel and various words and expressions were fairly popular with the Jewish homilists.

---

[23] Buber, pp. 416–17; Braude, pp. 129–30, 499.

Liturgy

As is now widely recognised, the process of standardizing the rabbinic liturgy made considerable progress between the Geonic period
and the high Middle Ages.[24] It will now therefore be of value to this
study to examine the manner in which the liturgical use of Psalm 93
developed during those centuries and what we may conclude therefrom
with regard to the history of its interpretation. Although the Mishnah
already makes reference to the recitation of Psalm 93 in the Temple
on Fridays, there is no clear-cut evidence that a similar custom was
practised in the talmudic synagogue. The references to Psalm 93:1 in
b. Rosh Ha-Shanah 31 and *b. ʿAvodah Zarah* 24b indicate that there
was a special interest in, and consciousness of, its liturgical possibilities
but one cannot be sure that this expressed itself in a formal inclusion
in the Friday morning liturgy of the day. The praise accorded to the
use of biblical verses on appropriate occasions, together with a specific
note about the psalms for Friday and Saturday (as recorded in the post-
talmudic tractate *Soferim* and cited above), would appear to indicate at
least a limited liturgical use of Psalms 92–93 by the late Geonic period.
One such use is widely recorded among Genizah manuscript fragments
reflecting the rite of the land of Israel before or just after the Crusader
period. It relates not to a daily recitation of an appropriate psalm but
to the use of Psalms 92–93 on the sabbath.

The two psalms were recited together not only in the evening but also
on Saturday morning. Although it is essentially the first one of these
that is strictly relevant to the sabbath, they were regarded virtually as
inseparable so that Psalm 93 was often recited immediately after Psalm
92. This also had an impact on the liturgical poems (*piyyuṭim*) for the
sabbath in which verses from both psalms were incorporated. What
is more, Psalm 93 also came to be widely used as an introduction to
the other blocks of psalms being recited on a festival, even when that
festival did not coincide with the sabbath. Although much of the rite of
the land of Israel disappeared after the early thirteenth century, there
are remnants of the earlier use of Psalms 92–93 on Friday evenings in
the Romaniote and Persian liturgies. According to Fleischer, there may
even be a hint of a use of a daily psalm, other than on the sabbath, in
some Genizah manuscripts, although this is by no means unequivocal,

---

[24] S. C. Reif, *Judaism and Hebrew Prayer* (Cambridge, 1993), pp. 122–52.

since many others do not appear to attest to such a custom. The rites of some late medieval oriental, North African, Provençal and Sefardi communities included the recitation of Psalms 92–93 before the statutory prayers on Friday evening, but this was not widely adopted by the Ashkenazi and other prayer-books until after the sixteenth century.[25]

The Babylonian rite and the prayer-books that follow it reflect a different situation. With regard to the daily recitation of an appropriate psalm, there is no mention of the custom in the early liturgical manuscripts of Naṭronai Gaon (ninth century) or Saʿadya Gaon (tenth century) while the text in *Seder Rav ʿAmram* may simply be a repetition of the Mishnah in *Tamid* 7:4 as a whole, rather than a text of which a different part had to be read each day. There are indeed some manuscripts of Saʿadya Gaon's prayer-book that record the use of Psalms 92–93 on sabbath morning but it is possible that these represent examples of Palestinian influence on the authentic Babylonian ritual.[26] The mishnaic passage from *Tamid* also occurs in the *Maḥzor Vitry*, emanating from Simḥah of Vitry of the school of Rashi, but there the custom is attached to the sabbath prayers and not those of the weekdays. In any event, the unreliability of the texts of the prayer-book of ʿAmram Gaon prevents us from assuming that he himself included it, in whatever form, in the ninth century. But *Seder Rav ʿAmram* does often reflect the customs of the post-Geonic period, typically of about the twelfth century, and such a dating for the introduction of the daily recitation of Psalm 93, with the other psalms listed in Mishnah *Tamid*, would match other evidence.[27]

Maimonides, for instance, records such a liturgical usage as that of "some folk" although it is unclear whether he is referring to those in his place of domicile in twelfth-century Egypt, those who emigrated there from the land of Israel, or the custom of Muslim Spain from where he hailed. Nevertheless, it appears not to have become widespread as

[25] E. Fleischer, *Eretz-Israel Prayer and Prayer-Rituals as Portrayed in the Geniza Documents* (Heb.; Jerusalem, 1988), pp. 38, 164, 167–78, 190, 192, 213; I. M. Ta-Shma, *The Early Ashkenazic Prayer: Literary and Historical Aspects* (Heb.; Jerusalem, 2003), p. 151.
[26] L. Ginzberg, *Geonica*, 2 (New York, 1909), pp. 114–17; I. Davidson, S. Assaf, and B. I. Joel (eds.), *Siddur R. Saadya Gaon. Kitāb Ǧāmiʾ Aṣ-Ṣalawāt Wat-Tasābīḥ* (Jerusalem, ²1963); E. D. Goldschmidt (ed.), *Seder Rav ʿAmram Gaʾon* (Jerusalem, 1971), p. 40; Fleischer, p. 197.
[27] S. Hurwitz (ed.), *Maḥzor Vitry*, 2 vols. (Nuremburg, ²1923), 1, p. 176; R. Brody, "Liturgical Uses of the Book of Psalms in the Geonic Period", in J. L. Kugel (ed.), *Prayers that Cite Scripture* (Cambridge, MA, and London, 2006), pp. 63–64.

early as that century, since Abraham ben Nathan of Lunel in his *Sefer Ha-Manhig* in the early thirteenth century draws attention to a "fine custom" that he has observed in the city of Toledo and its environs to recite towards the end of the prayers a psalm suitable for each day. Interestingly, the British Museum manuscript of *Seder Rav ʿAmram*, which dates from about the fourteenth century, expands each of the brief Psalm references in that mishnaic passage into the whole psalm text, giving the distinct impression that in the time of its scribe they were being recited individually on the specific day.[28] By that time, too, it has become widespread to include Psalms 92–93 among those added to the morning psalms on sabbaths.

Although the detailed liturgical history of the use of Psalms 92–93 remains unclear and more concentrated research remains to be done, it is possible to offer some tentative conclusions that will contribute to the present analysis. It appears to be safe to presuppose that Psalm 93 had a significant liturgical history among the Jews of the land of Israel as part of the collections of psalms for sabbaths and festivals that preceded the statutory prayers, while there was a more limited use in the Babylonian rite. In the course of the high Middle Ages it eventually won a place at the end of the daily prayers on Fridays. It also became customary in that era to add Psalms 92–93 to the sabbath morning psalms. Moreover, it appears likely that the ultimately widespread custom of reciting both Psalm 92 and Psalm 93 before the formal commencement of the sabbath evening prayers is a remnant of the Jewish liturgy of pre-Crusader Palestine. It was not until the late medieval and early modern period that the custom of reciting the whole of Mishnah *Tamid* 7:4 on a daily basis became widespread.

Especially important in the present context is the reason why Psalm 93 stubbornly remained attached to so many liturgical contexts where it might have given way to an exclusive use of Psalm 92 and why it even functioned as an introductory liturgical passage. Here N. Wieder makes an important point about its theological content. Having earlier cited numerous examples of texts being used in the liturgy because they stress the eternity of God, he draws attention to the phrases נכון כסאך מאז מעולם אתה (v. 2) and יהוה לאורך ימים (v. 5) and points out that

---

[28] E. D. Goldschmidt, "The Oxford Ms. of Maimonides' Book of Prayer", in his *On Jewish Liturgy: Essays on Prayer and Religious Poetry* (Heb.; Jerusalem, 1978), p. 205; Y. Raphael (ed.), *Sefer Hamanhig. Rulings and Customs. Abraham ben Nathan of Lunel*, 2 vols. (Heb.; Jerusalem, 1978), 1, p. 107; Goldschmidt (ed.), 1971, p. 40.

they refer to the two dimensions of eternity, the first alluding to the past and the second to the future.[29] He notes that Ibn Ezra also stresses the psalm's message about eternity. What may be added on the basis of the above findings is that other aspects of its theological messages also became sufficiently attractive to the worshippers to warrant its more extensive use in the regular liturgy.

Medieval commentaries

In the high Middle Ages, the Jewish exegetes' concern with making greater use of biblical texts for the application of Jewish religious law, theology and liturgy than for achieving deeper literary and linguistic understanding was reversed in a number of intellectual circles. Although earlier interpretations had not been without their interest in the basic sense of a biblical word, phrase or story, a significant change took place in the climate of Jewish thought that was precipitated on the one hand by the influence of Islamic (and some Christian) rationalists, philosophers and linguists, and on the other by a Jewish desire to demonstrate to Christians that the latter's illumination of the Old Testament by way of the New Testament did not represent an accurate explanation of the original sense of the relevant texts. Particularly in France, Spain, and Provence between the eleventh and fourteenth centuries, there developed a kind of exegesis that was at first not wholly satisfied with anything that was *derash* (applied sense) rather than *peshaṭ* (literal sense) and ultimately grew into an almost obsessive tendency to reject out of hand any explanation of the text that did not analyse it as a piece of literature.[30] The novel nature of this exegesis, as well indeed as the manner in which it so often speaks to the modern scientific mind, makes it a potentially attractive component in any current treatment of texts from the Hebrew Bible. The problem is that few of those who occupy themselves with such treatment are competent and familiar enough with the genre to allow them to exploit it in any adequate fashion. It

---

[29] N. Wieder, *The Formation of Jewish Liturgy in the East and the West: A Collection of Essays*, 2 vols. (Heb.; Jerusalem, 1998), 1, p. 125.

[30] For a brief summary of this part of Jewish exegetical history see S. C. Reif, "Aspects of the Jewish Contribution to Biblical Interpretation", in J. Barton (ed.), *The Cambridge Companion to Biblical Interpretation* (Cambridge, 1998), pp. 150–53.

may therefore broadly be found useful if some of the comments made in such circles about Psalm 93 are now summarized.[31]

Rashi

R. Solomon b. Isaac ("Rashi", 1040–1105) was the oustanding exegete of eleventh-century Franco-Germany who made great efforts to provide his students with a mixed diet so that they could taste and enjoy contextual as well as applied interpretations. He succeeded so well that he became for the Jews (and for some Christians) one of the best known and most widely used of the biblical commentators.[32] For Rashi, the psalmist is looking forward to a time when the world will be glad at the acknowledgement of God's sovereignty. Meanwhile, he complains about the arrogance of the nations towards God but expresses confidence that God's power will ultimately prove greater than theirs. He regards as thoroughly authentic the prophetic comments about God's holy habitation and is convinced that they will be fulfilled even if this takes a long time. Rashi also offers unadorned linguistic comments on the words דכים and נאוה. In sum, he sees the Psalm as a reference to the messianic age when God's authority and power will be established and welcomed, when the conceit of the nations will be shown to be vacuous, and when the words of Scripture will finally be implemented. The references to God's clothing are apparently taken as metaphors for his power and mighty waters as literary figures for the nations. The divine throne will in the future be as well established as it was in the past. A good example of his approach is to be found in his comment on v. 3:

> נשאו נהרות יי: God is here being addressed by way of appeal and complaint. The sense is "God, these nations who stream out like flowing rivers, noisily raise their voices and always increase the level of their low

---

[31] For the Hebrew texts, I have employed the excellent editions reproduced in *Mikra'ot Gedolot Haketer, Psalms*, part II, ed. M. Cohen, Ramat-Gan, Bar-Ilan University Press, 2003, 80–81.

[32] From among the extensive literature on Rashi see S. Kamin, *Rashi's Exegetical Categorization in Respect to the Distinction between Peshat and Derash* (Heb.; Jerusalem, 1986); G. Sed-Rajna (ed.), *Rashi 1040–1990. Hommage à Ephraïm E. Urbach* (Paris, 1993); A. Grossman, *The Early Sages of France. Their Lives, Leadership and Works* (Heb.; Jerusalem, 1996), pp. 121–253; M. I. Gruber, *Rashi's Commentary on Psalms* (Leiden and Boston, 2004), pp. 589–91 and 846, where the text differs slightly from the one used here (see n. 31 above).

growling, in order to behave arrogantly towards you." The root דכא always has the sense of "low and debased".[33]

Ibn Ezra

R. Abraham b. Meir Ibn Ezra (1089–1164), who was born in Spain but travelled widely in western Europe, was a enthusiast for the rational and the literal and would sometimes use these, often in a cryptic or elliptic style, to challenge long-established rabbinic traditions. He also made wide use of the physical sciences of his day, addressing himself primarily to the intellectuals rather than the more common Jewish folk targeted by Rashi.[34] For Ibn Ezra, the psalmist uses regal and military metaphors to describe God's power and the manner in which it ensures the continuing existence of the earth. That power is represented in the higher spheres by the throne of glory which has been occupied by God from eternity. Further indications of God's power may be identified in the movements of rivers and seas and in the winds which transform gentle waves into vigorous tides. The sounds emanating from the celestial spheres are even more powerful than these natural phenomena but only those with the required spiritual faculties can hear them. God's revealed message is even more reliable than those phenomena because of the eternity of his presence. The concluding reference to "length of days" may allude to this eternity or represent the psalmist's prayer that God's temple will last for a long time. Ibn Ezra has created links between what appear to be disparate elements in the psalm, essentially seeing it as a description of God's power in nature and revelation, and an affirmation of his eternity. He employs Neoplatonic cosmology to make the association between the lower and higher spheres and appears to polemicize against those who are incapable of receiving the divine

---

[33] לשון צעקה וקובלן זה. אתה יי הנה האומות השוטפים כנהרות נשאו קולם ויהמיון ואת דוך עמקי נבכיהם ישאו ויגביהו תמיד להתגאות נגדך. כל לשון דכא לשון עומק ושפלות.

[34] See, for example, F. Díaz Esteban (ed.), *Abraham Ibn Ezra Y Su Tiempo. Abraham Ibn Ezra and his Age* (Madrid, 1990); U. Simon, *Four Approaches to the Book of Psalms from Saadiah Gaon to Abraham Ibn Ezra* (ET Albany, NY, 1991 [Heb. 1982]); I. Lancaster, *Deconstructing the Bible. Abraham ibn Ezra's Introduction to the Torah* (London, 2003); E. Silver, "Ibn Ezra and his Commentary on Psalms", in the companion volume to *The Parma Psalter. A Thirteenth Century Illuminated Hebrew Book of Psalms with a Commentary by Abraham Ibn Ezra. A Facsimile Edition* (London, 1996), pp. 149–275. The text there differs slightly but not significantly from the one used here.

message. Ibn Ezra's comment on v. 4 demonstrates how he links the apparently disparate parts of Psalm 93:

> v. 4: מקולות: One thing that is even greater than the noise of many waters that are themselves powerful, such as the waves of the sea, is the power of God on high. This proves that sounds do emanate from the celestial spheres, as is reported in Ezekiel's vision (1:24), כקול מים רבים. But these sounds cannot be heard by those who are deaf to them, just as the awesome acts of God cannot be seen by those who are blind to them (Isaiah 42:18).[35]

Qimḥi

R. David b. Joseph ("Redaq", 1160–1235) came from a Provençal family of linguists and exegetes and the object of his commentaries was to synthesize what he regarded as all the best and varied parts of the Jewish exegetical tradition. His comments are clearly expressed and wide-ranging and it is not uncommon for him to make use of them in order to challenge Christian interpretations.[36] For Qimḥi, Psalms 93–101 refer to the messianic age. They begin by asserting that at that future time God will be acknowledged not only as equitable (as at the conclusion of Psalm 92) but also as the universal ruler, the only one "clothed in majesty" and "dressed as a warrior". Given that degree of acknowledgement, national leaders will no longer follow the example of Nebuchadnezzar, Pharaoh and the kings of Assyria and Tyre but will leave the earth secure and untroubled by war. God's eternal occupation of his throne of glory will also receive wide recognition. The rivers and seas of the psalm are metaphors for the armies of evil that will attack Jerusalem at the end of time since they are as noisy, as destructive and as troublesome as torrents of water. However noisy and powerful these hordes, God in his greater might will lay them low. The "reliable testimonies" refer to the prophetic oracles about the end of time which will then be truly fulfilled and seen by all to have been wholly authentic. The temple will never again be destroyed but will,

---

[35] יותר מקולות מים רבים שהם אדירים שהם משברי ים יותר אדיר השם במרום. וזה לאות כי לגלגלים קולות וכן כתוב ביחזקאל כקול מים רבים. ואלה הקולות לא ישמעו החרשים כאשר לא יביטו העורים מעשה השם הנוראים.

[36] J. Baker and E. W. Nicholson (ed. and tr.), *The Commentary of Rabbi David Kimhi on Psalms CXX–CL* (UCOP 22; Cambridge, 1973); F. E. Talmage, *David Kimhi. The Man and the Commentaries* (Cambridge, MA, and London, 1975).

in its great beauty, be the object of widespread pleasure and the site of universal pilgrimage. Qimḥi consistently supports his interpretations by reference to other prophetic verses and includes grammatical and lexicographical comments on the words דכים, תמוט/תכון, and נאוה. He relates the whole psalm to the novel circumstances of the messianic period, explains the roles of the various participants in these future events, and points to similar thoughts about universal recognition, the messianic age, and the role of the temple as expressed by the Hebrew prophets. His comment on the first part of v. 5 relates to the reliability of the prophetic message:

עדותיך נאמנו מאד: These testimonies are the scriptural words of your prophets which bear witness to your kingship and will then be truly fulfilled. The use of the word מאד indicates that no one at that time will have any doubt whatsoever about this. לביתך נאוה קדש: In this case the *alef* has a *ḥatef pataḥ* while in the other instances of this word in the Hebrew Bible (Ps 33:1, Isa 52:7 and Song 1:10) it is unvocalized.[37]

Me'iri

Menaḥem b. Solomon Me'iri (1249–1316), also from a Provençal family, spent his whole life in Perpignan and established a reputation as a lucid expounder of Talmud and Bible. Another synthesizer, with a relatively open mind towards Christianity, philosophy and contemporary science, Me'iri includes in his commentary on the Psalms both the literal sense and traditional religious teachings.[38] He sees here a creation psalm, the phrases about the powerful waters in verses 3–4 constituting a reference to the events described in Genesis 1:9 and to the defined areas of the earth as laid out by God. The phrases about the divine throne and the earth are also to be understood cosmologically, alluding to the various parts of the universe. God's majesty, unlike its human equivalent, is constructive rather than destructive and is relevant here because it is seen by all as a powerful and miraculous ability to exist eternally and to create a universe *ex nihilo*, with everything in its required form and totally perfect. The final verse makes an association between all the

---

[37] והם דבריך הכתובים על ידי נביאיך המעידים על מלכותך, יתקיימו אז מאד, כלומר שלא יהיה לשום אדם ספק בלבו אז בזה. לביתך נאוה קדש האל"ף מונעת בחטף פתח והשאר נחה בהם האל"ף.

[38] J. Cohn (ed.), *Commentarius Libri Psalmorum*: פירוש לספר תהלים (Jerusalem, 1936 [²1970]).

matters of religious faith known from Jewish tradition and belief in
God's creation of the world. Such a faith, in order to be perfect, must go
beyond what can be understood by the logical minds of humanity and
the psalmist is expressing the view that only those with such a level of
faith are worthy of sanctifying and beautifying God's shrine and praying
for the survival of the temple, when it is still standing, and, later, for
its restoration and permanence in the messianic age. In this preferred
exegesis, Me'iri is clearly anxious for the message of the Psalm to be
seen as theological, cosmological and doctrinal. He sets out for the
reader of the psalm the relative and related roles of God, the universe,
monotheistic humanity and pious Jewry. The act of creation is seen
to lead on to God's universal recognition and Jewish religious faith is
linked with the historical and eschatological fate of the Jerusalem shrine.
Having first expressed himself in these somewhat unique terms, Me'iri
then goes on to cite the alternative interpretation according to which
Psalm 93 refers to the messianic age. Although often expressed in his
own language, his comments here align to a great extent with those of
Qimḥi. There are, however, some variations. He defines the word מלך
as what would in modern times be called a prophetic perfect. The phrase
לארך ימים is regarded by him as an allusion to the messianic age. He
rejects the derivation of נאוה from the stem אוה and the consequent
rendering that links it to the pleasure to be taken by humanity in the
restored temple. Me'iri's introductory comment on Psalm 93 is a fine
combination of cosmology and theology:

ה' מלך גאות לבש: It seems to me that this psalm also alludes to the
creation of the world, particularly to the exposure of the land when "the
waters were gathered to one place" (Gen 1:9). These four words convey
the sense that the celestial and earthly beings will both recognise some
of God's powerful and miraculous ability and that he girded himself with
strength (התאזר עז) and might when he created the world *ex nihilo* and
when he permanently fixed the earth in the middle of the world בל תמוט
so that it can never move off in another direction.[39]

גם זה המזמור נראה לי שרומז על חדוש העולם ובפרט על הגלות הארץ בהקוות [39]
המים אל מקום אחד. ואמ' ה' מלך גאות לבש כלומ' עליונים ותחתונים יכירו כיצד
מעלתו העצומה ובו התאזר עוז וגבורה בחדשו העולם יש מאין ובהכינו תבל באמצע
העולם בל תמוט ותנוע לשום צד.

Issues

A broad assessment of the themes that are of interest to these medieval Jewish commentators will obviously be instructive. They wish to establish a context for the psalm and to relate it to the power and eternity of God, as well as to his revealed message. They contrast worldly and divine rulership, as well as Israel and the nations. Some elements of doctrine are noted but not expanded or significantly promoted, while there is little interest in practical *halakhah* or synagogal liturgy. Expressions are explained metaphorically for the sake of arriving at a literal meaning and there is a concern with cosmology as well as with the ultimate future and the status of the Temple at that time.

Conclusions

One must of course be wary of drawing any wide-ranging conclusions on the basis of such a limited range of sample material as that cited above. It does, however, draw one's attention to the fact that sources that are historically and religiously distant from each other may have a number of strikingly similar or even parallel statements to make or approaches to champion. This does not by any means imply that we may expect modern critical viewpoints among the ancient or medieval sources or that any interpretation of religious ideology offered within such viewpoints is to be judged in the same way as its earlier counterparts. What may nonetheless be stated with confidence is that a thematic analysis is as important and as revealing as an historical one. As Adele Berlin wisely expressed it, there are "crucial differences in the purposes of traditional exegetes and modern literary scholars but major similarities in the ways that they work with the biblical text".[40] Not only can modern interpreters of the Hebrew Bible find value in the traditional Jewish "treasure of lexical and grammatical observations" but they may also benefit from an "unlimited supply of raw material" throughout the rabbinic corpora.[41]

---

[40] A. Berlin, "On the Use of Traditional Jewish Exegesis in the Modern Literary Study of the Bible", in M. Cogan, B. L. Eichler and J. H. Tigay (eds.), *Tehillah le-Moshe: Biblical and Judaic Studies in Honor of Moshe Greenberg* (Winona Lake, IN, 1997), pp. 173–83.
[41] Ibid.

The summaries of the modern, ancient, early rabbinic and medieval exegesis of Psalm 93 offered above uncover as many common factors as divergent ones and illuminate the degree to which an early generation's contribution, whatever the variations of methodology, may well remain valuable to those interpreters who are tackling the same biblical text many centuries later. Sometimes it merely assists with a philological point or the explanation of a figure of speech; at others it may clarify the broader context or stress the centrality of a particular religious message. There are undoubtedly also occasions on which it simply inspires a knowing smile. In whatever way it aids the process of current exegesis, it will almost always, as John Emerton has consistently understood, prove itself worthy of the close attention that it demands in order for its own sense to become apparent to the contemporary reader. Consequently, I like to think that the discussions I have had with him over the years have played some role in advancing knowledge of some of the many scriptural texts that are challenging to our two intellects as well as close to both his heart and mine.[42]

---

[42] When this article was in proof, I received the latest issue of *Tarbiz* in which further evidence relating to the post-talmudic liturgical use of Psalm 93 is cited from Genizah texts by Uri Ehrlich; see his "*Ma'aseh Bereshit* and *Shir Shel Yom* in the Early Siddur: New Finds from the Cairo Geniza", *Tarbiz* 78 (2009), pp. 189–202.

GREGORY OF NYSSA:
THE SUPERSCRIPTIONS OF THE PSALMS*

Patrick D. Miller

Among the works of the fourth-century theologian, Gregory of Nyssa, is a treatment of the superscriptions that appear at the beginning of most of the Psalms (116 of the 150 Psalms). The superscriptions have been much discussed in modern Psalms interpretation, though there is little certainty about such important critical questions as to who is responsible for their addition to the psalms and when. It is generally agreed that they have little to do with the original authorship of the psalms or their content but belong more to the compilation and ordering of the psalms. Many of the superscriptions contain technical terms, musical or otherwise, whose precise definition is not always certain. Their significance for interpreting the psalms has been rather minor in modern Psalms study, symbolized best by their omission from the translation of the Psalms in the modern New English Bible, a move corrected in the later Revised English Bible.[1]

That was not always the case. Ancient Christian and Jewish interpreters took the superscriptions – or inscriptions, as Gregory and others call them – very seriously and often saw in them basic clues to the meaning and relevance of the rest of the psalm.[2] For the early interpreters, they were a kind of title for the psalm. Gregory's treatise on the superscriptions is a rich example of the possibilities explicit or implicit in them. Indeed, while most interpreters discuss these

---

* It is an honour to contribute to this celebration of the life and work of John Emerton, who has been my neighbour, friend, and colleague over many years. The depth and value of his scholarship is matched only by his gracious kindness to the many persons whose lives he has touched.

[1] Note the comment of Brevard Childs: "By the middle of the nineteenth century the Psalm titles, which had been thought to provide the key to psalm interpretation, had been almost universally abandoned as late, inauthentic, and insignificant" (*Introduction to the Old Testament as Scripture* [Philadelphia, 1979], p. 509).

[2] B. E. Daley, "Training for 'the Good Ascent': Gregory of Nyssa's Homily on the Sixth Psalm", in P. M. Blowers, A. R. Christman, D. G. Hunter, and R. D. Young (eds.), *In Dominico Eloquio – In Lordly Eloquence: Essays on Patristic Exegesis in Honor of Robert Louis Wilken*, (Grand Rapids, 2002), p. 195.

superscriptions in the context of commentary on the whole, Gregory reversed the process and discussed the content of many of the psalms via an interpretation of the superscriptions.[3] While the focus is on the inscriptions, the whole is a major work of Psalm interpretation that looks both at many individual psalms and also at the Psalter as a whole. It is a significant bridge between early church interpreters and contemporary theological interpretation of the Psalms.

Gregory's Psalms study consists of two parts. In Part I, he seeks first of all to identify the aim of the Psalter, which he finds revealed in the very first word of Psalm 1, 'ašrê, "blessed." That is, blessedness is the ultimate aim of the Psalter and of the virtuous life, and the Psalms provide a description of the way to achieve that blessedness. Psalm 1, as a whole, is central to identifying this goal and the way, which includes three things: rejection of the way of evil or wickedness, meditation on things that are sublime, and the likeness to God. These are aspects of the way of virtue that Gregory found in almost anything he studied, so it is not surprising that he uncovers them in the Psalter. Yet, his reading makes sense, especially of the first two parts of virtue, which are clearly evident in Psalm 1. The final one, likeness to God, which is the ultimate aim of the virtuous or Christian life, is evident for Gregory in the image of the transplanted tree (Ps. 1:3) "to which the life which has been perfected through virtue is likened" (I. 8).[4] Before going further, he elaborates on these dimensions of virtue, drawing upon Psalm 1 and other psalms, in the course of which he makes a powerful claim for the significance of music, its power to make the meditation on the words pleasant – like honey added to a bitter medicine – to subdue the passions, and to join the human community with the whole of nature and creation in the joyful praise of God.

In the rest of Part I, Gregory turns to the order of the Psalter, calling attention to the division of the Psalter into five parts or books and focusing on the first psalm in each of the books. This is because he sees in these five books stages in the ascent to the virtuous life and the initial psalms in each case as key directives. The first psalm in each book

---

[3] As far as is known, Gregory did not write a commentary on the Psalms and only one extant sermon on a Psalm exists, his homily on Psalm 6, referred to in the previous note.

[4] R. E. Heine, *Gregory of Nyssa's Treatise on the Inscriptions of the Psalms: Introduction, Translation, and Notes* (Oxford Early Christian Studies; Oxford, 1995), p. 85. Unless otherwise indicated, all quotations of the treatise are taken from Heine's translation.

is a pointer to the next step in the journey or the ascent. Perhaps his clearest explanation of this movement is at the beginning of his homily on Psalm 6, where he draws on the Psalms to make his point:

> Those who are "progressing from strength to strength," [Ps. 83:8 (LXX)] according to the prophet's words of blessing, and who are accomplishing good "ascents in their own hearts" [Ps. 83:6 (LXX)] first grasp hold of a good thought and then are led along by it towards a thought that is higher still; in this way, the ascent to the very summit takes place in the soul. So, "reaching out always to what lies ahead" [Phil. 3:13], a person never ceases to travel the good road upwards, always journeying through his lofty thoughts towards an apprehension of the things that are above.[5]

Psalm 1 is rightly seen not only as the introduction to the whole of the Psalter but also as introducing Book I.[6] From there Gregory discusses Psalms 42, 73, 90 and 107, with major attention to the last three. Psalm 73 is seen as a critical psalm in the way of virtue because "it examines especially how the justice of the divine judgment will be preserved in the disparity of life" (I. 43), in the light of the fact that, as the psalm makes clear, the person who has pursued righteousness often fares badly. The strategic location of Psalm 90 is especially important for Gregory because it is the only psalm identified with Moses, and one of Gregory's primary works is *De Vita Moysis*, in which he sees in Moses' life the stages of growth in virtue. Here he speaks of Moses as "the one who takes the lead for us in the fourth ascent [i.e. Book IV of the Psalter] and lifts the person who has achieved greatness through the three ascents previously discussed [Books I–III] to the level of himself" (I. 57). The imagery of movement and ascent along the way of virtue toward blessedness has its reflection in the Psalter itself in a body of texts that Gregory never got to in any detail: the Psalms of Ascents (Pss. 120–134) in Book V. There is much debate on what is meant by the expression "song of ascents", but one of the most plausible explanations is that these were psalms to be sung and prayed on the journey to the temple in Jerusalem. These psalms, therefore, provide an example of the kind of ascent or movement that Gregory has in mind,

---

[5] Daley, pp. 211–212. [References inserted in the text.] For an extended summary of how Gregory sees the stages of this ascent, of the spiritual life, through the books of the Psalter, see Heine, pp. 50–79.

[6] Cf. P. D. Miller, "The Beginning of the Psalter", in J. C. McCann Jr., (ed.), *The Shape and Shaping of the Psalter* (JSOTSup 159; Sheffield, 1993), pp. 83–92.

ascent in this case more into the presence of God than the likeness of God. Both movements bring one closer to God.[7]

Finally in Book V we are taken "to the height to the most sublime step of contemplation" (I. 76), and the beginning of Book V, Psalm 107, is commented on at length to make that point. Gregory rightly sees in this psalm a paradigm of God's way with us as it recounts the many kinds of things that happen to us in our "propensity for evil" but also "sets forth in many ways the assistance which we received from God for the good" (I. 78). The movement from the outcry of the human creature in pain to God's answer in help and redemption is central to the Psalter and elaborated at length in Psalm 107. As Gregory puts it: "What a marvel! One cry to God by way of correction changed everything to the good" (I. 82). And the "manner of their salvation, and the description is straightforwardly gospel" (I. 91). Here Gregory makes a move that he does easily in the treatise but not necessarily often. That is, he discerns in the Word the presence of God and in this case – where the text reads: "He sent out his word and healed them, and delivered them from destruction" (v. 20) – one sees "the living and animate Word being sent for the salvation of the lost" (I. 91). In response to this good news, Gregory exclaims: "What evangelist proclaims the mystery so plainly?" (I. 91). The comment is important. It shows Gregory's self-consciousness that he is indeed in another context than one of the New Testament Gospels while asserting how thoroughly the good news of God's saving grace in Jesus Christ is heard in these words. The character of the Psalm feeds this interpretation. While many interpreters, including the author, make connections between Psalm 107 and the exilic and post-exilic period, the text is much more open than that. It describes, as Gregory recognizes, the many human predicaments and the many times and ways God has answered the cries and prayers of the suffering – in this case the sinful (see v. 17) – and saved them out of their troubles. No particular historical event is in view in the text as we receive it; so inevitably it will be heard, and is to be heard, resonating with the whole of Israel and the Church's story. And while what this psalm relates does

---

[7] Other interpreters such as Origen and Augustine did see in the superscriptions of Psalms 120–134 reference to a spiritual ascent. At the beginning of his exposition on Psalm 120 in his *Enarrationes* Augustine says with reference to "song of ascents" that those who ascend are "they who progress toward the understanding of things spiritual".

not exhaust the experiences of God's saving grace, the Church has seen the good news centred and climaxed in "the living and animate Word being sent for the salvation of the lost".

At the end of Part I, Gregory notes that "the peak of good things" is reached in the last psalms: the praise of God (I. 114–115). Later he will make the observation that the Alleluia superscriptions are "found above all in the final chapters of the book of the Psalms" (II. 71), confirming that "praising God is appropriate for those who have already arrived at the goal of the virtuous way of life". In this way Gregory anticipates the observations of later interpreters that there is a clear movement in the Psalter from prayer to praise and the final word is praise.[8] The movement of the virtuous life is reflected in and directed by the movement of the Psalms.

In the second part of the treatise, Gregory turns to the subject indicated by the title, the inscriptions or superscriptions of the Psalms. There he first discusses and interprets the superscriptions at some length and then turns to ask about the psalms that have no superscriptions. Finally he discusses a number of psalms at some length in the context of the question about why the order of some psalms – according to their superscriptions – is at variance with the historical record as we know it from other books. In the middle of the whole there is an extended treatment of the word *diapsalma* (Hebrew *selâ*). In what follows, we shall look especially at the first part of Book II, the meaning and function of the superscriptions.

Consistent with the character of the treatise as a whole, Gregory sees in the superscriptions a double aim. One function is to help the reader understand better and more quickly what follows in the psalm because the superscription shows the aim of the Psalm. But the superscription also "in and of itself points to something which is achieved in relation to virtue in the meaning in its own words" (II. 11). The superscriptions, which contain different kinds of things but often some historical materials, are there not so much to give us facts as to lead us to what is good. This understanding of the functions of the superscriptions is what frees Gregory to explore historical connections while also

---

[8] E.g. C. Westermann, *Praise and Lament in the Psalms* (ET K. R. Crim and R. N. Soulen from *Lob und Klage in den Psalmen* [5th ed., Göttingen, 1977]; Atlanta, 1981), pp. 250–58; P. D. Miller, "The Psalter as a Book of Theology," in H. W. Attridge and M. E. Fassler (eds.), *Psalms in Community: Jewish and Christian Textual, Liturgical, and Artistic Traditions* (Atlanta, 2003), p. 88.

uncovering metaphors and resonances in the superscriptions that have to do with the way of virtue, that is, what Psalm 1 calls "the way of the righteous".

Gregory begins with the most frequent element in the superscriptions, the Hebrew expression *lam^enaṣṣēaḥ*, the meaning of which "is basically still unexplained",[9] although it is frequently read as referring to the leader of the singing or choirmaster. In Greek, it is translated as εἰς τὸ τέλος, "to the end", a translation Kraus regards as "completely enigmatic" but is generally associated with the Hebrew word *nēṣaḥ*, meaning "for eternity, everlastingness".[10] Gregory does not make a christological or eschatological move in interpreting this phrase, but rather turns to the way it was read by others in the early centuries, specifically Aquila, Symmachus, and Theodotion. Their translations all have "victory" as the key word, and Gregory takes this term as a rich metaphor to describe again the goal of the ascent along the way of virtue. It is thus a contest for those "who are contending by means of virtues in the stadium of life" (II. 15). Other terms appearing in the superscriptions with this expression are seen as giving further explanation of the metaphor, "suggestions and advice related to victory" (II. 18). Gregory concludes this discussion with the following summary:

> Anyone who makes a careful examination would discover, in respect to all such phrases, that they are cheers for the athletes shouted to the combatants by the trainer, that one might attain to *the end* of victory. And likewise, if some historical information is inscribed along with the phrase, *'unto the end'*, it looks to this same goal, namely, that we might be encouraged even more in the contests by means of the historical examples. This is the meaning of the phrase, *'unto the end'*. (II. 21)

Another of the superscriptions Gregory takes up is a *'al hašš^emînît*, occurring in the superscriptions of Psalms 6 and 12 and translated in the Septuagint as ὑπὲρ τῆς ὀγδόης, "concerning/above the eighth". Once again the Hebrew term may be musical, referring to an eight-stringed instrument, but there is no certainty. Because the Hebrew root for "eight" is embedded in the word, early Christian interpreters associated it with "the eighth day", or the "octave", as Gregory translates the superscription. While he does not spend much time on the meaning of the term in his work on the Psalm superscriptions, its theological

---

[9] H.-J. Kraus, *Psalms 1–50* (ET from *Psalmen 1–59*, 5th ed. [BKAT; Neukirchen, 1978]; Minneapolis, 1986), p. 29.

[10] Ibid.

and spiritual importance to him is evident by his homily on Psalm 6 where he devotes more than half of the sermon to the superscription. The eighth day was Sunday, the same as the first day of the week and so came to be associated with the resurrection and from that with the time of the new creation, the general resurrection, and the day of judgment. It is this latter meaning that Gregory appropriates, seeing in these two references to the octave a reference to the time when "the anticipated resurrection transforms our nature into another condition of life, and the fleeting nature of time ceases, and the activity related to generation and corruption no longer exists" (II. 53). The expression "for the octave", as Gregory translates the Greek, fits perfectly with his interpretation of the Psalms and the Psalter as the way of virtue/right-eousness, "for all the diligence of the virtuous life looks to the next age, whose beginning…is designated *octave*" (II. 52).[11]

The superscription *'al haggittît* (Pss. 8, 81, 84) is often thought to be musical, but its linguistic association with the word *gat*, "winepress", led to the Septuagint translation ὑπὲρ τῶν ληνῶν, which Gregory translates as "for the winepresses", developing a thick interpretation of the theology or spirituality he sees embedded in the image. He talks about the winepress as the workshop where the wine is made and the possibility of bad grapes producing foul wine while good grapes will produce wine "with a pleasant taste and a fine bouquet, increasing in beauty and fragrance for a long time" (II. 54). Longevity is important for Gregory because, as the length of the Psalter itself shows, the ascent to virtue is a long and arduous process. Every piece of the Psalter, including these obscure superscriptions, is to be read as part of – to use Brian Daley's term – "training for 'the Good Ascent'".[12] Gregory's work on these varied expressions is not an obscurantist endeavour. It is his effort to uncover every aspect of the Psalms' contribution to such training. The winepress imagery shows how much that is the case when one recognizes that "in the winepress of each soul (now the con-science is the winepress) the cluster of grapes of our deeds will stow away for us the wine for the life that follows" (II. 56). What is central for the image of the octave – the new age toward which the virtuous life aspires – is present also in the image of the winepress, which rep-resents the mind, the soul, and the conscience.

---

[11] For other places where Gregory puts some weight on the Eighth Day, see Daley, pp. 203–04.

[12] See note 2.

While his treatment of the superscriptions to this point does not hesitate to make reference to the New Testament, his interpretation is not very christological and his biblical sources are largely the Old Testament. Things become quite different when he ventures to explore why it is that some of the psalms have superscriptions in the Greek Septuagint but not in the Hebrew. His argument from silence is a heavily theological one. He does not say clearly whether these superscriptions have been omitted from the Hebrew or added to the Greek, though he seems to think the former, for their absence from the Hebrew text is because they are "ecclesiastical and mystical" and not accepted in the synagogue "because of unbelief" (II. 76). Arguments from silence (in the Hebrew text) even when made in relation to what is in fact spoken or written (in the Greek text) are very risky and subject to caution and scepticism. Certainly that is the case here. While Gregory draws on both the Psalms and the New Testament, his interpretation is in some instances typically christological and understandable as such but in other cases is more forced. The former is typified by a reading of "Rejoice in the Lord, O you righteous" (Ps. 33:1) as bidding Christians "to exult in the one who has come to earth from heaven" (II. 79). A more forced interpretive move is found in Gregory's interpretation of the Septuagint heading for Psalm 91 [Gk.=90]. It reads something like "Praise of a song". To account for its omission in the Hebrew as reflective of unbelief, Gregory says: "But the Hebrews hush up praise and command those praising the Lord to be silent. They attempt to prevent the children in the temple from praising the Lord for his benefits, as the Gospel has recorded their senseless pride" (II. 86), this with reference to Matthew 21:15–16.

While sometimes Gregory will interpret the psalms without inscriptions in the Hebrew more in relation to the ascent to virtue, the handling of this particular feature of Psalm superscriptions is generally in terms of "the disbelief of the Jews" making the psalm "unacceptable to the Hebrews" (II. 113).

Before turning to the psalms with more historical superscriptions, Gregory is drawn to consider the enigmatic word selâ, translated in the Greek as διάψαλμα. He does not try to translate the term but suggests that it is "a pause which occurs suddenly in the midst of the singing of a psalm in order to receive an additional thought which is being introduced from God" (II. 116). His elaborated interpretation is intelligible and, like so much of his interpretation, draws on images from human experience. For example, he says:

It often happens that, if people who are walking together or conversing with one another at banquets or meetings should suddenly hear a sound from somewhere, they stop their discourse and give their full attention to the sound, so that in the silence they may hear and know the meaning of the sound. Then when the noise has ceased they again take up their discussions with one another. (II. 115)

The interpretive image is all the more impressive because one of the plausible interpretations of the term *selâ* is "pause" or "interruption".[13] Gregory sees also in the way that Selah is laid out in the psalms a further indication of the movement and progress in the Psalter. The term appears in the earlier part of the Psalter but is no longer there in the later part, that is, in the final book, at least according to Gregory's reading.[14] He sees this as part of the progressive movement "to what is more sublime through each of the sections" (II. 118). As one reaches the peak, where there is only "the song of praise continuous and unbroken from beginning to end in each psalm", there is no longer need for such interruptions and interventions (II. 118). It is, he says, like nursing the "childlike and imperfect" with milk and "spreading the table with meat for those who are already perfect" (II. 120). "[T]he perfection by means of the *steps*...is in need of no addition" (II. 119).

The longest section in Gregory's treatise is his discussion of the psalms that have historical superscriptions, particularly Psalms 51–59, with which he concludes his study. While such superscriptions provide fruit for his reflections on the spiritual meaning of the psalms, as he seeks to show in some detail, his primary reason for taking them up is the fact that the order of the events in the superscriptions does not fit the historical sequence as laid out in the historical books. That incongruity would not be a problem except for the fact that the order and sequence of the movement on the way of virtue and righteousness through the psalms in "the good ascent" are central to his whole interpretation. Therefore, he is forced to make the case that the historical order is not of significance for the aim of the Psalms, although the historical references are helpful and important clues to what is involved in that progressive ascent. This is first suggested by the reference to

---

[13] For this and various other possible interpretations of the term *selâ*, see Kraus, pp. 27–29. Weiser also suggests that the term "was meant to denote a pause": *The Psalms* (ET of *Die Psalmen*, 5th ed. [ATD; Göttingen, 1959], OTL; Philadelphia, 1962), p. 22.

[14] As Heine notes (p. 159, n. 171), there are in fact two psalms (140 and 143) in Book V that contain the word Selah.

David's flight from Absalom in the heading to Psalm 3. The historical character and his story are not the focus of attention. Rather he is an *example* to show that "fleeing the approach of such a one is not insignificant for those who are under attack" (II. 140). Gregory then moves through the next nine psalms to show how the superscriptions and the content carry forward the sequence of the life in pursuit of blessedness and union with God. Absalom is referred to several times, still as a kind of representative figure: "For that same adversary, Absalom, as if he has been born again from ourselves, prepares the war against us" (II. 148). The spiritual and the historical may conflict but only in the sense that the spiritual interpretation does not depend upon precise historical order.

Having made his point with the Absalom superscription at the beginning of Psalm 3, Gregory moves on, first showing the sequence and continuing ascent to blessedness in several of the psalms in the 40s and then concluding at length with Psalms 51–59. There he engages in extended exposition often apart from the superscriptions but always assuming they have given specific instances in the life of David that become images and representations for those who later pray the Psalms. The order and movement of the Christian life through the order of the Psalms is not disturbed by the historical inconsistencies in the order of the events referred to in the superscriptions. He notes, for example, that the matter having to do with Doeg the Edomite mentioned in the superscription of Psalm 52 actually occurred much earlier than the David and Bathsheba incident that is mentioned in the heading of Psalm 51. This is not a problem for Gregory. The historical order is transcended by the order given in the movement of the Psalms:

> For what great benefit is it to me to learn first that about the *Edomite*, and then to be taught that about *Bathsheba*? What virtue is there in this? What sort of ascent to that which is superior? What teaching that produces desire for things sublime? But if, after I have learned all the mysteries related to the deeper sense which the Word contains in the fiftieth [i.e. Psalm 51], and with that I am taught the antidote which has been given to us for the destruction of the adversary, I mean the antidote of repentance, so that by means of this I am always accustomed to and exercised in victory against the enemy, behold how I proceed consequently to the next ascent, exchanging victory for victory. (II. 178)

In other words the order given in the historical notes is a spiritual one and its teaching is evident if one thinks of it in regard to the progress on the way of virtue.

Brief as this presentation of Gregory's treatise may be, it is sufficient to suggest connections with more recent interpretation of the Psalms. One may start with the observation that the Psalmic superscriptions have received increasing attention in various commentaries and other studies of the Psalms, though that is primarily with regard to the ones that have historical references, with regard to David especially but also others such as Moses (Psalm 90) and Solomon (Psalm 127). In his commentary on Psalm 3, James Mays concludes with an extended discussion of the superscription, "A psalm of David, when he fled from his son Absalom". J. L. Mays gives a significant portion of his discussion of the psalm to the significance of the heading. It is, in effect, the chief interpretive clue to the theological meaning of the psalm. Citing the early interpreters, he sees this heading and other narrative headings, which are a major focus of Gregory in his treatment of the superscriptions, as not so much historical notices as "permission and encouragement to heuristic reflection", which leads to theological, pastoral, and homiletical intimations.[15] Erich Zenger and Frank-Lothar Hossfeld uncover many connections between the historical inscriptions in Psalms 51–59 and elsewhere and the narratives of the books of Samuel, Kings, and Chronicles, as does Mays.[16] Often this involves resonances between expressions in the psalms and elements of the narratives. The interpretation is not quite the same as Gregory's, who seeks to see how the incident referred to in the superscription helps the reader appropriate the psalm and does not pursue all the literary affinities that may be uncovered.

A contemporary approach that reminds one of Gregory's frequent *allusion to David as the representative of progress on the way of virtue* may be found in Brevard Childs's interpretation of the references to David in the superscriptions. Gregory writes of David that he "shows kindness to human nature both by means of those psalms in which he prefigures our salvation symbolically, and by means of those in which he indicates the manner of repentance to mankind" (II. 177). In his *Introduction* Childs says with reference to the psalm titles or

---

[15] James L. Mays, *Psalms* (IBC; Louisville, 1994), p. 54.

[16] E. Zenger and F.-L. Hossfeld, *Psalms 2* (ET of *Psalmen 51–100* [HTKAT; Freiburg, 2000], Hermeneia; Minneapolis, 2005). Contrast this extensive examination of the connections between the psalm and the historical context suggested by the superscription and the commentaries of earlier modern interpreters, such as Gunkel, Kraus, and Weiser, for example.

superscriptions that "David is pictured simply as a man, indeed chosen by God for the sake of Israel, but who displays all the strengths and weaknesses of all human beings.... An access is now provided into his emotional life". Then he lays out the significance of this:

> The effect of this new context has wide hermeneutical implications. The psalms are transmitted as the sacred psalms of David, but they testify to all the common troubles and joys of ordinary human life in which all persons participate. These psalms do not need to be cultically actualized to serve later generations. They are made immediately accessible to the faithful. Through the mouth of David, the man, they become a personal word from God in each individual situation. In the case of the titles the effect has been exactly the opposite from what one might have expected. Far from tying these hymns to the ancient past, they have been contemporized and individualized for every generation of suffering and persecuted Israel.[17]

This is not a depiction of the ascent to the peak, as Gregory would interpret the Psalter. It is, however, a spiritual reading of the Psalms and the function of David in the titles.

Gregory's vision of the sequence of the books of the Psalms as a guide to the way of virtue, the ascent to blessedness, connects in other ways with contemporary interpretation. His attention to *the five books*, the sense of some *movement or sequence* as one moves through them, and *the importance of the psalms at the beginning and end* of the books anticipates what is one of the dominant strains in contemporary Psalms studies. An early and representative contribution to this focus on the books and the movement discernable as one reads through the Psalter and from one book to the next is Gerald Wilson's monograph – followed up by numerous essays – *The Editing of the Hebrew Psalter*.[18] He identifies a movement from book to book, with the whole focused on kingship, the kingship of David and his descendants and the kingship of God. It is important to note that with Wilson, as with others

---

[17] Childs, p. 521. I have tried to make a similar point in the following way: "The ascription of psalms to David is not simply to give an author's identity but to receive them from the lips and heart of one who in many respects was as much a representative human being as any figure in the Old Testament.... In the psalms of David we see our own image, our own profile, and indeed, in one of the psalms (Psalm 102), which is like so many of the psalms of David that it could have been listed as one of them, the superscription says that it belongs to an anonymous afflicted one, faint and pouring out complaint before the Lord – someone like David, like me, who is undone and pours out his or her heart in anguish, and indeed anger and complaint before the Lord" (P. D. Miller, *Interpreting the Psalms* [Philadelphia, 1986], pp. 26–27.)

[18] G. H. Wilson, *The Editing of the Hebrew Psalter* (SBLDS 76; Chico, CA, 1985).

who follow his lead, the psalms at the seams of the books are especially important for discerning the movement and progress from book to book. He summarizes at one point as follows:

> So the covenant which YHWH made with David (Ps 2) and in whose promises David rested secure (Ps 41) is now passed on to his descendants in this series of petitions in behalf of "the king's son" (Ps. 72)....
>
> With the addition of Book Three and its concluding Ps 89, a new perspective is achieved. Here (Ps 89) the concern with the Davidic covenant is made explicit....
>
> At the conclusion of the third book, immediately preceding the break observed separating the earlier and later books, the impression left is one of a covenant remembered, but a covenant *failed*. The Davidic covenant introduced in Ps 2 has come to nothing and the combination of three books concludes with the anguished cry of the Davidic descendants....
>
> In my opinion, Pss 90–106 [Book IV] function as the editorial "center" of the final form of the Hebrew Psalter. As such this grouping stands as the "answer" to the problem posed in Ps 89 as to the apparent failure of the Davidic covenant with which Books One–Three are primarily concerned. Briefly summarized the answer given is: (1) YHWH is king; (2) He has been our "refuge" in the past, long before the monarchy existed (i.e. in the Mosaic period); (3) He will continue to be our refuge now that the monarchy is gone; (4) Blessed are they that trust in him![19]

While Wilson sees the steps in the movement of the Psalter signalled especially in psalms at the end of the books, others have pointed out that psalms at the beginning of the books play a role in their sequence and movement,[20] a point that Wilson recognizes in specific instances, such as the way in which Psalm 107 responds to the conclusion of Psalm 106.

This focus on the psalms at the seams of the books of the Psalter, their beginnings and endings, as clues to what is going on in the books they introduce or conclude is a sharp echo of Gregory's attention to

---

[19] Wilson, pp. 211–15. For a variation on Wilson's approach that sees the books more as representing theologically prominent stages in the history of ancient Israel, see B. Janowski, "Die 'Kleine Biblia': Zur Bedeutung der Psalmen für eine Theologie des Alten Testaments", in E. Zenger (ed.), *Der Psalter in Judentum und Christentum*, (HBS 18; Freiburg, 1998), pp. 403–04.

[20] E.g. J. C. McCann Jr., "Books I–III and the Editorial Purpose of the Hebrew Psalter", in McCann (ed.), pp. 93–107. One should note also how Walter Brueggemann in his very broad sense of movement in the Psalter regards Psalm 73, the opening psalm in Book III, as the pivotal psalm of the Psalter in its movement from obedience (Ps. 1) through the depths of the laments into the gratitude of praise: see his "Bounded by Obedience and Praise: The Psalms as Canon", *JSOT* 50 (1991), pp. 63–92, repr. in P. D. Miller (ed.) *The Psalms and the Life of Faith* (Minneapolis, 1995), pp. 189–213.

these same psalms, including the opening and closing psalms of the Psalter.[21] In both his and Wilson's approach, there is a sense of movement and progress as one goes through the Psalms, the significance of which is often indicated by the psalms at the seams. When for instance, Gregory identifies Book V as "the mountain-peak of the fifth ascent in which there is, as it were, a complete consummation and recapitulation of human salvation" (II. 77), he devotes his whole discussion of this claim to an extended exposition of the opening psalm, Psalm 107. For Gregory, however, the progress is less a literary and theological one about the Psalter, that is, about the kingship of God or a theological reading of Israel's history, than it is a spiritual and mystical movement of the reader-Christian, a blueprint for that ascent to the blessedness that comes in the likeness of God. That does not mean, however, that his reading of the Psalms as they show the way is not theological. In fact, in his exposition of Psalm 90, with regard to verse 4, he asks explicitly: "What, then, are we taught doctrinally in these words?" (I. 62). His extended exposition of this psalm is at every point an appropriation of its teaching for understanding God's ways with us and what is involved in walking or ascending the path of virtue. The difference is his placing the reader in the shoes of the psalmist/David. Even in that regard, there are serious efforts within contemporary Psalms study to identify the openness of the Psalms to an identification of the reader's experience and that of the Psalms. I have suggested that the difficulty of pinning down the historical or cultic specifics lying behind the psalms, a task that has occupied much of modern study of the Psalms, is a reflection of the openness of the psalms.[22] That openness and the powerful poetic images of the Psalms have throughout history facilitated what Gregory saw – and many others after him have echoed – about the ready address of the psalm to the contemporary reader in any time and place, evoking an appropriation that is shaped by both human experience and the larger framework of Scripture.[23]

---

[21] Gregory's focus is more on the opening psalms of each book, but he also looks at how the book concludes the step on the way that it is set to describe, as, for example, in his discussion of Psalm 41 (II.157).

[22] Miller, 1986, p. 51.

[23] A related notion seems to be evident in Dorothea Erbele-Küster's appropriation of the notion of the empty spaces or gaps in the lament psalms (D. Erbele-Küster, *Lesen als Akt des Betens: Eine Rezeptionsästhetik der Psalmen* [WMANT 87; Neukirchen-Vluyn, 2001]). See the comment of Hermann Spieckermann, drawing on the

The sense of movement through *groups of Psalms* within the five books, which Gregory lays out particularly with regard to Psalms 1–12 and 51–59, has its resonance with a similar focus on psalm groupings in contemporary Psalms study. The author has tried to show the connections and movements in Psalms 15–24, for example.[24] A great deal more important work has been done in this regard by Erich Zenger and F.-L. Hossfeld, evident throughout their commentaries on the Psalms but also worked out in even more detail in a number of articles.[25] They have uncovered many of the linguistic connections and interactions among the psalms in small groupings, but they have also sought to show how different groups of psalms have a movement and a unity to them, for example, in Book One where they seek to demonstrate the following groupings: Pss. 3–14 (the suffering existence of the poor and the righteous), Pss. 15–24 (the Lord delivers the righteous), Pss. 25–34 (the Lord delivers the poor), and Pss. 35–41 (the suffering existence of the poor and the righteous).[26]

The noticeable difference between Gregory's accomplishment and the echoes or resonances that I have sought to illustrate here is that he brought them together. Assuming the openness of the psalms for identification with ordinary human experience through the language and metaphors or the empty spaces is one thing, but doing that in relation to an interpretation of the superscriptions and putting it all together in an interpretation of the movement of the Psalter and the significance of the Books and their beginnings and endings as well as the progress through groups of psalms – see, for example, his treatments of Psalms 1–13 and 51–59 – is a major accomplishment not fully duplicated in contemporary interpretation.

---

work of Erbele-Küster: "Das in den Texten betende Ich ist eine Leerstelle, die von dem Beter durch Identifikation gefüllt werden will" (H. Spieckermann, "Psalmen und Psalter: Suchbewegungen des Forschens und Betens", in F. García Martínez and E. Noort (eds.), *Perspectives in the Study of the Old Testament and Early Judaism*, [VTSup 73; Leiden, 1998], p. 146).

[24] P. D. Miller, "Kingship, Torah Obedience, and Prayer: The Theology of Psalms 15–24", in Miller, *Israelite Religion and Biblical Theology: Collected Essays* (JSOTSup 267; Sheffield, 2000), pp. 279–287 (first published as "Kingship, Torah Obedience, and Prayer" in K. Seybold and E. Zenger [ed.], *Neue Wege der Psalmenforschung: Für Walter Beyerlin* [HBS 1; Freiburg, 1994], pp. 127–42).

[25] See, for example, their commentary on Psalms 51–100 (n. 16) and E. Zenger, "Der Psalter als Buch: Beobachtungen zu seiner Entstehung, Komposition und Funktion", in Zenger (ed.), 1998, pp. 1–57.

[26] See the treatment of these psalms in the introduction to Zenger and Hossfeld, *Die Psalmen 1–50* (NEchtB 29; Würzburg, 1993).

THE BOOK OF PSALMS IS FULL OF ERRORS.

Professor Welhausen, the Famous German Savant, Who Is Translating This Part of the Scriptures for the Great Polychrome Edition of the Bible, Has Found That Most of the Passages in the Psalms So Familiar to All Christendom Are Serious Mistranslations.

PSALM I.

PSALM I.—NEW VERSION.

1 Happy the man who follows not the counsel of the wicked,
Nor treads the path of sinners,
Nor sits in the company of scoffers,
2 But delights in the Law of JHVH,
And on that Law meditates day and night;
3 He is like a tree planted by the water-side,
Which brings forth fruit in due season
And whose leaf never withers;
All that he does, prospers.
4 Not so the wicked; not so:
They are like chaff which the wind scatters away.
5 Therefore the wicked cannot stand in the judgment,
Nor sinners in the congregation of the righteous.
6 For JHVH gives heed to the course of the righteous,
But the course of the wicked is ruin.

PSALM I.—ACCEPTED VERSION.

1. Blessed is the man that walketh not in the counsel of the ungodly, nor standeth in the way of sinners, nor sitteth in the seat of the scornful.
2. But his delight is in the law of the Lord; and in his law doth he meditate day and night.
3. And he shall be like a tree planted by the rivers of water, that bringeth forth his fruit in his season; his leaf also shall not wither; and whatsoever he doeth shall prosper.
4. The ungodly are not so; but are like the chaff which the wind driveth away.
5. Therefore the ungodly shall not stand in the judgment. And sinners in the congregation of the righteous.
6. For the Lord knoweth the way of the righteous; but the way of the ungodly shall perish.

PROF. J. WELHAUSEN, OF GOTTINGEN UNIVERSITY.

PSALM XIX.

PSALM XIX.—NEW VERSION.

For the Liturgy. Psalm of David.
1 The heavens recount the glory of God,
And the firmament proclaims His handiwork.
2 Day after day utters it the day,
And the night shows knowledge to the night.
3 Their voice sounds on through every land,
To the end of the world, their speech.
11 Is there He has prepared a tent for the sun,
3 And thence he comes forth, as from the bridal chamber, the bridegroom,
And rejoices like a hero, to run his course.
4 From one end of heaven he sets out,
And to the other holds his winding way,
And nothing from his fervor can be hid.
7 The Law of JHVH is perfect, refreshing the soul,

PSALM XIX.—ACCEPTED VERSION.

1. The heavens declare the glory of God; and the firmament showeth his handywork.
2. Day unto day uttereth speech, and night unto night sheweth knowledge.
3. There is no speech nor language, where their voice is not heard.

PROF. WELHAUSEN'S DISCOVERY.

The accepted version of the Book of Psalms in the Holy Bible is full of errors!

This startling discovery has just been announced by Professor J. Welhausen, of Gottingen University, who is the leading Hebrew scholar of Europe. He has carefully gone over the oldest existing Bibles, in Greek and Hebrew, and has found that most of the passages in the Psalms, so familiar to every Christian, are gross mistranslations. His discovery will create a profound sensation throughout the world wherever Christianity is preached.

The Sunday Journal here presents to its readers the first and exclusive account of this colossal discovery. Professor Welhausen is one of the forty famous professors of Semitic literature who have undertaken the laborious task of translating the Bible into English without fear or favor, bringing to bear upon their work the light of recent discoveries and paying no heed to former translations or revisions. Only one book has been completed thus far, namely Ecclesiastes, which was translated by Professor Paul Haupt, of Johns Hopkins University, and a full account of which was published exclusively, at the time, in the Sunday Journal.

The advance sheets of Professor Welhausen's translation have just been secured. This translation was revised by Professor Haupt and arranged in rhythmical form by Dr. Horace Howard Furness, the famous Shakespearian scholar, both of them, as well as the translator, being religious men. The extracts printed here will show how, for several centuries, all the world has misunderstood many of the best known Psalms.

DR. FURNESS, THE SHAKESPEARIAN SCHOLAR.

PROF. PAUL HAUPT, OF JOHNS HOPKINS UNIVERSITY.

PSALM II.

PSALM II.—NEW VERSION.

1 Why do the heathen rage,
And the peoples devise what is vain?
2 The kings of the earth confederate plots
And the princes take counsel together
Against JHVH, and against His anointed;
3 "Their bonds we will break asunder,
Their cords we will cast away from us."
4 He in the heavens laughs,
At them the LORD mocks.
5 Until in His wrath He speaks to them,
In His fury affrighting them—
6 "It is not I who my king have established
On Zion, holy mountain of mine!"
7 JHVH's decree I make known:
Thus He has said to me: "Thou art my son,
I have this day begotten Thee;
8 Ask, and, as a heritage, I give thee the heathen,
The ends of the earth shall be thy possession.
9 With a staff of iron shalt thou break them to pieces,
Like a vessel of earth, dash them to fragments."
10 Be wary, therefore, ye kings!
Ye rulers of earth, be advised!
11 Wait ye on JHVH with fear,
Submit yourselves to Him with trembling
12 Adopt a modest demeanor, lest He be angry, and ruin seize you!
For His anger is easily kindled.
Happy all they who in Him put their trust!

PSALM II.—ACCEPTED VERSION.

1. Why do the heathen rage, and the people imagine a vain thing?
2. The kings of the earth set themselves, and the rulers take counsel together, against the Lord, and against his Anointed, saying,
3. Let us break their bands asunder, and cast away their cords from us.
4. He that sitteth in the heavens shall laugh: the Lord shall have them in derision.
5. Then shall he speak unto them in his wrath, and vex them in his sore displeasure.
6. Yet have I set my King upon my holy hill of Zion.
7. I will declare the decree: the Lord hath said unto me, Thou art my Son; this day have I begotten thee.
8. Ask of me, and I shall give thee the heathen for thine inheritance, and the uttermost parts of the earth for thy possession.
9. Thou shalt break them with a rod of iron; thou shalt dash them in pieces like a potter's vessel.
10. Be wise now therefore, O ye kings: be instructed, ye judges of the earth.
11. Serve the Lord with fear, and rejoice with trembling.
12. Kiss the Son, lest he be angry, and ye perish from the way, when his wrath is kindled but a little. Blessed are all they that put their trust in him.

PSALM VIII.

PSALM VIII.—NEW VERSION.

For the Liturgy. On GIHIH. Psalm of David.
1 O JHVH, our Lord!
How glorious is Thy name over all the earth!
And in the heavens, how Thy glory shines!
2 Thou createst, from the mouths of children and of sucklings a power,
Because of Thine enemies,
To silence the foe and the revengeful.
4 When I see Thy heavens, the work of Thy fingers,
The moon and the stars which Thou hast ordained,
5 What is man that Thou takest thought of him,
And a son of man that Thou heedest him?
6 Thou hast made him in rank little less than divine,
Thou hast crowned him with glory and honor.
7 Thou hast given him dominion over the creatures of Thy hand;
8 All sheep and oxen, yea, and the beasts of the field;
The birds of the air and the fishes of the sea.

PSALM VIII.—ACCEPTED VERSION.

1. O Lord our Lord, how excellent is thy name in all the earth! who hast set thy glory above the heavens.
2. Out of the mouth of babes and sucklings hast thou ordained strength because of thine enemies, that thou mightest still the enemy and the avenger.
3. When I consider thy heavens, the work of thy fingers, the moon and the stars, which thou hast ordained;
4. What is man, that thou art mindful of him? and the son of man, that thou visitest him?
5. For thou hast made him a little lower than the angels, and hast crowned him with glory and honour.
6. Thou madest him to have dominion over the works of thy hands; thou hast put all things under his feet:
7. All sheep and oxen, yea, and the beasts of the field;
8. The fowl of the air, and the fish of the sea, and whatsoever passeth through the paths of the seas.
9. O Lord our Lord, how excellent is thy name in all the earth!

PSALM XXII.

PSALM XXII.—NEW VERSION.

For the Liturgy. To the tune of The Hind of the Dawn. Psalm of David.
1 My God, my God, why hast Thou forsaken me?
Far aloud from mine invocation, from my wailing entreaty.
2 By day do I call, O my God, yet Thou dost not answer,
And by night do I find me no rest.
4 Yet Thee are the Holy One, Thy throne is held on Israel's songs of praise.
5 On Thee our fathers built their trust,
They trusted, and Thou didst deliver them.
6 On Thee they called, and they escaped;
They trusted, and were not disappointed.
7 No man am I, but a worm, A by-word of the people, and of all sorts despised.
8 All they that see me laugh me to scorn; they shoot out the lip, they shake the head, saying,
9 He trusteth on the Lord that he would deliver him; let him deliver him, seeing he delighted in him.

PSALM XXII.—ACCEPTED VERSION.

1. My God, my God, why hast thou forsaken me? why art thou so far from helping me, and from the words of my roaring?
2. O my God, I cry in the daytime, but thou hearest not; and in the night season, and am not silent.
3. But thou art holy, O thou that inhabitest the praises of Israel.
4. Our fathers trusted in thee: they trusted, and thou didst deliver them.
5. They cried unto thee, and were delivered: they trusted in thee, and were not confounded.
6. But I am a worm, and no man; a reproach of men, and despised of the people.
7. All they that see me laugh me to scorn: they shoot out the lip, they shake the head, saying,
8. He trusted on the Lord that he would deliver him: let him deliver him, seeing he delighted in him.

WELLHAUSEN ON THE PSALMS*

Rudolf Smend

In 1898, or shortly before,[1] the American *Sunday Journal* devoted a whole large page to the Bible, or to be more exact, to the Psalms. The headline runs: THE BOOK OF PSALMS IS FULL OF ERRORS. And the subtitle: "Professor Welhausen, the Famous German Savant, Who Is Translating This Part of the Scriptures for the Great Polychrome Edition of the Bible, Has Found That Most of the Passages in the Psalms So Familiar to All Christendom Are Serious Mistranslations." The page is dominated by drawings showing the heads of three scholars, each of them against the background of a page from the Psalter. In the middle, and above the two others, there is the profile of a curly head, with a slightly hooked nose, side-whiskers, and unframed spectacles, attached by a cord. Underneath is the name: PROF. J. WELHAUSEN, OF GOTTINGEN UNIVERSITY. Anyone who has ever seen a picture of Wellhausen, or has even a vague idea of what he looked like, notices at once: this cannot be him! Wellhausen had neither curls nor glasses, but he had a strong, straight nose, and a beard. We find all these features best reproduced in the portrait on the left-hand side below, which really does correspond to one of the best-known photographs of Wellhausen dating from that period, and which probably provided the model for our portrait here.[2] But in the *Sunday Journal* the caption for this drawing is PROF. PAUL HAUPT, OF JOHNS HOPKINS UNIVERSITY. The riddle is easily solved. The captions or, to be more correct, the pictures have been reversed. The central figure who is called "Welhausen" is in fact Paul Haupt (1858–1926), the German-born predecessor of William F. Albright as Professor of Semitic Languages at the Johns Hopkins University. This becomes obvious, if further

---

* Translated by Margaret Kohl.
[1] Cf. here below. The page I have in front of me does not show the date because the margin has been cut off. The name of the newspaper is mentioned in the article itself.
[2] Reproduced, for example, in A. Duff, *History of Old Testament Criticism* (London, 1910), p. 25.

proof is needed, from a comparison with the relevant photographs.[3] On the other hand, the third head, on the right-hand side below, is quite correctly captioned: this is DR. FURNESS, THE SHAKESPEAR-IAN SCHOLAR. Horace Howard Furness (1833–1912) was the publisher from 1871 onwards of the multi-volume Variorum Edition of Shakespeare, his son, Horace Howard Furness junior (1865–1930), being his assistant and successor in the work.[4] If the reader's mistrust has already been awakened by the mix-up of the portraits of the two main figures, and if this mistrust has been accentuated by the fact that the *Sunday Journal* consistently spells Wellhausen with one "l" instead of two, he will turn with a double portion of suspicion to the article itself. This runs as follows:

> "PROF. WELHAUSEN'S DISCOVERY
> The accepted version of the Book of Psalms in the Holy Bible is full of errors!
> This startling discovery has just been announced by Professor J. Welhausen, of Gottingen University, who is the leading Hebrew scholar of Europe. He has carefully gone over the oldest existing Bibles, in Greek and Hebrew, and has found that most of the passages in the Psalms, so familiar to every Christian, are gross mistranslations. His discovery will create a profound sensation throughout the world wherever Christianity is preached.
> The Sunday Journal here presents to its readers the first and exclusive account of this colossal discovery. Professor Welhausen is one of the forty famous professors of Semitic literature who have undertaken the laborious task of translating the Bible into English without fear or favour, bringing to bear upon their work the light of recent discoveries and paying no heed to former translations or revisions. Only one book has been completed so far, namely Ecclesiastes, which was translated by Professor Paul Haupt, of Johns Hopkins University, and a full account of which was published exclusively, at the time, in the *Sunday Journal*.
> The advance sheets of Professor Welhausen's translation have just been secured. This translation was revised by Professor Haupt and arranged in rhythmical form by Dr. Horace Howard Furness, the famous Shakespearian scholar, both of them, as well as the translator, being religious men. The extracts printed here will show how, for several centuries, all the world has misunderstood many of the best known Psalms."

---

[3] For example *NCAB* XXII, 158; B. O. Long, *Planting and Reaping Albright* (Pennsylvania, 1997), p. 128.

[4] Cf. *NCAB* VIII, pp. 396f.; XXIII, pp. 205f.

As examples the *Sunday Journal* prints five psalms (1, 2, 8, 19 and 22) side by side in the "accepted version" and the "new version", and at the beginning in each case points to one difference or another, beginning at once with אַשְׁרֵי, the first word in Ps 1. The new version (Wellhausen) translates this as "happy", whereas the old version had "blessed", that being "the version of the religious enthusiasts who made the King James translation". In Ps 2:12 Wellhausen replaces the Masoretic text's נַשְּׁקוּ־בַר ("Kiss the Son!") as "corrupt" by the conjecture קְחוּ מוּסָר (Wellhausen adds the word "perhaps"), and he therefore translates: "Adopt a modest demeanor." Here the *Sunday Journal* explains that the "kiss" of the earlier English translation was an example of "the interpolation of unimportant words…that do not exist in the original". But in this case the word, for all that, appears in the Masoretic text! In Ps 8:2 the Sunday Journal considers the traditional "babes and sucklings" to be "not an accurate translation of the Hebrew words" (עוֹלְלִים וְיֹנְקִים), unlike Wellhausen's "children and sucklings". This may be correct, but examples of this kind hardly provide a basis for the assertion that Wellhausen "found that most of the passages in the Psalms, so familiar to every Christian, are gross mistranslations", and that "his discovery will create a profound sensation throughout the world wherever Christianity is preached". Not that Wellhausen never "created a profound sensation", more even than any other single Old Testament scholar in modern times. But in 1898 the sensation already lay twenty years in the past, and applied to his Pentateuchal criticism and his *History of Israel*; and of that sensation "the world wherever Christianity is preached" did not take much notice. When Wellhausen was sent the page from the *Sunday Journal* he laughed heartily over it.

Now, it would be quite mistaken to deduce from this somewhat curious side-effect of Wellhausen's English-American translation of the Psalms, and its minor influence compared with his Pentateuchal criticism, that the Psalms did not mean much to him. He was a pastor's son, and had undoubtedly been thoroughly familiar with the Psalms from childhood. And the first lectures he heard given by his later teacher the great and eccentric Heinrich Ewald (six hours a week during his second semester, the winter semester of 1862/63) were on the Psalms; and they deeply impressed him. It was probably actually these lectures which directed the whole of his studies towards the Old Testament. He later said about them: "In the exegesis of the psalms [Ewald] proceeded very thetically and did not entangle us in scruples and doubts. He paid no attention at all to deviating opinions. At the beginning he named some of the more recent commentaries, giving his opinion of them, and finally, after he had brushed them aside as a whole, remarked that he had no further need to confute them in detail. 'From now on I shall simply say at the very beginning what is correct.' But the explanation often took him a good long way away from the matter in hand. While rejecting the view that Ps 45 is an allegory, he first began to talk about Talleyrand, who, as a proper allegorist, thought that language was there to conceal meaning; then he moved on to Louis Napoleon and his Mamelukery, and finally arrived at Garibaldi, the leader of a robber band and a rogue. It will readily be understood that his lectures were not to everyone's taste…In spite of that, one could learn sufficient from him. For anyone who had ears to hear, valuable hints were dropped in passing. I remember, for example, his polemic against the Hegelian sequence: 1. epic, 2. lyric, 3. drama; whereas according to his own view lyric was the original form and remained the essential one in poetry."[5]

It is true that, during his university studies, Wellhausen in his reading concentrated pre-eminently on the law and the prophets, and that it was this which in 1867 made him an adherent of Graf's hypothesis about the sequence of the sources of the Pentateuch[6] – the hypothesis which he himself made victorious, with such far-reaching consequences, through his work right up to the Prolegomena of 1878. But when he applied in 1867 for a post at the Theological Hall of Residence in Göttingen (a post which was to provide the basis for this work and for his academic career), he chose as subject for the treatise he had to submit: *De Justitia dei erga singulos quid sentiat Vetus Testamentum* – "What the Old Testament thinks about the justice of God towards individuals."[7] This is a subject of central importance in the Psalms, but in the book of Job as well; and consequently the treatise (the very first of Wellhausen's which we possess) is for the most part an exegesis of Psalms, a smaller part being an exegesis of Job. And here one of Wellhausen's elemental interests as a Christian and as a theologian emerges.

---

[5] J. Wellhausen, "Heinrich Ewald", in *Beiträge zur Gelehrtengeschichte Göttingens. Festschrift zur Feier des hundertfünfzigjährigen Bestehens der Königlichen Gesellschaft der Wissenschaften zu Göttingen* (Berlin, 1901), pp. 61–88 [p. 64].

[6] J. Wellhausen, *Prolegomena to the History of Israel*. Transl. by J. M. Black and A. Menzies (Edinburgh, 1885), pp. 3f.

[7] University Archives, Göttingen, Theol. SA 0056.2.

He did not choose this subject fortuitously, but because his heart was in it. "His life was never easy and happy, and he did not take it lightly", testifies his colleague Ulrich von Wilamowitz-Moellendorff.[8] For him, the question about divine justice will not have been a merely theoretical one, and both in the question as well as in the possible or impossible answer, he will have been helped by the Psalms (and by Job).

As university teacher, he interpreted the Psalms five times in all between 1873 and 1898, in lectures of four to five hours weekly (he lectured on Job six times, among these lectures being his very first, given in 1870–71, and his very last, given in 1913). But he came to feel that the Psalms "were not well suited for interpretation in a four or five-hour weekly lecture course, because of their great similarity and their lack of a continuous context; whereas they are excellent material for classes on exegesis". And so when he was in Greifswald he took them as the subject for his Hebrew seminar classes. In the summer semester of 1875, he took selected psalms, and in four following semesters, from the winter of 1878/79 until the winter of 1880/81,[9] he went through the whole Psalter from beginning to end, generally with good accompanying work by the students.[10]

In these classes Wellhausen did not confine himself to a pure reading of the text. He discussed problems arising from the content with his students. "Thus the attempt was made to define some important and frequently occurring concepts, e.g., the idea of judgment and of justice, sin and punishment, wrath, and so forth." Twice Wellhausen announced subjects for essays for which, according to the Greifswald rules, a prize of money was offered. The first was "Who is speaking in Psalm 22?" Wellhausen found that all the three essays that were handed in were "not bad"; the one he liked least was one which came out in support of "Hitzig's utterly foolish view that the speaker is Jeremiah". The second subject was: "In what way does the forgiveness of sins find expression in the Psalms?" One student handed in an essay with which Wellhausen was not very satisfied, because the writer "did not keep his eye firmly and exclusively on the subject, but made it the occasion for expressing all kinds of general views about the Old

---

[8] U. von Wilamowitz-Moellendorff, *Erinnerungen* (Leipzig, 1928), p. 189.

[9] During the summer semester of 1880 Wellhausen was working in libraries in Leiden and London.

[10] I am following his reports in the files of the theological faculty in the University archives in Greifswald (Th.F.59–65).

Testament, usually taken from books written by the undersigned [i.e. Wellhausen], ideas which have been imperfectly digested and are quite out of place here". But he remarked self-critically, "Perhaps the subject was too difficult."

Unfortunately none of the manuscripts of Wellhausen's lectures has survived, including his lectures on the Psalms. However, there are a number of surrogates with the help of which we can gain a rough impression of what he said. We have already mentioned the first of these: the English translation of the Psalms in Paul Haupt's *Sacred Books of the Old and New Testaments*. He explained the way this translation came into being in a letter written to William Robertson Smith in Cambridge on 31 March 1892: "I have let myself be captured for the Psalms by Paul Haupt, and have just finished my manuscript and sent it off to him. It would have been better if I could have published it separately, for I shall find myself here in mixed company. But I have to keep my word. The reason I promised was that I wanted to be forced to revise and edit my old lecture manuscript on the minor prophets. But that will appear separately. I felt that it was a pity to throw the manuscripts away, but on the other hand I did not really want to keep them, in case they were published by other people after my death." Writing about the undertaking for which he had let himself be "captured" he adds: "The Americans are dreadful people. It is not enough for them to invade the house. They also demand contributions for all kinds of periodicals, want to have my photograph, etc., etc. Paul Haupt [Wellhausen knew him from his earlier days in Germany] is the proper Yankee. He has also turned Quaker, and is a real business man."[11] The book is Part 14 of the series. On the first, general, title page stands "Translated by J. Wellhausen" and according to the second, special, title page the book includes "Explanatory notes and an appendix on the music of the ancient Hebrews", also "by J. Wellhausen, D.D." The translator of the notes is stated to be John Taylor, and the translator of the appendix J. A. Paterson. Of course the translation of the psalm texts is not Wellhausen's either. Also according to the second title page, the translator is H. H. Furness, the Shakespearian scholar, to whom the first general title page also ascribes "assistance" with the whole Haupt edition. However, as we saw, according to the *Sunday Journal* Haupt "revised" Wellhausen's

---

[11] Cambridge University Library Add. 7449/D826.

English translation, and Furness merely "arranged [it] in rhythmical form". We may probably assume that both Haupt and Furness contributed to the English version, Haupt as exegetical expert and also as native German speaker, and Furness as English stylist. Wellhausen will hardly have "translated" into English. His German translation was available to Haupt and Furness, and from that they constructed the English version, which Wellhausen then looked through. Wellhausen's German text has probably been lost – lamentably, since Wellhausen was a highly gifted translator, as we can see from his translation of the Gospels. Of course I cannot permit myself any opinion about the English version, but I enjoy reading it, and like to remember that behind it is not merely Wellhausen, but William Shakespeare too, with whom Furness was most of all concerned.

As emerges from the letter to Robertson Smith, the "explanatory notes" which follow the translation of the Psalms are a revision of Wellhausen's early manuscript, that is to say the manuscript which he usually took as the basis for his lectures on the Psalms from 1873/74 onwards. He gave these lectures once more in the summer of 1891, no doubt in connection with the "revision" for the "notes", his idea being that he would afterwards throw the manuscript away. Following Haupt's advice, he kept the notes as brief as possible, since according to Haupt the work was intended to be for the general reader; Wellhausen, he said, should keep his scholarship for periodical articles. But after Wellhausen had finished, sometime in 1891, Haupt changed his plan and asked Wellhausen to provide more detailed notes after all. But for this Wellhausen "felt no inclination".[12] There was a second factor in addition. Haupt decided "to precede the translation by a critical edition of the Hebrew text". At first Wellhausen refused to provide this, realizing "that the means [for establishing a critical text] were lacking". He of all people was very much aware of both the attraction of the project and the problems involved, for in 1871 he had examined the text of the books of Samuel with the intention of "offering a contribution to some future [critical] edition of the Old Testament".[13] The "Yankee" Haupt had fewer inhibitions in this respect and was more optimistic, and it is to this that we have to thank for the "Polychrome" or "Rainbow Bible", the Hebrew equivalent of the "new translation"

---

[12] J. Wellhausen, *Skizzen und Vorarbeiten*, VI (Berlin, 1899), p. 165.
[13] J. Wellhausen, *Der Text der Bücher Samuelis* (Göttingen, 1871), p. III.

which was all that had been originally planned. However, Wellhausen remained sceptical, unlike a whole series of "eminent Biblical scholars of Europe and America" (as the title now runs, not only in the English but also in the Hebrew series). And in view of his reluctance, Haupt declared that if he did not want to take on the edition, then they would get someone else, who would work from Wellhausen's translation. However, Wellhausen, as he wrote, "could not take this risk and had no choice but to set about providing a text corresponding to my translation and to extract the critical notes from the exegetical ones with which they were combined." He added the warning: "So my Hebrew text must be used only as a help in understanding my translation. It is in no way intended to be a proper critical edition."[14] Wellhausen was always a rapid worker, and in no time he provided the Hebrew text together with the "notes" belonging to it, and sent it to Haupt in the spring of 1892 together with the translation. In the series that now appeared, the text was published in 1895, and the translation in 1898. This three-year delay seems to have kept Wellhausen from throwing away his old manuscript in the meantime, as he had planned. Instead he gave his psalm lectures (four hours weekly) for the last time in the winter semester of 1897/98. Also in 1898, in the sixth volume of his *Skizzen und Vorarbeiten*, he published *Bemerkungen zu den Psalmen* ("Comments on the Psalms") in which he further developed some points from the notes to the English translation, and "corrected and appended"[15] other material. He probably now really did throw away the old manuscript. But by a happy chance it was not lost completely after all. For some time before, his friend R. Smend had copied parts of it (the exposition of Psalms 47–90); and this transcript has been preserved. So for a whole section of the Psalms, several of them important, we are not dependent on the surrogate of few and shorter notes.

In the history of scholarship, Wellhausen's work on the Psalms is disadvantaged due to the circumstance that, like the commentaries by Cheyne (1888), Duhm (1899), Buhl (1900) and Briggs (1906–07), it preceded the great caesura brought about towards the beginning of the twentieth century by Assyriology and Egyptology on the one hand, and by genre research (Gattungsforschung) on the other. My teacher

---

[14] Wellhausen, *Skizzen*, p. 163.
[15] Wellhausen, *Skizzen*, p. 163.

Walter Baumgartner liked to tell how in 1912 he visited Hermann Gunkel for the first time, hoping to become his pupil (as he then in fact became). Gunkel examined him a little, and asked him: "What is the first thing we have to ask about a psalm?" Baumgartner answered: "Its date." Of course, for Gunkel, this was the wrong answer – his first and most important question was: "What is the genre?" as was afterwards true for the whole of twentieth-century scholarship. If Gunkel had been able to examine Wellhausen, he would have failed too. For during the whole time he worked on the Psalms, he could not have known Gunkel's relevant work, which began with his *Ausgewählte Psalmen* ("Selected Psalms") in 1904. So he was unable to respond to it either positively or negatively. What he might have known, however, was something else: in his commentary on the Psalms of 1811, W. M. L. de Wette already anticipated the essentials of Gunkel's insights a whole century before him. A psalm commentator of our own day, talking about de Wette's book, remarks that one must ask "why any commentaries on the psalms were written at all afterwards".[16] The answer is an obvious one: it was because de Wette's commentary was unknown. Gunkel did not know it – he read only the commentaries that appeared after about 1850.[17] And unfortunately Wellhausen did not know it either, or not sufficiently well, unlike de Wette's critical work on the Pentateuch and the history of ancient Israel, which anticipated so much in his own *Prolegomena* of 1878 that he could say: "You can already find everything I have done in the Old Testament in him."[18]

So for Wellhausen the "classic" commentary on the Psalms was not de Wette's, and not even the one written by his teacher Ewald, although Ewald's lectures impressed him as a student. It was the commentary by Justus Olshausen (1853), who, as Wellhausen "gratefully acknowledged", "gave [his exegesis] its direction in general".[19] Olshausen (1800–1882), a very interesting figure, stressed that he was no theologian. He was a Professor of oriental languages, first in Kiel

---

[16] K. Seybold, "W. M. L. de Wettes Arbeit an den Psalmen", in H.-P. Mathys and K. Seybold (eds.), *Wilhelm Martin Leberecht de Wette. Ein Universaltheologe des 19. Jahrhunderts* (Studien zur Geschichte der Wissenschaften in Basel. Neue Folge 1; Basel, 2001), pp. 62–78 [p. 64].

[17] Cf. H. Gunkel, *Die Psalmen* (HKAT; Göttingen, 1926), p. VI.

[18] Cf. R. Smend, *From Astruc to Zimmerli*, Transl. by M. Kohl (Tübingen, 2007), p. 43.

[19] Wellhausen, *Skizzen*, p. 165.

and then in Königsberg. Finally, he became responsible in the Berlin government for all the Prussian universities. He was a harsh critic of the Masoretic text, for the delightful reason "that I love and revere the singers of Hebrew antiquity too much to sacrifice the glory of their legacy to the form of the text passed down by human hand, and for that reason deficient".[20] Olshausen also took up a very critical viewpoint with regard to the date of the Psalms: he considered that most of them belonged to the Maccabean period, that a few could be pre-exilic, but that hardly "a single fragment in the collection can be attributed with any degree of certainty to the first kings, as it might be David or Solomon."[21] Even apart from his critical stance, his commentary was disregarded among theologians because its author, as he himself stressed in his foreword, was not a theologian but a Professor of oriental languages, who was not called upon to participate in the disputes of the theologians, and who therefore confined himself to philological interpretation.[22]

Referring explicitly to Olshausen, in his *Bemerkungen zu den Psalmen* of 1899 Wellhausen appealed for both restraint and freedom where textual criticism was concerned. In the past the text, which was held to be unblemished, had been "explained again and again, all and everything had been explained", so that the biblical text had ceased to be submitted to the claims of normal human speech". Scholars believed that they could understand "even what was linguistically and factually impossible". Here restraint was called for. "The exegete's primary duty is not to pretend that the indigestible is digestible. He requires a fine palate rather than a strong stomach." Moreover he could not be expected to rectify what had been shown to be corrupt. Emendation was "an awkward business". But nevertheless it was indispensable as a makeshift, if one did not wish to stop short at a pure negation.[23] In Wellhausen's practice, this means, on the one hand, that more often than other people he simply dispenses with a pretence of understanding – that is, he allows words or phrases to stand, as "unintelligible", "not translatable", "doubtful", or "corrupt", or even deletes them. On the other hand he is daringly free with conjectures – in full awareness of

---

[20] J. Olshausen, *Die Psalmen* (KeHAT; Leipzig, 1853), p. III.
[21] Olshausen, *Die Psalmen*, pp. 7f.
[22] Olshausen, *Die Psalmen*, p. I.
[23] Wellhausen, *Skizzen*, p. 165.

their uncertainty and their character as "makeshift". It is clear – and this was Wellhausen's intention – that the result was objection and discussion; and he generally had no difficulty in revising his suggestions.[24]

In the debate he was also reproached with failing to make use of metrics to aid his textual criticism. Budde in particular was pained by his ignoring of the halting rhythm in the song of lament, which he had discovered in the Book of Lamentations and found in the Psalms too.[25] But Wellhausen was and remained sceptical here, if only because we know so little about the pronunciation of ancient Hebrew.[26] Of course in his Hebrew and English text in the *Sacred Books of the Old Testament* he brings out the strophic structure of some of the Psalms, and they are all set in *stichoi*; but this may partly have been in order to comply with Haupt's intention and the form given to the text by Furness. When Wellhausen occasionally translates a psalm on his own, he does not set the *stichoi* or verse lines over against each other, but prints the text continuously, as if it were prose. It occurs to me in this connection that Wellhausen seems to have been one of the rare people who never wrote a poem in his life, not even for someone's birthday, even if the birthday was an eightieth one.

In his *Israelitische und jüdische Geschichte* he translated two psalms completely, and hence in prose, Psalm 87 and Psalm 46, adding to the latter the explanation that it was "the unsurpassed model for Luther's *Ein feste Burg* ('A safe stronghold')", this being the classic hymn of the German Reformation. Psalm 87 is incorporated into the chapter about the second half of the Persian period,[27] Psalm 46 into the chapter on the period of Alexander and his successors.[28] This brings us to the question about the date of the Psalms – the question which the young Baumgartner, in nineteenth-century fashion, saw as the primary one. The nineteenth-century discussion centred largely on an overall view which was then new, and which Eduard Reuss summed up in the

---

[24] Cf. especially K. Budde, Review of Wellhausen, *The Sacred Books of the Old Testament*, 14, *ThLZ* 21 (1896), pp. 561–64, and F. Baethgen, *Die Psalmen* (HKAT; Göttingen, 1892), passim, with Wellhausen's reactions in his *Skizzen* of 1899.

[25] Budde, *ThLZ* 21, p. 564.

[26] Wellhausen, *Skizzen*, p. 164.

[27] J. Wellhausen, *Israelitische und jüdische Geschichte*, 1st edn. (Berlin, 1894), p. 162 n. 1, 7th edn. (Berlin, 1914), p. 192, n. 1.

[28] Wellhausen, *Israelitische und jüdische Geschichte*, 1st edn., p. 182, n. 1; from the 2nd edn. (1895), p. 200, n. 1 onwards in the chapter about Jewish piety (7th edn., 1914, pp. 194ff.), which makes no distinction.

radical and somewhat vague formula that the prophets were earlier than the law, and the Psalms were later than both.[29] Wellhausen intervened in this discussion, giving a sharper form to Reuss's formulation in the terse statement: "It is not a question whether there be any post-Exilic Psalms, but rather, whether the Psalms contain any poems written before the Exile." Wellhausen first made this statement in print in 1878,[30] the same year in which in the very first sentence of his *Prolegomena to the History of Israel* he narrowed down the problem about the historical "placing" of the "law of Moses" to the question "whether that law is the starting-point for the history of ancient Israel, or not rather for that of Judaism, i.e., of the religious communion which survived the destruction of the nation by the Assyrians and Chaldaeans".[31] The two questions are very similar, but the one about the age of the Psalms is not so much of an either-or, and Wellhausen does not give it as much attention as he does the question about the age of the law, which at that time occupied a much more important position on the agenda. Where the Psalms are concerned, Wellhausen contents himself with a general explanation: "The Psalter is a part of the Hagiographa. It is the Hymn-Book of the Second Temple. The titles of the Psalms presuppose the musical service described in the Book of Chronicles, and the David of these titles is the David of the Chronicler...The so-called Psalms of Solomon (63–48 B.C.) do not differ from the canonical ones in any essential characteristic, and the fact that there are such is a proof of the late date at which Jewish poets continued to write Psalms."[32] A final general argument is surprising, coming from the pen of Wellhausen of all people: "The strong family-likeness which runs through the Psalms forbids our distributing them among periods of Israelitish history widely separated in time and fundamentally unlike in character."[33] How does this fit in with Wellhausen's maxim that a fine palate is of more use to the exegete than a strong stomach? For after all Wellhausen shows his mastery both in the Old and the New Testament pre-eminently through his ability to detect, with the help of

---

[29] E. Reuss, *Die Geschichte der Heiligen Schrift des Alten Testaments* (2nd edn., Braunschweig, 1890), p. VII.

[30] F. Bleek, *Einleitung in das Alte Testament*, 4. Aufl. bearbeitet von J. Wellhausen (Berlin, 1878), note on p. 507; cf. J. Wellhausen, *The Sacred Books* (1897), p. 163.

[31] Cited here according to the English edition (1885), p. 1.

[32] Wellhausen, *The Sacred Books*, p. 163, cf. Bleek-Wellhausen, *Einleitung*, note on p. 507.

[33] Wellhausen, *The Sacred Books*, p. 163.

literary criticism, differences behind many a "family likeness", indeed seeming uniformity, and to give the detected parts a profile, a historical or, as it is usual to say nowadays, a diachronic one. Here it is not only surprising to see the extent to which he views the whole Psalter as a (relative) unity. It is also astonishing that within the individual psalms he – of all people – dispenses almost entirely with literary criticism. Gunkel and his pupils, and his pupils' pupils, did nothing to advance beyond this abnegation. Their interest lay elsewhere. Today, it would seem that things are changing: individual psalms are also seen to have their history, a history of development (*Fortschreibung*) and revision which literary criticism can help to elucidate – but that only in parenthesis.

In psalm criticism, the question of the "Maccabean Psalms" was always almost a shibboleth. De Wette first supposed that these psalms existed, but then drew back in response to Gesenius's objection. Wellhausen's teacher Ewald entirely denied their existence, as did Gunkel later. Conversely, R. H. Kennett, one of the predecessors of John Emerton as Regius Professor of Hebrew in Cambridge – and incidentally a follower of Wellhausen – assigned all 150 psalms at a single stroke to the "Maccabean" years 168 to 141 (or 134) B.C.[34] Wellhausen, here again learning above all from Justus Olshausen, did not take so radical a view. He frequently noted points suggesting the Maccabean period,[35] but did not always follow this up consistently with a firm date. He often rather left open the early Hellenistic or even the Persian period as possibilities; and we have already seen his placing of Psalms 46 and 87. In the case of Psalm 46,[36] and in some other instances, he also set about refuting the arguments for a pre-exilic or exilic date. The most important of these other examples is Psalm 137 ("By the waters of Babylon"), which some who dispute the existence of pre-exilic psalms are inclined to consider the oldest of all, as being "a folk song deriving from the period of the Babylonian exile":[37] but, so Wellhausen counters, "here the Exile is no longer present but past; the poet is *remembering* those times. But in truth he is merely fantasizing; he does

---

[34] R. H. Kennett, *Old Testament Essays* (Cambridge, 1928), pp. 145, 217 *et passim*.
[35] Cf., for example, the notes (in Wellhausen, *Skizzen*) on Pss. 44, 59–63; 68; 74–76; 79; 83; 102; 110; 118; 124–126; 149.
[36] See Wellhausen, *The Sacred Books*, p. 184.
[37] Cf. B. Duhm, *Die Psalmen* (KHAT; Tübingen, 1922), p. XIX.

not remember them in reality."[38] The most difficult problem for those who contest the existence of pre-exilic psalms is of course the so-called royal psalms. Wellhausen was not accustomed to gloss over difficulties, as we can see from his note on Ps 20. "The person who is addressed is the anointed one of v. 7, the king of v. 10. Accordingly, it would seem that this psalm (and, on the same grounds, the following one) belongs to the days of the kingdom of Judah. This, however, would remove the two psalms entirely out of the sphere to which the Psalms, as a whole, belong, and there are hardly any other points suggesting an earlier date. On the other hand, they cannot be dated as late as the period of the Maccabean kings (105–63 B.C.), who were hardly called kings in the sacred tongue. This we cannot understand."[39] Wellhausen therefore admits the existence of an unsolvable crux, and lets it stand as such. On the other hand, he has no problem in reckoning with a king belonging to the Hasmonean dynasty in Psalms 61–63, for example, which are not classic royal psalms, but whose Maccabean background is plausible. And – to take a final example – this is entirely so in the case of the famous royal psalm 110, which proves its late date by its reference to the "extremely late" Melchizedek chapter Genesis 14.[40]

Even more characteristic of Wellhausen, but very problematical, is what he thought about the origins of psalm poetry or, to be more precise, his ideas about its relationship to the prophet Jeremiah. As we know, there are points of contact between some psalms and certain passages in the book of Jeremiah, especially the "Confessions", which have repeatedly prompted the theory that Jeremiah was the author of these particular psalms. T. K. Cheyne did not have much difficulty in refuting this theory.[41] But Wellhausen outdid it by far with his own thesis, which embraced the whole Psalter: "Without Jeremiah the Psalms would not have been written."[42] Wellhausen described Jeremiah as "the last and in some respects the greatest of the prophets", because of the very fact that his proclamation earned him mockery and persecution. "His scorned prophecy was for him the bridge to an inward

---

[38] Wellhausen, *Skizzen*, p. 185.
[39] Wellhausen, *The Sacred Books*, p. 171.
[40] Wellhausen, *The Sacred Books*, p. 207.
[41] *The Origin and Religious Contents of the Psalter* (London, 1891), pp. 122, 135f., 230, 244f.
[42] Wellhausen, *Israelitische und jüdische Geschichte*, 1st edn., p. 106.

contact with the Deity. Out of his position as mediator between Yahweh and Israel, and since Israel would have none of such mediation, a
private religious relationship grew up between him and Yahweh...in
which...he...himself in all his human frailty, poured himself out
before Yahweh...His experience was perpetuated and repeated in the
experience of the devout who came after him...He is the father of true
prayer, in which the humble soul gives utterance to both its subhuman
misery and its superhuman confidence, its fearfulness and doubt, and
its unshakeable trust. So out of prophecy there crystallized not merely
the law but, in the end, individual religiosity as well."[43]

In saying this Wellhausen gave precise form a second time to
Reuss's formula about the relationship between the Prophets, the Law
and the Psalms, but he did so in a way which could not remain unan-
swered. Starting from an exegesis of the book of Jeremiah and the
Psalms, Gunkel's pupil Baumgartner, whom I have already mentioned,
worked out the confutation during Wellhausen's final years; it was
published in 1917.[44] Today, in the context of the generally more critical view of the book of Jeremiah, it would probably have to be restated
in modified form. Equally problematical is the more fundamental side
of the matter: the individualism which Wellhausen maintains here
and elsewhere, and in which he was a child of his time and which
is so remote from us. Very interestingly, he varies his thesis about
Jeremiah and the Psalms in the note on Ps. 31:13 in Haupt's *Sacred
Books* as follows: "Jeremiah is the model followed by the congregation
of the pious in later days; one might almost call him the nucleus out
of which the congregation developed. The Israel that had gone before
was summed up in him; the new Israel grew out of him. He exercised
a larger influence than anyone else in forming the pietism of post-
Exilic times."[45] It is unknown whether in his German text Wellhausen
used the term *Pietismus*, but he must at least have approved the term
"pietism" in the English translation. Although he was the son of an
orthodox Lutheran pastor, Wellhausen felt less and less at home in the
German Lutheran church as time went on. He therefore voluntarily
renounced his theological chair in order to become a professor of oriental studies, unlike his friend Robertson Smith, who took a similar

---

[43] Wellhausen, *Israelitische und jüdische Geschichte*, pp. 105f.
[44] W. Baumgartner, *Die Klagegedichte des Jeremia* (BZAW 32; Gießen, 1917).
[45] Wellhausen, *The Sacred Books*, p. 178.

step, but not voluntarily. Wellhausen did indeed remain in his church, but as a completely passive member, and there are hints that he found smaller groups more congenial and more in accord with his leanings – groups which we might characterize in religious or theological terms as pietist, and institutionally as congregationalist. In this respect and in others too, we may perhaps assume that he would have felt at least as much at home in England as in Germany. Where ancient Israel is concerned, or, to be more correct, the Judaism of the Second Temple, his sympathies, entirely analogously, were not on the side of the law and the official institutions. They lay with the devout men at prayer in the Psalms, or at least with many of them. He generally understood the "I" of the Psalms as a collective entity (although here too the Gunkel school thought differently),[46] but this "I" originated in an individual, the prophet Jeremiah in his relationship to God, and it could at all times become again the "I" of an individual – the "I", for example, of the seeking and – if not always, yet often – finding, devout scholar Julius Wellhausen.

---

[46] Cf. E. Balla, *Das Ich der Psalmen* (FRLANT 16; Göttingen, 1912).

INDEX OF BIBLICAL REFERENCES

INDEX OF AUTHORS